The Life and Explorations of Frederick Stanley Arnot; the Authorized Biography of a Zealous Missionary, Intrepid Explorer, & Self-denying Benefactor Amongst the Natives of Africa

THE LIFE & EXPLORATIONS OF
FREDERICK STANLEY ARNOT

FREDERICK STANLEY ARNOT

A photo taken on Paddington Station platform in June, 1913, when leaving for Africa for the
last time.

THE LIFE & EXPLORATIONS
OF
FREDERICK STANLEY ARNOT

THE AUTHORISED BIOGRAPHY OF A ZEALOUS
MISSIONARY, INTREPID EXPLORER, & SELF-
DENYING BENEFACTOR AMONGST THE
NATIVES OF AFRICA

BY

ERNEST BAKER
AUTHOR OF "THE RETURN OF THE LORD," &c. &c.

WITH ILLUSTRATIONS & A MAP

NEW YORK
E. P. DUTTON & COMPANY
PUBLISHERS

PRINTED IN GREAT BRITAIN

PREFACE

I HESITATED long as to the form the Life of Arnot should take, alternating between a descriptive narrative and a transcript of his diaries and letters. As I read and re-read these I felt something of the spell that the diaries of David Brainerd, Henry Martyn, and Murray McCheyne have exercised over so many, and I felt that it would be better for the most part to allow Arnot to tell his own story. So I have made a plentiful use of his own words, believing that the result of combining the two methods will be the addition to our literature of a story that will be both interesting from a narrative point of view, and stimulating and inspiring from the devotional standpoint. In the use of letters I have not specified, except on occasions when I have deemed it necessary, to whom they were addressed.

Arnot must be reckoned, not only amongst the greatest saints and missionaries of modern times, but also amongst its greatest travellers. He made nine journeys to the centre of Africa. Without reckoning the tens of thousands of miles that he had to travel on the ocean to get to Africa and back, without counting the journeys around the coast from port to port, and without including the long distances he was able to go in the latter part of his life by train over railways that had then been built, it is estimated that he covered 29,000 miles in all by foot, in hammocks, on the back of donkeys or oxen, or in canoes. This is a record that has probably never been surpassed in Africa, and it is doubtful if many have equalled it in other parts of the world.

I am greatly indebted to the hearty co-operation of Mrs. Arnot, the widow of F. S Arnot, for the loan of diaries, letters, and other papers, and for numerous articles and booklets written by Arnot from time to time. Mrs. Arnot's counsel has been invaluable in deciding what to include and what to eliminate.

Some of the material has of necessity appeared already in Arnot's principal books, *Garenganze, Bihé and Garenganze,* and *Missionary Travels in Central Africa,* and grateful acknowledgment is hereby made both to Mrs. Arnot and the publishers of these works for permission to use the material contained therein.

Miss Ray Arnot, Arnot's eldest daughter, who assisted him in his later years in his literary work and correspondence, has been a great help in correcting place-names.

Then a word must be said for the great traveller's mother, Mrs. Arnot, who is still alive, and, at the time of writing, is eighty-six years of age. She resides in Glasgow and has followed with great interest the progress of this Biography, and has trusted letters of her son to the mercy of the seas, infested in war time with the deadly submarine. Glimpses of him, in a tenderer and more vivid light, can thus be given to the public than could be obtained from a perusal of his journals and letters, which were written with a view to publication.

ERNEST BAKER.

JOHANNESBURG, SOUTH AFRICA.

CONTENTS

LIST OF ILLUSTRATIONS

THE LIFE & EXPLORATIONS

OF

FREDERICK STANLEY ARNOT

CHAPTER I

BEGINNINGS

FREDERICK STANLEY ARNOT came of a good stock. His great-grandfather, on his paternal side, was the Rev. William Arnot of the church now known as the Arnot Memorial Church, Kennoway, Fifeshire. A book of sermons entitled *Law and Grace*, written by him, was greatly esteemed by his fellow ministers at the time of its publication. This William Arnot was a great friend of the Rev. John Newton, the well-known hymn writer. A letter by this famous preacher written to Mrs. Arnot on the occasion of the death of her husband has been preserved, and was read by Fred as a boy with great and reverent interest.

The grandfather of the future missionary was also a William Arnot. He was a publisher in Edinburgh, and connected with the Bible Society in that city. He was alive when Fred was born, and daily remembered his grandsons in prayer.

Fred's own father was also named William, and at the time of his (Fred's) birth—which took place on September 12th, 1858, at 8 Bunbank Terrace, Glasgow—had a shipping connection with Australia.

His mother was the youngest daughter of Neil Macdonald, of Macdonald and Dunn, sewed-muslin manufacturers of Paisley. Mr. Macdonald died before his daughter's marriage with Mr. Arnot. His grandparents belonged to the islands of Skye, from which they fled at the time of the rebellion in connection with Prince Charlie.

When Fred was about four years of age his parents removed to Hamilton. Here he attended the Gilbertfield School, where,

B

at the age of six, at the Annual Prize Distribution, he heard Dr. Livingstone, who had just returned from exploring the Zambesi. His interest in Africa began then.

As Hamilton was the home of Livingstone a friendship sprang up between the Arnots and the Livingstones; and on Saturday afternoons Fred used to play with the children of the great traveller. On these occasions they frequently rummaged in the corners of an old attic where many of the curios brought from Africa were kept, and where also the Doctor's books and letters were stored. On one of these occasions Annie Mary, Livingstone's daughter, read to them one of her father's letters in which he told of the cruelties practised by the slave traders. Though only a boy Fred there and then determined that " he would go and help that great man in his work." That resolution was always kept in mind, and it governed his studies and thoughts. Africa became the centre around which his mind revolved. Whenever his home lessons included geography, no matter what part of the world was the subject, he generally finished up with Africa. Asked on one of these occasions how, if no one gave him the money, he would get there, he replied that he would swim.

Arnot's father was brought up in the Free Church of Scotland, but when Fred was about ten years of age he became exercised about baptism and meeting to break bread every Lord's Day. As the result of this he joined an assembly of Brethren in Hamilton. At the same time he worked in connection with the Evangelisation Society, and had charge of a work in a little hall called " Back of the Barns," where he carried on a very successful Gospel effort. In this he was helped by members of the assembly in the town, and also by some well-known Brethren from Glasgow.

In 1870 Mr. and Mrs. W. Arnot removed to Tayport, Fifeshire. Here the father initiated a meeting for the breaking of bread which was first held in a cottage, and afterwards in a small hall in the village.

As early as his eighth year Fred realised his need of a Saviour; and in 1869 he found peace through repeating and believing, at two o'clock one morning, the message of John iii. 16.

Whilst in his early teens he was baptised at the " Mid Wynd " meeting in Dundee, the late Mr. Scott interviewing him regarding his religious experience, after which he was received into the meeting at Tayport where his father was the principal speaker.

Young Arnot commenced Christian work early. He accompanied his father in open-air work, and took part in the meetings when he was only fifteen. A Tayport man afterwards remarked : " We used to think he took too much on himself preaching to us men, but now I see the lad was father to the man."

At the shipbuilding yard in Tayport he spent six months learning how to use tools ; and frequently in later years he would say that the training he received here was very useful to him in Africa.

In 1876 the family removed back to Glasgow, when Fred entered a wholesale linen merchant's warehouse. There he was once asked to invoice some goods wrongly. He refused, and after a time of anxiety was commended by the head of the firm for acting in accordance with his conscience. In his further business life he travelled much in different parts of Scotland, and in following his tracks to-day one learns how much he was loved and how well he has been remembered.

In order to fit himself for his work in Africa Arnot would frequently take cross-country journeys guided only by the compass. On one occasion he was in a lonely part and in a district of which he was ignorant. He asked his way to the nearest railway station. A coal miner directed him, and as the distance was considerable, and as this stranger knew the nature of the inhabitants, and also saw a few suspicious characters on the road, he called two of his sons, who were also miners, and told them to follow Arnot and guard him till he reached his destination. This they did. In after years in Central Africa, when welcoming a party of missionaries sent to reinforce him, Arnot was told by one of the new arrivals of the incident. and the narrator added : " I am one of the sons who followed you to guard you, little thinking that I would become a missionary and meet you in Africa."

In his spare time the future missionary learnt to make shoes, to cut out cloth, and sew it as a tailor. He learnt how to take a watch to pieces, and to put it together again, and practised working as a blacksmith and as a joiner. He also acquired a certain amount of medical and surgical knowledge which on several occasions stood him in good stead, both as to himself and others. To all this he added a careful systematic study of the Scriptures, the result of which was that all his addresses were edifying as well as suggestive.

In Glasgow Arnot was connected with the meeting of Brethren held in Parkholm Hall, Paisley Road. By this assembly he was commended to God for the work to which he had consecrated himself, the elder brethren being particularly hearty in their approval of his enterprise, having carefully marked his diligence in summer pioneer Gospel work in Scottish and English districts.

Arnot was twenty-three years of age when he started for Africa. Many of his relatives were opposed to his going in the simple way of trusting his temporal affairs to God, wishing him to take a University training and to go out in connection with a recognised society. But this he did not feel called to do. He went, as he believed, and as the results showed, at the call of God. Several friends shared his desire to evangelise the natives of the Dark Continent. These helped in providing his outfit, and in equipping him for his expedition. But being the agent of no organisation his resources were very slender. To this fact he himself said, upon returning seven years later, he owed his escape from some of the troubles befalling travellers furnished with a large stock of goods; and, being without the helps and comforts possessed by them, he was obliged to share the lives of the natives in a way that gave him a better knowledge of them than he would otherwise have obtained.

His intention when leaving was to make for the Zambesi, and to follow up one of the smaller affluents, and so get on to the watershed on the north, where he expected to find a mountainous and healthy country. He had been much impressed with the heavy death rate, often as high as 50 per cent, of African missionaries, due to the fact that the mission stations were dotted along the banks of the great rivers. His idea, therefore, was to find a big inland ridge where healthier conditions would be possible, and which would be a centre for missionary work.

On July 19th, 1881, Arnot sailed by the *Dublin Castle* for South Africa, accompanied by one who purposed to be his companion in the work.

Arriving at the Cape on August 13th, Arnot and his friend were much refreshed by meeting with a band of earnest Christian workers who showed much interest in their enterprise. With these the question was considered of making their way into the interior from Cape Town, but they were led to conclude that Natal offered a more advantageous starting-point, so they proceeded to Durban in a small coasting steamer. They were much impressed by meeting on this vessel four natives from Delagoa Bay who urged them to start work there, promising to build them a house and a chapel, and to give them food and drink. When little hope of their settlement in that centre was given the reply came: " Ah ! white man bring brandy to Delagoa Bay, and guns and powder, but white man no bring chapel to Delagoa Bay."

Durban was reached on August 20th. The next day was a Sunday, and the visitors worshipped in the evening in the little Congregational church near the pier, where the Rev. David Russell (since known as the South African Evangelist) was the preacher. The text on that occasion was: ' Verily I say unto you, there is no man that hath left house, or brethren, or sisters, or father, or mother, or wife, or children, or lands, for My sake, and the gospel's, but he shall receive a hundredfold now in this time, houses, and brethren, and sisters, and mothers, and children, and lands, with persecutions ; and in the world to come eternal life." The word was like a drink from the brook by the way to hearts that were already beginning to feel something of the loneliness to which they were committed.

The first trial came here. The health of Arnot's companion broke down, and acting under medical advice he felt he must abandon the journey to the interior, so Arnot had to proceed alone.

CHAPTER II

THE next step was Maritzburg, where Arnot was detained for three months. The country was still in an unsettled condition, due to the Boer War of 1880-1, and preparations for a journey to the Zambesi were difficult. The time, however, was well spent. Mission stations in the surrounding country were visited and much useful information gained. Opportunities for preaching to his fellow-countrymen were also seized, and many visits to the sick in the hospitals gladly paid.

It was in this place that Arnot had the first of his many marvellous escapes, and learnt how near he could be brought to death and yet preserved without a hair of his head being touched. Going to a meeting, when a tremendous thunderstorm was raging, he was startled by an electric ball falling just at his feet. The small stones and dust caused by its contact with the ground flew all around him. The shock passed through his whole body. Those who saw the ball of fire fall said it seemed to come right down where he stood, and they described the noise when it struck the ground as like the crash of a cannon-ball. Arnot was none the worse for the occurrence and was able to conduct the meeting.

Arnot made many friends in Maritzburg, and from these he received valuable assistance in fitting himself for the long journey before him. The help was not only with word but with means. He was persuaded to buy a rifle, as he was told by reliable persons that he would be unable to secure natives to travel with him unless he had a gun with which to obtain meat.

The decision was made during this waiting time to proceed to Shoshong, the capital of the Bamangwato in Bechuanaland, under the rule of the chief Khama. Here he would be for a while amongst some of his countrymen, and have at the same time the best opportunity of learning the Sechuana language, which is the basis of most of the dialects of the interior tribes.

Arrangements were made to travel with a transport rider who was taking a number of waggons to Potchefstroom, and with these Arnot left on November 20th. The waggons started from the Natal capital on the 19th, reaching the top of the hill above the town the same evening. Arnot did not join them till the next morning when some of the Christians of the city accompanied him up the hill to say good-bye. Sixteen Kaffir drivers soon put the oxen and the heavy waggons into motion.

Now that the country is intersected with railways it is interesting to read Arnot's description of the travelling of his day. "Inland journeys from Maritzburg," he said, "are made by means of ox-waggons, each carrying between three and four tons weight of goods, and drawn by from 16 to 20 oxen. Four or five waggons, however, generally travel together, as the roads in many places are hilly, and in others so marshy that more than one team of oxen is required to get the waggon along. It does look stupid to see so many oxen drawing one waggon over the level roads about town; but when one sees them out in the country dragging it through a quagmire, with great boulders of stone hidden in the mud every few yards, and then up a tremendously steep hill, one wonders how they manage to get along at all. Sometimes as many as 70 oxen have to be yoked to one transport waggon We hope to make eight or ten miles a day, without many stoppages, if the rivers are fordable."

Day after day, after leaving Maritzburg, the train of bullock waggons passed the soldiers returning from Northern Natal in consequence of the settlement after the Boer War. Leaving the town of Ladysmith on their right they went up the Van Reenan Pass, through the Drakensberg Range, to the Free State. Arnot's sleeping accommodation was on the ground under one of the waggons, which he confessed was a little trying with a drenching rain, and with four degrees of frost before the morning. For three days a terrific storm of wind and rain kept them prisoners, and Arnot remained for most of that time wrapped in a sheep-skin kaross, lying under one of the waggons sharing coffee and "scoff" with the drivers, for the white man in charge had ridden off to the nearest hotel.

Most of the time on the road was spent with the Kaffirs only, and as he understood but little of their language as yet he was consequently shut up to " converse only with Him whose ear is ever open to us. This," Arnot says, " has turned my solitude into a very precious time, and I can say to His praise that I never felt more free from all care and anxious thought than now. I wonder how it is that Satan has so managed to blindfold me in the past, that my whole life has not been one note of praise. Oh ! stir up every child of God you meet to praise our God more. We little know how much we rob Him by our sad hearts and dull, thankless lives. The Lord has been teaching me a little of the awful sin of unthankfulness. Two great reasons why God gave up those of old to uncleanness and darkness were, that they glorified Him not as God, neither were thankful."

Travelling in the Free State was easy except for occasional deep sloughs of black mud when the drivers had to inspan forty or more oxen to one waggon at a time. Proceeding via Harrismith and Heilbron, and crossing the Vaal River, Potchefstroom was reached on December 23rd.

For a few days Arnot camped on the Market Square in his small patrol tent, 6 ft. by 3 ft. The fort recently garrisoned by the British was just outside the town and was to him a centre of interest. This had been besieged by a large force of Boers, and had held out in ignorance for some time after peace had been concluded. Evidence of recent happenings were to be seen in the neighbourhood ; remains of horses, oxen, and even natives, lying in the vicinity. Arnot was shown a dug-out provided for the only woman in the garrison, and also a spot where a young soldier fell who had been found sleeping whilst on duty in the trenches, and who was condemned to be shot. Rather, however, than be killed by his own countrymen he jumped upon the parapet and was immediately shot down by the Boers. " If," says Arnot, " our Captain so treated His sleeping soldiers, who would stand ? How gentle were His words when He found His disciples sleeping for sorrow, ' Why sleep ye ? ' "

Suitable lodgings were soon found in the town, and for six weeks Potchefstroom was his centre. He made extended tours on horseback from this place to many of the Dutch farms, carrying Scripture portions with him. In the course of these tours he was entertained by Mr. (afterwards General) Cronje and his wife, and also by General Joubert. These helped and cheered him much in his work amongst the Boers.

At Potchefstroom Arnot met a Mr. Webb, who had been a missionary amongst the Baralongs, but, owing to a deficit of eighty thousand pounds in funds, the Society he represented had been obliged to retrench and dispense with his services. Consequently he had resumed his trade, which was that of a blacksmith. As a return for help in his occupation Mr. Webb gave Arnot lessons in the Sechuana language. Writing from this centre Arnot said : " Potchefstroom is a lovely place, with such a lot of fruit of every description. The young man with whom I lodge has a large garden and I have undertaken to dry his fruit for him as he has not time. I have been busy with the apricots during the last few days, opening them up and laying them out on reeds to dry in the sun. Peaches and figs come next ; so with this, learning the Sechuana language, and helping Mr. Webb in his business, I am kept pretty busy. The other day I walked out to the British fort just outside the town, where for three months a constant fight was kept up. It is surprising to see the amount of labour and toil they must have gone through in throwing up the immense earth mounds, and in digging the long deep trenches. Eighty-five of our men fell in these trenches, and they are buried here and there very much as they fell."

A letter of introduction to a friend in Klerskdorp resulted in an introduction, in that town, to Mr. F. C. Selous. This famous hunter was making arrangements to go to Shoshong, and when he found that Arnot wanted to reach the same place he gave him a cordial invitation to accompany him, which was joyfully accepted. Returning to Potchefstroom to get his belongings Arnot found that the woman who did his washing had left with all that he had entrusted to her, and that the Hollander, who had permitted him to graze his mule on his ground had ridden off with it to Kimberley.

Writing home Arnot said : " Klerksdorp is a nice little place. There is no doctor in this neighbourhood so I have been kept busy in prescribing as best I could. I was very

successful with one man, and also with a little girl who had
been afflicted for some time with a most distressing complaint
When I left she was eating well and running about with the
rest. I was asked to stay in the place as a doctor, which of
course I refused to do, although I could make a good thing of
it financially. I find that if the healing of bodily sickness were
not kept strictly in the second place it would soon get the first
place with me, and would at once absorb all my attention."

Prior to this Arnot had had other experiences of the need of
doctors amongst the scattered populations of the veld, as the
following letter dated, Potchefstroom, January 20, 1882, will
show : " I have just returned from another of my mad freaks.
I had intended to visit the chief Monsoia, and was on the lookout for a horse for hire, but failed entirely, so gave up the idea
in the meantime. A day or two afterwards an Englishman
came and offered me the use of a big white riding mule for a
very reasonable hire. So I accepted his offer and went. I
heard before I started that the Boers were doing what they
could to get up a fight among the Kaffirs, but reports here are
so absurd at times, and so little to be trusted, that I thought
I had better go on and see for myself, and I am glad I did so,
for I now understand the true condition of affairs in that part.
If Joubert succeeds in driving off the 200 rebel Boers, who
have joined Moshite and Monchabie, Monsoia will soon right
himself, as England has pledged herself to support him, and
has at present a military agent staying with him, so it will
only be a question of a very short time till things are settled.
It took me three days to reach Lichtenburg, a distance of 76
miles, which was awfully hard work on a zigzagging mule.
I had a very good reception at Lichtenburg. There are some
ten or twelve English people there, and they nearly all turned
out, with a few English-speaking Boers, to see the visitor, and
to hear his news. I was asked if I was a doctor, or knew anything about medicine. I told them I knew a little. I was then
first invited to go out and join the camp of the rebel Boers,
and then to come to Lichtenburg as doctor, as the nearest
medical man they had was a German missionary, some 30
miles away, and who practices homæopathy, in consequence
of which they are in love with the system."

The route followed by Arnot and Selous led them through
Lichtenburg and Zeerust ; and, again, as in Natal, Arnot met

men returning from war. This time it was the Boers who had
been in conflict with the Baralongs, one of the Bechuana tribes,
and they had with them large droves of cattle which they had
captured from the natives.

Before reaching Zeerust Mr. Selous pressed on ahead to the
Limpopo, where he spent some time in collecting natural
history specimens for the British and Continental museums.
This left Arnot alone for a time. The season was so hot that
progress had to be made at night. On one occasion Arnot
says he had to walk for five hours through thick bush, in front
of the waggons, with a lantern to trace the road, and when no
road could be found he had to use his compass.

The journey from Zeerust to the Limpopo was much enjoyed,
the river being described by Arnot as a " beautiful river indeed.
The wild animals," he said, " became more numerous here—
lions, leopards, etc. ; but with a scherm of thorns all round at
night, and a large fire blazing, there is no danger. When the
nights are dark they keep one awake with their roaring. I shall
be glad when we reach Bamangwato, and I can get settled down
to the language. I feel so useless, and sometimes impatient,
when so many all round sadly need the Gospel, and I cannot
converse with them."

A long continued drought in these parts compelled the
travellers to remain for a fortnight at this spot for the sake
of water for the oxen, and whilst here the waggon was daily
visited by Bushmen, of whom Arnot says : " These men are
supposed to be the lowest type of humanity. They live in a
most primitive fashion ; the whole company will sleep in a
little hollow in the ground under a bush ; they come round the
waggon for any scraps of meat and offal thrown away. Growing no grain, they live on wild fruit, and on animals which they
kill with their poisoned arrows. Their little children at once
proved the connection of these people with the whole human
race. Their ways at play, and their sweet ringing laugh, are
the same as those of our own children at home."

Heavy rains falling, the journey was made across the dry
desert lying between the Limpopo and Shoshong, the latter
place being reached on March 11th, 1882, after thirty-six days'
travelling from Potchefstroom.

Arnot stayed in Shoshong for three months, and had in that
time a wonderful and an encouraging object lesson of the power

of the Gospel over an African chief. Shoshong was then the capital of the Bamangwato, and Khama had been in power for ten years, long enough to demonstrate what a Christian ruler with autocratic power could do for his people. No other South African chief has ever attempted one half of what Khama has done for those under his rule.

The late Mr. Hepburn was one of the greatest influences in Khama's life, and he and his devoted wife were at Shoshong at the time of Arnot's visit. They showed much kindness to the visitor, and he profited much from his intercourse with them. A friendship was formed which became one of the most valuable of the many fellowships made by Arnot in Africa. Something of his opinion of Hepburn may be gathered from the following : " The record of Mr. Hepburn's life work, *Twenty Years in Khama's Country*, is a most inspiring book, and might well be placed in the same category as the lives of Brainerd and Henry Martyn." Mr. Hepburn gave Arnot lessons in Sechuana daily for two months until he and his family left for England on furlough. With the language Arnot made rapid progress, and in return for the help given to him by Hepburn spent a part of his time in teaching English to the two sons of his friends. He was also kept busy in doctoring the natives, and on Sundays he conducted services for the white residents (the traders and their wives) to the number of fourteen. Just at that time traders were in Shoshong from Lake Ngami, the Matabele country, and from the Zambesi.

Concerning Shoshong itself, Arnot wrote : " There is a great amount of sickness and death in the town ; and no wonder, when one thinks of 20,000 people being crowded together as close as they could well be packed. Two persons can scarcely walk abreast between the houses, which form such a perfect maze to me, that when visiting the sick I have to be guided in and out. Their idea is that this plan affords greater protection from their enemies. The town is sadly in need of a hospital as there is nothing more difficult than to attend to people in the midst of such a mass of filthy humanity. The surgical cases are the most trying, of which I will not harass you with particulars Yesterday, however, I was called upon to cut a young man's leg off that had got fearfully smashed. I was just preparing to put him under chloroform when he began to sink rapidly, and died in a few hours. There is another similar case, which I have taken on hand, and which is causing me a good deal of anxiety. Still, God has helped me wonderfully. Once I master the language I will not lay myself out for this sort of work, but meantime I rejoice at the opportunity of getting among the people. I think I have already gained the confidence of some who at first treated me with suspicion.

" The moral condition of Shoshong is in many respects most exemplary. Since coming here I have not seen an intoxicated person, either black or white, which could not be said by anyone for the same period, in any other town in Africa where the white man trades. The chief, Khama, has put down the drink traffic most effectually. Not only has he forbidden it among his own people, but he will not allow the liquor to pass through his country ; consequently none has passed into Central Africa from this side for some years, unless it be a very small quantity occasionally smuggled in. If a trader is found out once bringing drink into the place, even for the use of the white people, he is turned off Khama's territory, and never allowed to enter it again.

" In many respects Khama is a noble chief, and it would be well if other rulers imitated his unselfish Christian policy. None of his people are allowed to want, if he can help it. If they are too poor to buy, he provides them with a stock of cattle, the increase of which belongs to the poor man ; and thus Khama has distributed during the last few years thousands of cattle to such of his people as have suffered through loss of crops, cattle disease, etc.

" Although he has stopped all beer-drinking amongst his people, and put down many of the revolting heathen customs in which formerly they delighted, yet they all like their chief, and would almost to a man die for him.

" Now and then Khama gets up hunts on a large scale to kill the larger kinds of game. These hunting parties go far into the desert, and often suffer greatly from want of food and water ; but the chief is always the first to go without his share, and will not help himself until all are supplied, so that there is not the slightest grumbling on the part of his followers.

" In spite, however, of all the chief can do, very revolting practices are carried on secretly among his people—such as the murdering of children. A deformed child is at once put to death ; twins are seldom allowed to live. If any peculiar circumstances happen at the birth of a child, or any suspicious omen occur, such as the call of certain animals or birds, the child is murdered. The ordinary way is to pour boiling water down the child's throat, and carry the body out to the wolves ; they also cast out the old people. Some of them still cut their bodies, use enchantments, etc., but their heathen customs are not openly observed. (This was written in 1882)

" I can, nevertheless, say confidently that one would see more vice and open immorality on a Saturday night in the High Street, Glasgow, than would be seen in twelve months.

" The clothing of the people is scanty, but sufficient. They are naturally civil and polite to each other, and when addressing an older or superior person, finish every sentence with ' my father,' or ' my mother.' Both young and old address me as ' my father,' and often as ' my lord ' ; but it is merely civility.

" Shoshong is built and ordered after the manner of a military camp, and everything is done by word of command. The gardens are tilled at the word of the chief ; the crops cannot be gathered in till the order is given. Each man is supposed to be able to muster a gun or so many spears. The people in the town live together in what might be called regiments, the huts of each regiment being clustered around the hut of its captain ; and around the town there is a double row of outposts, extending a long way into the veld.

" I have seen two turn-outs of the army since I came. On one occasion an attack was expected from the Matabele. When the report first came every man at once armed himself, and all began jointly to get themselves into training for fighting. For several mornings in succession they had a grand race of six miles. It was a strange sight to see ten or twelve thousand men, in all sorts of fantastic dresses, running along as hard as they could, all the time shouting and boasting of what they could do.

" The other day as the wife of one of the residents was recovering from an attack of fever she took a great longing for a pheasant, and could scarcely eat anything else. Her husband could not leave her to go and hunt for one, so I started off in the afternoon and walked to some hills 12 miles away where I shot one pheasant and one guinea-fowl, and returned in time for tea, doing 24 miles in six hours. So you must not think of me as a weary-looking, white-faced character wandering through the country. I am much heavier in weight and stronger every way than I ever hoped to be in this country. Ah, well ! This little brag is just *en passant* by way of giving you confidence, you know."

CHAPTER III

FROM the time of Arnot's arrival Khama was very friendly to him, and promised to help him on his journey to the Zambesi with guides and servants, whenever he was ready to go. It was eventually decided to take the desert route to the north. Khama told Arnot that he was sending Tinka, his chief hunter, to the Mababi, at the extreme north of the Kalahari desert, and that he could go with him if he choose. He promised him every help and comfort in travelling with Tinka, who was a man of experience and knew every inch of the ground, and had strict orders not to run any risks in trying to cross the desert. Khama also placed one of his waggons, with a span of oxen, at the disposal of Arnot to take him as far as the Mababi, which was as far as they could go without being hindered by the tsetse fly. " Wherever this insect is found," Arnot wrote, " the ox, the horse, and the European dog die from the effects of its bite, although human beings and wild animals do not suffer. Donkeys too are supposed to be immune."

Khama also sent orders by Tinka that on reaching the Mababi Arnot was to have as many Basubia men as he needed to assist him on to Panda-ma-tenka, which would be the next stage of his journey, and where he could easily get guides to take him across the Zambesi.

The trek north began on June 8th, 1882. In addition to the waggon loaned by Khama to take his supplies as far as the Mababi, Arnot bought three donkeys for the transport of his belongings beyond that point. From the journey from the Mababi to the Batoka, north of the Zambesi, and back (for at that time his intention was to return to Shoshong by October or November before the unhealthy season set in), Arnot only took one suit of clothes, one knife, one fork and spoon, one plate, one cup, some soap, beads, calico, wheat-meal, tea, sugar, coffee, a little powder and lead, all of which was packed into six sailor bolster bags which a Glasgow sailmaker had made for him.

Khama and his wife joined in the farewell, the chief expressing the wish that God would be with him to save him by the way, and to bring him back in peace. His wife said with tears : " May God go with you, and remain with us, and fill you with blessing." A number of native Christians gave him presents for the way. First one and then another appeared by the side of the road with bundles and bags of food and supplies for the journey. The half-coloured butcher of the town rolled a bundle into the waggon, saying : " These sausages are well spiced, sir ; I have been up all night making them ; hang them to the roof of the waggon." " Nothing," said Arnot, " could have been finer or more encouraging than the way those natives seriously owned the claims that the Gospel had upon them and the way they did their utmost to speed me on."

The experiences of the desert journey are best told in Arnot's own words :

" June is not a good month for travelling in the Kalahari desert. The water holes and pans begin to dry up, the ' frost by night and the sun by day,' wither the grass. As we zigzagged about from water hole to water hole it seemed that we were constantly on the brink of dire disaster. Usually the guide would report that there was only water sufficient for half of our oxen, so it was necessary to outspan a mile or so to the windward of the water holes. Nothing could surpass the beauty of those desert nights, when for hours I would sit listening to the natives or trying to exercise the Sechuana that I had learned at Shoshong. For the first few weeks, trees, rugged hills and great dry river beds covered the country.

" There are many wild animals all over the country through which we have to pass It is only in hunting these, however, that there is any real danger. Every night, when travelling, the natives cut down a lot of thorn bushes, and make with them a thick fence, called a ' scherm,' and two large fires are placed at the opening, thus forming a complete protection. Very seldom will a lion break into a ' scherm,' although at times they walk round it all night. The principal danger is in travelling by night, and where water is scarce one is compelled to do so ; but if the party is kept well together, and not allowed to

c

scatter, there is very little danger, as a lion will not attack a company."

" Once when travelling up the Crocodile River (on the way to Shoshong) during the night I was walking behind Mr. Selous' waggon, and a young man was driving some loose cattle not far from me. On reaching the halting place, towards morning, the cattle came up all right, but the young driver was not with them. Search was made in all directions, but without result, and we came to the conclusion that a lion had carried him off, even though he was but a little distance from the party.

" Yesterday (June 13th) we sent the oxen ten miles off to get a drink. Poor animals ! they suffer much from thirst. The hunters too have suffered from hunger. They have as yet not been fortunate in finding game, and have had to go for days with only a little corn, although it is the king's special hunting party. Because of the famine which threatens Shoshong they started with but a small quantity of food, counting on getting some on the road.

" I am writing (June 18th) in the centre of the north-east part of the great Kalahari desert, hoping to meet some native at the Botletle River going down to Shoshong. We are losing no time by the way, as we shall not have any water for nearly two days and two nights. I have a fair supply of food with me ; for after I had laid in, as I thought, a reasonable store, I found on starting that a bag of rusks, a large loaf of bread, a small crock of butter, some oranges from the Transvaal, a water melon, etc., had been sent to the waggon for me. I am beginning to know my fellow travellers a little more. Tinka is undoubtedly a decent fellow, and I think a true Christian. At first, however, I felt a peculiar sense of loneliness in finding myself surrounded by black faces, with no one near to whom I could speak in my own tongue, but I have got over that. Two other companies of hunters, going on to the Botletle River, have joined us. They are a wild lot, and, away from their own town and chief, seem to enjoy their liberty immensely. The camp at night would make a fine picture on canvas : ten or twelve fires, and round each a crowd of black faces, some of the men singing, talking, laughing, scolding, and others tearing antelope's bones to pieces. All around is pitchy dark, made doubly so by the shade of the dense forest and bush.

" We have just got to another well, which is, however, almost dry, and have travelled 40 hours from the last water, during which we only stopped for five hours, the oxen have been without water for three days As there is not water enough for the oxen and donkeys they have to go half a day further on. I was glad, I assure you, to lie down and get a little sleep. The endurance of these people astonishes me. Some of them walked the whole time ; and walking two days and a night through loose sand is no easy thing. The first day we stopped two hours for meals, during the night two hours for sleep, and two hours the next day for food. Tinka as yet has no certain news as to water beyond the Botletle River, so it is not clear whether we shall go on or not. I am getting into training by walking a long distance every day, and I can endure a good deal of thirst The natives drink a lot of water, and seem to suffer if they are without it for a day.

" We have got thus far (Letlakani Water, June 21st), but are all very tired. The waters were so very low, and so few and far between that we had to push on, the oxen not being able to get more than one drink at the different wells. Poor animals ! They do look knocked up, their necks all raw with the galling of the yoke. The wells are very deep, so that to water a span of oxen is no light task, the men having to climb up and down with pails of water. I am busy at making boots, and have successfully finished one, which fits admirably (not to speak of appearance) ; the soles are giraffe hide, the uppers, I think are buffalo, and are stitched with narrow strips of zebra skin.

" We reached the Botletle River on June 22nd. We stay here eight days altogether, and are outspanned in a most deso-late spot. Behind is the great Kalahari desert, and before us is a great stretch of reeds. A strong wind is constantly blow-ing from the desert, bringing with it clouds of white sand ; but better to have a wind, charged with sand, than one charged with malaria from the reeds.

" I thought a short account of my first effort at ' village work ' in the interior would interest you, so will tell you some-what about it. At home in eight days one could accomplish a good deal, but not so here, the distance being very great. A meeting is called for this (Sunday) evening at which I am ex-pected to speak ; it will be my first attempt. I am very doubtful as to how I shall make myself understood. Tinka asked me last night to have meetings all along the river, as the people understood Sechuana, which he thinks I speak well enough ; it will depend upon how I get on this evening. Nothing would be a greater pleasure to me, as many of the people in these towns have never heard the Gospel.

" This (Sunday) evening around three fires we met for prayer and reading   I got on pretty well, and most seemed to understand me.   Tinka and the Bamangwato understood every word. All listened with eyes and mouth wide open ; so I am much encouraged, and shall have meetings at all the little towns we come to.   To pray in another tongue seems very strange to me, more so than speaking in it to the people.   I can scarcely describe the sense of relief felt, after straining to understand the language for four months, to find that I am able in a measure to tell the story I had come to make known.   God has helped me much more than my heart will acknowledge.

" On Monday I got a young Christian from Shoshong, named Ramosi, to accompany me.   Like most native Christians, he can read and preach the Gospel pretty well.   We intended visiting three villages.   The first we came to was Makoako, and to reach it we had a long, tiresome walk, first through deep sand, and then for some miles through reeds by a narrow winding path in which there was scarcely room for one to walk. Arriving at Makoako about midday, we found nearly all the inhabitants asleep.   Taking our seats in the kotla (the place of public meeting) we awaited our audience.   Those near awoke the others, and soon they all came trooping out of their little huts.   They listened closely.   The faces of most, however, showed that they were more occupied with criticising than assenting ; still, it is ours to sow, and God's to give the increase. The next village we reached was a small one.   The men were all away hunting, and the women out working, so we passed on. We were not, however, able to reach the third village, for my feet were sorely blistered, and so were Ramosi's.   He said the road was killing him.   Turning our course for the waggon we reached it after again crossing the stretch of reeds.

" Tuesday was a very stormy day, the sand blowing all round in great clouds, and we did not venture out ; my feet were also too sore.   On Wednesday we started again on the donkeys for a village called Sosineu, which we reached about midday, and found it quite a town.   As we entered, the donkeys caused a great sensation.   I suppose it was the first time such animals had been seen there. The people are Makalako, from the Matabele country. They all understand Sechuana well, but are wild and savage looking. Taking our seats in the kotla, one of the headmen sent a messenger to call the people, and he went round shouting in a most frantic manner. Every time he reached the climax of his sentence he threw his arms into the air and jumped up, as if he were calling the people to a war dance. His cry was for all the people, men, women and children, to come for ' Sunday ' In a short time a large crowd gathered, the men sitting in one large ring, the women in another, and we continued the meeting for fully two hours. I had of course to keep very closely to passages of Scriptures, such as the Lord's words in John x. The Shepherd giving his life for the sheep was an illustration that seemed to grip their attention. It was one they could understand even better than people at home. They have, however, little idea of what sin is ; but the Spirit of God is able to convince of sin, and may please to use a very feeble word for that end. Ramosi spoke very earnestly on the same subject. It was evening ere we reached the waggon

" In the Kalahari desert, through which we have just come, wandering bands of Basarawa or Bushmen, Bakalahari, and Bakalaka are found, all runaway remnants of tribes and races living in the countries adjoining. Certainly these wild men appear to us to be in a very degenerate condition, but their faculties and senses are sharpened to a remarkable degree. As they move about they allow nothing to escape their notice ; they ' read ' the path, and can tell, not only the name of an animal that may have crossed it during the night, but the time of night that it happened to pass. They also seem to know instinctively where water is likely to be found.

" Crossing the Botletle we moved on slowly, finding a fair supply of water, but the trees were very close together in places and my axe was kept very busy. At Tontgaru we rested for several days ; our Bushman guide assured us that for ten days or so beyond we should find no water in any of the pans. My men shot the game down and feasted to their hearts' content, loading up the waggon with dried meat. Giraffes, ostriches, wildebeeste, elephants, and many other species, come round the water at night to drink. We spent our last day at Tontgaru cleaning and filling our water barrels, setting aside one keg for Khama's hunting horse that Tinka had brought with him. In the cool of the evening the oxen were inspanned, and without a word we quietly moved away into the long stretch that lay before us The sand proved to be unusually heavy ; the dry air and blistering sun seemed as if they would dry us all up like so many Egyptian mummies, in spite of the pint of water we allowed ourselves three times a day.

" We are now getting well north, and I feel somehow nearer home by being again in sight of the ' Great Bear ' constellation. It is, however, much warmer here. This is the coldest month of the year ; yet during the day it is very hot, about 85° in the shade ; but the nights are decidedly cold. I get on pretty well with the people ; we have prayer and reading every night and morning, and on Sunday in the afternoon. I do not under-stand the language sufficiently to appeal personally to their hearts. I could not be in a better school, however, for learning the words and idioms of the people ; yet it would be a treat to meet someone with whom I could speak in my own tongue.

' I did not tell you in my last that when I was at the Bot-letle River there was much fever, and many of the natives died of it. Three of our company were ill, but I had not even a headache. My sleeping accommodation is not the best, rough but comfortable. When travelling I always sleep with my clothes on. In Setobi I have a very faithful and trusty servant ; he takes charge of all my property, and looks after my clothes and goods as though they were his own. Nearly all my spare time is occupied in getting up the Sechuana grammar, and in learning portions of Scripture in Sechuana. It is difficult to read by the fires, and candle light is too expensive for much reading, so that I spend the dark evenings mostly in thinking. Taking it all round my days pass very pleasantly indeed, and also very quickly. There is nothing that I want that I have not got."

" Since leaving the Botletle we have been travelling through a wild but beautiful country teeming with game of all sorts. I have installed Setobi as my huntsman. The game is large and not difficult to shoot so that he is well able to keep the pot going. It is surprising, however, to see how much these people can eat. Tinka shot two giraffes on Saturday. The flesh was brought in late at night. On Sunday morning they began dividing and cooking, and by Sunday evening only a few bones and a few strings of meat hung up to dry were all that were left of nearly one-and-a-half tons of meat. There were only 20 eaters. My own appetite in fact surprises me, but of course I am living entirely in the open air, and walking a good deal every day. I can take a hearty meal of two or three pounds of meat and never dream of eating anything with it.

" I will tell you lots of wild beast stories when I come home. But I do not think you would like them so well if you heard the beasts themselves howling round all night. My ! the roaring and yelping of some of those animals in a pitch-dark night at one's very ear does make one jump and grasp one's gun almost instinctively. There is a terror in the roar of a lion which quite petrifies its victim, and it has somewhat the same effect on the animal nature of man."

It was on July 13th that the party started from Tontgaru Water, which is quite close to Kama-Kama on Livingstone's route Arnot's narrative proceeds : " Here we took in our final supply of water and started across the thirst-land for the Mababi flats. Tinka having sent on some men to look for water, we went on for three days and nights with scarcely a stop. It was hard work, the bush being so very dense. I calculated that we travelled 40 miles in 24 hours, or about 30 miles as the crow flies, in a N.W. by W. direction.

" On the third day we fell in with traces of the disaster that befell the great Boer trek of 1878-9, when only a remnant of some 200 families survived. Waggons, Scotch carts, and other vehicles, ploughs, and bones of horses were scattered along the trail. On the fifth day the bones of oxen lay white around the large trees, where the poor animals had died in scores and hundreds. Then came the graves of the voortrekkers themselves, young and old.

" Our oxen at last showed signs of collapse, so we sent them on without the waggon. Fortunately for us a company of wandering Bushmen came along, and at our urgent request and fair offer of pay, they began to look round for signs of water. Fixing on a place where a certain bulbous root grew, the little men began with vigour to scoop out the sand with their hands until an inverted cone-shaped hollow of about nine feet deep had been made in the loose sand. Then one Bushman, who looked like the master water-finder of the company, took several lengths of reed in his hand and slid down head first to the foot of the hole. Taking one length of reed, the end of which had already been stopped up with grass to prevent the sand entering, he pushed it little by little into the ground. Then he added a second length of reed to the first, making a workman-like joint with a lump of gum. To the end of the second reed he now applied his mouth, and after sucking and blowing for some time, looked up over his shoulder with a smile of satis-faction. He had tasted water, he said, but we would have to wait. Six hours or so later he slid down the hole, taking with him this time a tortoise shell, and, again applying his mouth to the reed, sucked up a mouthful of water at a time, squirting it out of the corner of his mouth and filling the tortoise shell. We all drank heartily and thankfully, and in the course of the next day he managed to fill our smaller kegs with the frothy liquid.

" The oxen and the donkeys did not return until Wednesday evening, having had to go two days' journey before they found water, and then only a little pan of surface water which they emptied. We found afterwards that, between that and the Mababi River (two days further on), there was not a drop to be had. The cattle could not have gone a day further, as they had already been six days without water—the longest time they have been known to live without it—so that but for that little pan of water, which was found almost unexpectedly, we should have lost both oxen and donkeys, and as Tinka says, ' very few of the people with us would have got through ' ; for when the oxen returned that evening, the Masaroa sucked out of the ground the last drop of water they could procure.

" As for myself, a very little more of that sort of fare would have been too much for me. I do not mean that I suffered seriously from thirst, but I got into a very reduced state.

" After giving the cattle a night's rest, we started early on Thursday morning for the Mababi, Tinka and the other huntsmen of the company riding on to find the nearest water, as we had only a very limited supply in the waggon. I had but a pint and a half for a four days' journey ; nor had we any meat, no game having been killed in the desert. I had meal with me, but could not cook it for want of water, so my staple supply was a few dry peaches which I had brought from Sho-shong. On Friday, July 21st, we were still a long way from the Mababi River. I had finished my supply of water the day before, and the natives declared that they were all dead.

" My conviction was that we should not suffer from thirst much longer. I was lying back in the waggon, and had just mentioned to the Lord that promise: 'Their water shall be sure,' when a young man of the company asked me if I wished to drink. Three Masaroa, sent by Tinka, had brought three calabashes full of water for us, so that we all had a drink. The next thing was to try and find a little food. Setobi was too much knocked up to go and hunt, so I started with one of Tinka's men to look for something. We walked a long way through thick wood but got nothing; and then finding we were too far from the waggon to be sure of meeting it again, we decided to make for the Mababi River.

" After wandering along through thick wood and bush, and patches of long, reedy grass, we struck a footpath leading in the direction of the river. Just as the sun was sinking I shot an antelope ; it rolled over, then got up and ran into some bush. The man who was with me said it would soon die, but that we must push on as the river was very far away yet. So on we went, the night setting in clear, so that we could see the path. On and on we walked for a long time, till at last through the trees we saw the fires of a camp of Masaroa Bushmen.

" All had gone to sleep in circular holes about the size of large cart wheels. A small fire burnt in the centre. Hearing us approach, the men sprang instantly to their feet with their weapons in their hands, but seeing that I was a friend and not a lion or a Matabele warrior, they made room for us to lie down beside one of their fires. Towards morning lions came round and disturbed the camp. A few nights before a lion had dragged a woman off from one of the sleeping groups. The men ran after the brute with tufts of burning grass in their hands, compelling him to drop his prey ; and now that I had come along they wanted me to dress her wounds. Before I left the neighbourhood she was able to walk about again and to see to her domestic duties

" At the first streak of dawn all are astir in these Bushmen encampments Even the little children scatter like wild things to gather berries, or a red tree seed for their morning's pottage. The women dig up edible roots and bring water from distant water holes in the entrails of one of the larger animals, or in ostrich eggs held together in a roughly made net bag. Tortoise shells are used as cooking pots unless their men folk are rich enough to buy clay pots from the Bechuana. The men hunt big game, using a small bow and poisoned arrows. One night a hyena had the audacity to come near to some Bushmen sleeping a short distance from my waggon. They rose in an instant and were after him with their spears. It was a clear moonlight night, and we saw the hunters racing along, one on each side of the savage animal, probing him with their spears, and nimbly avoiding his side rushes, and the snap of his powerful jaws.

"Next morning I started along the river, which we found was close by, to some Basubia towns. On the way I met Tinka returning. He wished to wait for the waggon so I gladly sat down with him, and it came along during the day. These nine long, long days I shall not soon forget."

In visiting the villages in this district, Arnot says : " I was very well received at the first one. The people all turned out to listen to the Word, and then brought me three baskets of corn. But at the second my reception was a saucy one, and the people were not much inclined to listen to ' this new thing ' ; at first, in fact, they refused altogether. I asked them if they would hear me if I returned. This they promised to do. As I was moving off they changed their minds, and said they would hear me now. The tardiness of the older men in allowing me to read the Word of God, and to speak, seemed to have a good effect in rousing the curiosity of the young men, for they listened eagerly. One man doubly repaid me for all their grunts by a deep sigh, which seemed to come from his heart, and told what the lips could not have spoken."

CHAPTER IV

FIRST EXPERIENCES WITH CARRIERS

AS Tinka and his men were unable, owing to the prevalence of the tsetse fly, to proceed beyond the Mababi flat Arnot had to make his own arrangements for carriers. The first of many trying experiences in engaging and governing a body of natives in Central Africa now came to him. From the villages of the Basubia Arnot succeeded in engaging fifteen porters. His party, including five others not employed by him, but who availed themselves of the opportunity of company in crossing the thirst-land which lies between the Mababi and the Chobe River, started on July 31st, 1882. Arnot, with these twenty natives, and his three donkeys, started off in bright spirits.

"The first march," he says, "was very tiresome, being across the bed of reeds and marsh into which the Mababi River flows—an immense bed of slush, and of reeds which towered a long way above one's head, and at times were so close together that one could not see his neighbour a few steps on before. We found the ground, or rather the layer of rotten reeds and sand, very difficult to walk over, and we sank at times almost up to our knees. I thought we should never get the donkeys through; but by about four o'clock in the afternoon we managed to get on to solid ground, and made for a Masaroa town, where we expected to find water. The water pit being nearly dry there was nothing for the poor donkeys. We remained there for the night, as I expected the the waters in front would also fail us, and I had made up my mind not to leave until my donkeys had a good drink. The Masaroa kept on drawing water, and scarcely left us enough to drink; still I waited patiently, and after midnight, when the water had gathered again, I sent out six men who emptied the pit, and brought enough for the donkeys.

"*August 1st.*—We were up before daybreak and off as

quickly as possible, having a long and probably dry tramp before us. We got on well to-day, having to go over good firm ground, though the bush was very thick and thorny. Before sundown we chose as comfortable a looking place as possible, and in about half-an-hour's time the men made a kotla. The Basubia know well how to make one snug for the night. They cut down branches of trees and stick them in the ground, forming a half circle, bring wood for the fire (we burn no less than seven big fires all night), and cut grass to sleep on. Then the bundles are brought and laid down at my head, and Setobi puts the kettle on the fire. After supper, leaving a little in the pots for an early morning repast—we cook but one meal a day—I read to the men in Sechuana and pray. It does not take much rocking to send me to sleep.

"*August 2nd.*—Made a good start this morning, and walked a long way ; the sand was very heavy, but we pushed on hard, expecting to get water at a place called Caucon. Arriving at the pan we were disappointed to find that elephants had been there before us, and that they had drunk up all the water. This is rather a serious fix, as the donkeys, being almost done up with carrying heavy loads, refuse to eat, and drag along painfully , besides, our drinking water is exhausted, and we are fully 60 miles from the River Chobe. Two of the men set to work digging a well at the foot of the pan, but after going through a little damp mud, turned up nothing but dry white sand. After prolonged consultation (and, I assure you, I earnestly consulted the Lord in the matter), I decided not to go on further, but the next morning to send the men out in all directions in search of water. The lives of the whole party depended on our finding water on the morrow, as already most of us were much exhausted, having gone over 70 miles of rough, weary country in the last three days.

"*August 3rd.*—Early this morning I sent Setobi with six men and the donkeys in the direction of the Sambuti River, hoping to find water thereabouts. Another party set out in the direction of the Caucon Hill to dig a well in a hollow there, while I ' remained by the stuff ' with a Basubia. We have only about half a pint of water, which at the present moment is worth more to me than half a ton of gold. I am hopeful that Setobi will find water ; if he does not he need not return ; but all is well for it is in my Lord's hands. As yet I have lacked no good thing, and am persuaded He will not leave me now. His presence and His promises are better than water.

"*Afternoon.*—Those who had gone out to dig for water returned without finding any, and, looking very downcast, they all began sucking away at the damp mud close by. I tried to suck some water out of the mud, but it was something like the dregs of a farmyard ; so I gave up, and returning to the kotla fell asleep ! I had not slept long when one of the men awoke me with ' Monare ! look ! look ! ' and I saw at some little distance a string of men coming, each with a calabash full of water over his shoulder. Setobi had met a party of Tinka's Bushmen hunters who were following the spoor of the elephants. The Bushmen took Setobi to one of their secret water stores, where the donkeys got a drink, and enough water was also left to succour us. I need not say how thankful I felt for this deliverance.

"*August 4th.*—We were a little longer in starting this morning as I had to readjust the men's bundles ; they were beginning to complain about the weight of them. We made about 80 miles to-day over heavy sand, passed the Gorgoli Hills, and camped in the midst of a very dense forest, as we found we could not get through it before sunset.

"*August 5th.*—Had a long tramp to-day through a beautiful country, thickly wooded and full of game. During the last few days I have seen quite a lot of giraffes , the country here is full of them. We arrived in the evening at a pit with a little water in it, which we reached after some digging. The men are getting very troublesome, fretting about their loads, and demanding gunpowder ; in fact, they made quite a revolt this afternoon. Bringing their loads to me, they laid them down, saying they would not go further, but would return home unless I gave them my powder. I sat down beside the stuff, looked at them awhile, and soon they began to shoulder their sticks. I said it was all right, and bade them ' Samæa sintly,' i.e. ' Go pleasantly.' This rather amused them ; their scowling faces relaxed a bit, but they began again, trying with their threatenings and impudence to rouse my temper. I answered all their talk with ' I hear you,' until they gradually subsided. You see I am getting a taste of some of the difficulties of travelling in this country. In the evening the man who had been the most troublesome, and had led on the others, seemed somewhat sorry for the way he had spoken to me, and began saying what great respect he had for missionaries. I shall watch him closely in future. Another cause for grumbling turned up in the evening. The food supply was running short, as we had shot no game, and I had to serve out a small allowance.

" *Sunday, August* 6*th*.—I was compelled, for the sake of food for the men, to move off this morning. Going in front to look for game, I came across a large troop of zebras, and also found an ostrich's egg, which will serve for my dinner. We camped about eleven o'clock, and I sent five men out to hunt the zebras.

" We are now close to the Chobe River. I shall never forget the effect that the first sight of that great stream had, not only upon myself, but also upon the poor men with me. What a feeling of disappointment came over me when I found that I was satisfied with only a few cups full, whereas I felt I could have drunk buckets full. This morning, before starting, the men had a sort of religious service over their guns. Laying their firearms (six in all) down in a row, they all sat around them, and one began to sing a dirge and to tap each gun, while the rest were keeping time by beating the palm of one hand with the fist of the other. They then sprinkled the guns with water, and finished up with a long shout. This they repeated twice, saying it was to make their guns kill well.

" This evening the men returned with a young zebra. Now, at last, I have found out the reason why they have gone on so unwillingly for a day or so, and are loth to go down and camp on the Chobe, as I would wish. ' Did not the marauding Barotse,' they say, ' live across the river ? If they should happen to see our fires would they not come over and kill us all ? ' They have been hearing from the Masaioa that the Barotse are vowing destruction on the Basubia who fled to the Mababi, saying that when the rains fall they will come down and kill them all. It seems that the Barotse have been victorious over the Bashukulumbe, and are now scattering in all directions the inhabitants north of the Zambesi. The last news is that they are among the Batoka in the hills, and are killing them off. Oh, the terribleness of war ! When I was in Natal, the Boer War was threatening to break out again, and feeling was running high. I had scarcely arrived in the Transvaal when war broke out among the natives over the border, and I ran a narrow escape of being commandeered for military service. On arriving at Shoshong, the first news I heard was that the Matabele were expected, and that in all directions the cattle of the Bamangwato were coming in. The morning after my arrival there all the men of the town were turned out on parade to prepare for immediate action, but news came in in a few days that the Matabele had turned. At Mababi I heard of ravages and bloodshed, quite near, by a company of the Matabele. The Masaroa of a whole town, whom Tinka was expecting to come and hunt for him, were massacred; and had the Matabele troop been a little stronger they would have come on to the Mababi. Now that I am nearing the Zambesi, reports of war and bloodshed increase more and more.

"*August 8th.*—A fair supply of zebra flesh has been brought in by the men, and all round the camp to-day flesh, cut in long strips, is hung on long poles to dry. A troop of zebras passed close to our camp, and my three donkeys seeing them started after them at full gallop, and soon joined them, when the troop made off. Setobi, and the other Bechuana, went in pursuit of them Hour after hour passed by with no news of the donkeys, and I confess I felt very uncomfortable, as the men seemed ready to leave me at a moment's notice. With my donkeys gone, and myself a hundred miles from any inhabited part, what could I do ? Greatly to my relief, just as the sun was setting, the donkeys appeared with the two Bechuana. We are surrounded for miles and miles with thick woods, and it looked a hopeless task to follow them. ' Bob,' however, did not seem to take so well to his new companions as the other two donkeys did, and withdrew from them. Ramatlodi, the Bushman, made up to him, and, wisely mounting, whipped him up. ' Bob ' made off at a run, kept most faithfully to the spoor of the other two donkeys and the zebras, and after a long run got up with them. The donkeys were by this time fighting with the zebras, and kicking each other. When Ramatlodi showed himself, the zebras scampered away, and the donkeys submitted to be driven back. The man had gone fully twelve miles after them.

"*August 9th*—After drying about 200 lbs of flesh I got a start this evening, and camped close by the Chobe, which flows into the Zambesi.

"*August* 10*th*.—During the night I lost my faithful dog Judy. She was barking away at my side, and I looked up and told her to be quiet. In a short time she began barking again ; then followed a deep growl with a rush, and poor Judy squeaked her last. I had scarcely time to look up ere a tiger had cleared the fires, and was off. The brute must have been very hungry to have ventured so near for a supper. These tigers, properly leopards, are very plentiful and destructive, and, in fact, though not so powerful, are more dangerous than lions.

" We had a good day's journey along the Chobe to-day ; on the whole the ground was good for walking, but we had to wade through one lagoon. We just get glimpses of this great river, the reeds are so tall and thick. It is, however, a refreshing sight to see such an immense body of water rolling along. The men are fond of their river, and have been singing away at their old canoe songs, which are very musical and plaintive.

"*August* 11*th*.—The river is now running in one broad, deep channel close to the path. It is quite a treat to walk along the thickly wooded bank, clad with all sorts of tropical creepers and flowers. The trees are full of monkeys, baboons, and beautiful birds. Every now and then a troop of antelopes scamper past, and on the river are all kinds of rare and splendid water-fowl. To-day I saw an immense hippopotamus rolling about in the water. Everything is the perfection of beauty and symmetry ; and the fearful, suspicious way in which my men creep along declares that ' only man is vile.' They are in mortal dread of their lives. We sighted a town on the other side of the river, and this disturbed them greatly. At first they refused to sleep at the place I had chosen for the night, and wanted to hide in the forest. They declared that the Barotse would cross during the night and kill them all. Talk as I will I cannot lessen their fears. They refuse to go along the river any further, and say that unless I turn from the river and make for Leshuma across the sand-belt they will forthwith desert. I refused at first, but when I saw that they really meant it I gave in

"*August* 12*th*.—After a restless night on the part of the men we started early this morning along the river for one short march. It was most impressive, yet I must say I could not help laughing to see how the men stole along through the high grass, glancing every now and then across the river, fearing that they

F. S. ARNOT, AGED 23

At the time of starting on his first journey to Africa.

F. S. ARNOT, AGED 31

After his eventful journey from Natal to Bihé and Benguella, and the sources of the Congo and Zambesi.

might be seen by their dreaded enemies. At last we turned from the river inland, or, speaking more correctly, west by one point north. The sand was very heavy, and reflected the heat of the sun painfully. We pushed on hard, hoping to reach a Masaroa well in the evening. We had a most tiresome walk, and shortly after sunset arrived at a well, very deep, but with nothing in it.

"*Sunday, August* 13th.—I sent three men to dig the well deeper, hoping to strike water, so that we might rest to-day, but it was in vain, so off we started. The sun was very hot, yet we could not wait, and walked on without resting to take breath more than five or ten minutes at a time. At last we reached a well with some water in it, which, after a little digging, proved sufficient for the night. I feel as if I were lying on raw flesh because my back is so sunburnt.

"*August* 14th.—About midday, as we reached a hill-top, we came in sight of Leshuma with the Zambesi in the distance. I sat down to rest a bit, and wondered at the grace and tenderness of my God who had brought me thus far. I sang the hymn, ' Simply Trusting,' and it filled my soul—not that my trust has ever been so real as the words of the hymn express, but I felt it was no vain thing to trust the Lord, even though my measure had been very small. Above all, there is a fullness of joy in proving the Word of God, in finding that the same wondrous grace of God which gave us promises is able to fulfil and does fulfil them to us. At length, after a long two months' journey from Shoshong I have reached the Zambesi River without a blister on my feet, and, but for my sorely burnt skin, in perfect health. The sun has in no way affected my head.

"*August* 15th.—The Basubia would not go down to Leshuma until Ramatlodi and I went on to see if the way were clear. I found Leshuma, which had been a trading station, nearly deserted ; only a few Masaroa women and children were there. I sent to let the Basubia know that the way was certainly clear enough, and they stole down, deposited their bundles, and forthwith demanded their pay. They wanted to return at once, and refused to go to Panda-ma-tenka. Ramatlodi also wished to go back, so that I was left with three donkeys, Setobi and a boy, to go on to Panda-ma-tenka. No natives were living near ; they had all fled before a scouring band of

D

Matabele. After a deal of talking I paid off the men, giving each of them fully ten charges of powder, caps, half a bar of lead, and half a yard of cloth, which is big pay. How I was ever to reach Panda-ma-tenka I did not know. After paying all off, I gathered them together, and, mustering all my Sechuana, gave them a long address, speaking for fully an hour. I finished by showing them how cruel they were in forsaking me with little food by me, and no means of getting to Panda-ma-tenka. I should have to leave all my goods to be stolen by the Masaroa, or I should have to burn them ; how would they answer to Khama when called upon to account for their actions, and how would they answer to God for leaving His servant to perish in the desert ?   Ramatlodi was the first to give in, though he was previously bent on returning   He, no doubt, felt the force of my remarks in speaking of Khama, and what he would think of his actions.   He said he would not leave me but would go to Panda-ma-tenka.   Then three Basubia said they would not leave, and two Masaroa, who before refused my proffered hire, offered their services ; so that with Setobi I have my full complement of carriers. I will drive the donkeys myself, so that we shall get along famously.   My purpose is to take a straight line from here to Panda-ma-tenka.   The temptation is certainly strong to go round by the Victoria Falls ; but as neither the time nor the money I have belongs to me, I do not feel justified in adding three or four days' journey for mere sightseeing.

" This evening, since the Basubia who refused to go further have departed, a much happier feeling seems to be among my men. I have served out as liberal a supply of food to them as I can, and they are talking of how well they will get along. We have three days' desert between this and Panda-ma-tenka, but the men say they are willing to travel day and night if I like.

"*August* 16*th.*—Last night we made a good long journey, and towards morning slept a few hours. The road, though through thick bush and sand, is easily followed. I was up and off before the sun rose, and towards midday we lay down in the shade a short time. A small abscess has formed under my toe, causing much pain ; but with a long stick as a crutch, I have managed to keep up with the rest. The night was dark, and the road bad, but we kept on, expecting at carry fresh

start to reach the Gezumba pan before halting. At last we
gave in, and lay down beside some thick bush for shelter,
knowing we were not far from water.

"*August 17th.*—My toe being very painful, I started before
the others and hobbled along. A half-hour's walk brought us
to the Gezumba pan, which is within three hours' walk of
Panda-ma-tenka. But for my toe I should go on, but shall
rest to-day.

" This is the quickest march I have yet had, doing 60 miles
in one day and two nights. The distance was considered by
the Bushmen, from whom I got directions as to the road, to be a
three days' journey. I hope the donkeys feel grateful. I
certainly felt anything but fresh to-day ; the painful shuffling
on the outer edge of my foot over the last 20 miles has strained
all the muscles of my body. I lanced the toe to-day, and shall
get along nicely to-morrow.

"*August 18th.*—Felt alright this morning, and was able to
walk with comparative comfort ; so I set off before the rest,
and reached Panda-ma-tenka about midday. It is a little
clump of huts on the top of slightly rising ground, surrounded
by low marsh. The Jesuits have built a comfortable-looking
house and chapel. The rest of the people live in huts, among
whom are Mr. Blockley, a trader, also a Dutchman, and the
wives and families of three or four Hottentot hunters, who at
present are out hunting Mr. Blockley received me very
kindly, and gave me a grass hut to live in as long as I may
remain here In a short time my men and donkeys arrived,
and I settled with them as liberally as I could. I also sold my
donkeys, and packed all my belongings in loads suitable for
the shoulders and sticks of the carriers I should engage here.
The natives in this district divide the load they carry into
two equal parts, fastening them on to the two ends of a stick
in Chinese fashion."

CHAPTER V

ARNOT wrote from Panda-ma-tenka on August 18th, 1882 : " The missionary, M. Coillard, from Basutoland, with his heroic wife, had already visited the Zambesi, and had sent messengers up to the Barotse Valley, asking permission from Liwanika to be allowed to return with a party and begin work in his country. Liwanika sent him a warm invitation. Coillard then left for South Africa and Europe in order to raise the interest of his friends and supporters in this great Upper Zambesi field. On M. Coillard's return from Europe to South Africa the Gun (Basuto) War broke out, so that he was unable to proceed at once to the Zambesi ; but, hearing that I was passing through Natal on my way to the interior, he wrote asking me to assure Lewanika, if I should succeed in reaching his country, that he had not forgotten his promise and hoped soon to leave Basutoland for the Barotse. It was my ambition to cross the Zambesi and reach the highlands beyond, without going up the river to the Barotse capital, but Mr. Blockley assured me that this was impossible, that the only road open to anyone crossing the Zambesi was that which led to the capital. So adding this report to M. Coillard's request I came to the conclusion that He Whom I sought to serve was directing me to go to the Barotse.

" I accompanied Mr. Blockley in a waggon journey he was about to make to the junction of the Zambesi and the Chobe Rivers, as he was going there to buy corn from the natives living on the north bank. It was pleasant to be in an ox waggon again."

" *August 25th.*—Off as early as possible for the Zambesi. The path lay through a thickly wooded tropical valley, full of rich herbage. We reached the river about midday, but as the wind was very strong and the water rough, the old man in charge of the ferry would not answer our call for some time ; so I was able to look round and take a good view of the river. We rested at the point where the waters of the Chobe and the Zambesi meet. The Zambesi at that point is as broad as the Clyde at Dumbarton, and is very deep from bank to bank ; the Chobe is a little narrower. Late in the afternoon the old man started in his canoe, but instead of coming over to us he went a long way up the river and crossed to the island of Inparairie. However, he came down after a time and landed where we were. After talking and waiting he agreed to ferry us over for so much. Three trips took us and our bundles across in his cranky canoe. Everything got wet, and I had to sit down in water. The edge of the canoe—the trunk of a tree shaped a bit and hollowed out—was scarcely a handbreadth from the water, and all the little waves came right in, so that Setobi had a hard half-hour's work in baling out the water.

" The boatman understood that I was a servant of Mr. Blockley's, and so took me on board his craft without any questions. We had not got far, however, when Mr. Blockley's boy, who was rowing in front, told him I was a Marute, i.e. a teacher. Much alarmed at this, the old man wanted to take me back again. The boy seemed to understand the difficulty, for he put matters right by assuring him that I was not one of the Panda-ma-tenka Marutes (the Jesuits who are staying there), but quite different. After a good deal of explanation on the boy's part, the boatman pushed on and took me across. Mr. Blockley came in the next boatload, and was able to pacify the old man. It seems that he has orders not to allow the Jesuits to cross the river until the chief sends down word. After settling with the boatman, we set off for the next nearest town, intending to sleep there.

" The north bank of the river rises steep from the water's edge, so our way lay uphill. As the sun was setting I had a grand view of the river, and of miles upon miles of country stretching far south, beautifully undulating and thickly wooded. We arrived at a little Batoka town in the evening, and were well received. The people showed us into a reed yard, with a hut in the centre for our use, but we preferred, as the night was fine, to sleep on the open ground. They gave us a goat to kill, and food for the men, at the same time bringing a supply of firewood and making a grass hut. The reception these Batoka gave us was so simple and kindly that they quite won my heart. I felt I had not thought of them in vain, and, without going another step, would willingly have settled amongst them ; but they are a conquered people, and therefore I must see the king of the country ere I can settle in it.

" *August* 26*th*.—After Mr. Blockley had bought a little corn that was brought here, we set off for the town of Mogumba, the chief of this part of the river. We found it partly deserted through failure of crops, all the men being out hunting, and Mogumba at Shesheke. His chief wife, however, entertained us to the best of her ability.

" We left Mogumba in the afternoon, and after walking ten or twelve miles, lay down under some trees growing by a clear stream of water, trusting to big fires to keep the lions off us. Tired out, however, with the long walk through grass and bush, we all fell asleep and the fires went out. But God guarded His reckless, would-be servant. For it so happened that we had lain down beside a game pit, and towards morning my men ran out and speared a huge lion that had fallen into it. There was no doubt but that I and my men had taken the place of the bait that allured this monster to his destruction.

" *Sunday, August* 27*th*.—Most of the boys who had offered their services ran off early this morning, so I remained at Mbova until evening, and went a short distance with two men who were willing to go with me. I might as well have remained until Monday, but was anxious to get out of Mbova as quickly as possible, hoping to get a good night's sleep. That town lies in the middle of an immense marsh, and at night it swarms with mosquitoes ; it is also a regular malaria swamp all the year round. I slept at night by the side of a small river in the middle of a thick wood

" *August* 28*th*.—After some trouble I started this morning, and got on well for a time. It is very pleasant sailing along this immense river. After a few hours, however, the boatmen landed me on the bank, and quietly set to work landing my stuff. I could not believe Shesheke was so near, but they assured me it was near to some trees close by, and that they landed me to avoid a long bend in the river ; so I let them go, and found out their deceit, to my sorrow, afterwards. The two boys I had with me as carriers were from the same town as the boatmen, and were privy to the plan. After a long six hours' walk, mostly through a labyrinth of broken down reeds, with mud and slush underneath, I arrived at Shesheke, and was glad to find Mr. Westbeech there. (Mr. Westbeech was the first South African trader to visit the Zambesi Valley) Welcoming me kindly he said that he had been detained for several weeks, much against his will, but was now expecting to be off at once.

" Having been introduced to the headmen of the town, I told them my errand, and they listened attentively. Their answer was that I was so far welcome, and that I had perfect liberty to go on to the king, but that the king's headmen were tired of teachers coming to the country and running away again Their spokesmen referred to M. Coillard's visit, and said he promised to return, but had not come. They heard last year that he was coming, and they hear again that he is coming now, but they do not see him. They then spoke of the Jesuits, and how they had deceived them. As to my coming amongst them, they said they did not know what I meant to do, whether I would just see the chief and run away again, or remain.

" This tribe, or rather these tribes, are governed by the king and his headmen, who have a voice in most affairs. They seemed determined not to be cheated any more. I tried to assure them that my intentions were sincere in coming amongst them, and that I was now willing, if I got permission, to remain with them. That pleased them better : in fact the whole tribe have been waiting for some teacher, and were compelled to think about receiving the Jesuits, although they did not like them. Boats are expected from the king every day to take them up.

" The headmen had a long talk over matters, and had Setobi with them to question him all about me. They told me in the afternoon that, as headmen of Shesheke, they had decided to receive me as a teacher into their country, on the understanding that I would not run away and leave them.

" After a good deal of talking, it was arranged that Mr. Westbeech should go on to the king and tell him of my desire, and get him to send boats down to Shesheke ; and that I should first return with a boat, which the headmen would place at my disposal, to Panda-ma-tenka, and fetch the things I had left, and a few supplies to last me some months among the Barotse.

" The week I was at Shesheke I had several companies in
my little reed yard listening; and one evening I overheard
one man—a young headman, who had attended regularly—
going over what he had heard. ' The good Shepherd; He gave
His life for the sheep' (followed by exclamations); then,
' Eo Mora oa Modimo ' (' He is the Son of God ')—this he
repeated—' Mora oa Modimo ' (' Son of God ! Son of God ! ')—
and he passed on. Not liking to disturb his thoughts I left him
alone, thanking God in the depths of my soul that these
words had for the time got a place in his mind and made him
think. He is a bright, thoughtful, young man, 24 or 25 years
of age.

" *Sunday, September 3rd*, 1882.—A letter arrived to-day
from the Jesuits who had come down to the Leshuma ferry,
asking for boats to take them to Shesheke. The headmen sent
word that they must wait until a reply came from the king in
answer to a message they had sent by Mr. Westbeech. I have
spent a pleasant week here, and have got on well with the
people. Shesheke is a town of slaves, three-fourths of the
population being the absolute property of the other fourth.
The people like to come and hear me read out of the Sechuana
Testament, and they ask all sorts of childish questions. Their
ignorance, to a man, is absolute, and their depravity complete.
Human sacrifices, burning of witches, cutting the flesh, etc.,
are the outcome of a religion of dark superstition.

" *Sept. 5th.*—Left Shesheke in a boat for Mbova. Slept the
first night on a reed island, the second on a mud-bank, as the
lions were too troublesome for us to sleep on the mainland.

" *Banks of Zambesi, Sept. 6th.*—As my big diary letter is not
altogether the quite homely letter of a fond son to his mother,
but is more a record of facts, I write this in addition. I am
now down on my way from Shesheke by boat to Leshuma, and
will walk from there to Panda-ma-tenka, and have stopped
to-day to give my men a feed. There is quite a famine all
along the river just now, so I halted this morning and shot
a gnu close to the river, which means a lot of fresh meat. I
have been compelled against my inclination to take the shooting into my own hands as Setobi was wasting all my ammunition and bringing little in. And travelling at this famine-
time is out of the question without a good deal of game meat.
Travelling on the river is very pleasant work indeed. It is a

lovely river. The size of it would cause one to expect nothing
in the way of soft beauty, but some of the inland scenes, and
beautifully banked spreading sheets of water, surpass description. The boat I am travelling in is the usual hollow tree, but
my men make me very comfortable so that I have nothing
to do but to lie back with an umbrella over me and read, or
enjoy the beautiful river scenery. Those boatmen give me no
trouble whatever as Ratua sent a man in charge with them.

" I have often written to you in former letters about the
Jesuits. You know how much I was exercised about them,
and their great exertions to close the whole country up against
the messengers of the Gospel. Another week or two and they
would have succeeded. Their presents were prepared. Everything was ready for making what would I fear have proved
to be a too successful overture. They only waited for a supply
of corn. Now, how was it ? Was it mere chance work that I
arrived at Panda-ma-tenka at this very time, and that two
days after my arrival Blockley, much against his will, was
compelled to cross the river and come up some distance in
search of corn, taking me with him ? How was it that Westbeech was detained at Sheshcke 25 days waiting for a boat
(the only man in the country who could interpret for me), and
that when the talking was finished his boat arrived ? It had
only been a few miles away all the time in some reeds. As
Mr. Westbeech said, my coming now had preserved all the
Barotse kingdom, and in fact nearly all the country north of
the Zambesi, and south of the Kafue River, for Protestant
missionaries. It is, however, too soon to say so yet, but if such
should prove to be the case, I am sure you will rejoice with me.
Not that I have done anything, for indeed I have done nothing
but simply move on, but in the might and power and wisdom
of our God.

" *Sept. 8th.*—My men tried to frighten me into dealing out
to them some extra rations. Coming up to a small reed-
covered island, they all landed, professing to be tired ; and as
it is not safe to sit in their canoes when they stop—the crocodiles having a trick of coming alongside slyly and whisking one
into the water with their tails—I got out with the men, spread
my mat, lay down, and read a book that had interested me.
My men stole back to the boat and suddenly pushed out to
mid-stream and feigned to be paddling off, saying they would

not return unless I promised them more pay. I lay perfectly
still, however, never even looking at them or letting them
know that I heard. The book, I remember, was very interesting. I had got it from Mr. Westbeech, and it contained the
lives of Scottish Covenanters. After having pulled down-
stream for some miles, going out of my sight, they returned in
about an hour's time and entreated me to enter the boat.
I professed to be annoyed at their importunity, shut my book,
and got in ; and off we went, the men rowing as they had not
done since we started, in order to make up for lost time.

"God has not opened up my way so far, to leave me now ;
this I know. He does not so work. 'The kingdom of God is
not meat and drink, but righteousness, peace, and joy in the
Holy Ghost '—not earthly comforts, but heavenly and spiritual
things. My greedy flesh shrinks from banishment for ' a little
while ' from kith and kin, but there are ' better things ' remaining to me. Let my one desire in this life be to possess to
the full those ' better things ' at whatever cost to the lesser.
' Ye shall burn no leaven, *nor any honey*, in any offering of the
Lord made by fire ' (Lev. ii. 11) It is ours then to lay aside
the honey of this life, and let Him Who filleth all things fill us
with Himself.

"I used to like a quiet walk through the woods, and enjoyed
the solitude, but I cannot do so here ; the lions are too numerous and very dangerous. During this week I have heard of
two persons being killed by lions close by. The Lord, however,
has wonderfully preserved me from wild animals, though they
have been very near to me at times.

"I am now in the hands of the raw Zambesi native, the
noisy, drum beating, quarrelsome forest and river negro ; so
different from the quiet and stealthy Bushman, or the more
thoughtful Bechuana, whose one business it is to mind sheep
and cattle. Although these river men have a bad character,
and are fond of blackmailing and plundering, yet again and
again one or other brought me milk, meal, or some such delicacy
from a distant village when they saw that I could hardly eat
the boiled corn, dried elephant's flesh and putrid meat stolen
from the crocodiles' larders, which was our usual fare.

"*September 12th.*—I reached Panda-ma-tenka again yesterday, after a long, dry walk of 85 miles, mostly through heavy
sand, from the junction of the Chobe and Zambesi, which took

us two days and a half, and not a drop of water did we find
for the last 70 miles   The last night and day I suffered a
good deal, but thank God for the strength given to take me
through.

" The heat just now is very great, and will be until the
rains fall. I fain hoped to get a week's rest here, but the
carriers who came with me from Shesheke refuse to stay an
hour longer than to-morrow afternoon. They are in terror
of their lives, lest the Matabele should come and kill them ;
so I have been working night and day making up bundles of
cloth, beads, food, etc., and start off to-morrow post haste.
To a casual observer, my hastening so to get away would seem
like impatience ; but I cannot get other carriers, and must
go. Were I to delay too long, they would simply take up their
weapons and march off without even giving me warning. The
last six weeks of almost constant travelling on foot, through
a rough-and-ready country, has reduced me to a bit of bone
and muscle—a sort of walking machine. Yet I enjoy the
greatest natural blessing—perfect health. I am writing this
when I ought to be sleeping, but hope to snatch time on the
way down to the river to write more.

" Quite a famine is raging ; all over the country people are
dying of starvation. It has often been hard to get food, and
I have lived mostly on the flesh of game dried in the sun.

" *September* 14*th.*—Started again for Shesheke, feeling a
little unwell ; as we went on matters did not improve, and
my men grew very troublesome. For most of the road, as I
have said, there is no water, and my carriers seized all the
water we had and demanded payment of it from me. Setobi
was getting sick. At last, on the second day, after having gone
about 40 miles through the desert, I had to lie down, and very
soon became unconscious. I was by this time in a high fever.
The men went on and left me and Setobi, who was as helpless
as myself. Fortunately a little boy had remained behind with
me, so I sent him, young as he was, through 30 miles of dangerous country to tell Mr. Blockley. He was a brave little chap,
and night for him had no terrors. For two nights and a day
I tossed about, suffering agonies from thirst and the blazing
sun. Vultures hovered overhead by day, and a gazelle looked
at me pitifully, and at night the hyena whooped at a distance.
On the third day I heard the crack of Blockley's whip a long

way off, and knew that my messenger had not failed me and that help had come."

Writing from Shesheke at the end of October Arnot said: "For five weeks I lay at Panda-ma-tenka; then, hiring Blockley's Scotch cart, I trekked to the Zambesi ferry. My men, I was told, had gone on to Shesheke, so I crossed the river hoping to overtake them on foot. But the fever had left me so weak that I could not follow the path, but wandered off it, and was unable to call back my guide. At last night came on. The path lay over a sharp hill covered with large boulders, in the midst of which I completely lost my way, wandered about from right to left, then lay down between two boulders, where I found myself fairly comfortable, as the stones were still radiating heat. I had not lain long when I heard a footstep in the distance On looking up, and watching in the direction from which the sound came, I saw the figure of a man, with a gun over his shoulder, walking along slowly in the direction I had come from. I called, and he at once replied and came over to me, when I found that he was one of the Bushmen I had hired at Leshuma, and that he was out in search of me. With his help I was able to reach Mbova shortly before midnight. The natives there provided me with a hut to sleep in, and brought food; but it was fully ten days ere I recovered the use of my limbs.

"Upon arriving at Shesheke I lay so still that my men thought I was dead. They drew my blanket over my head, and went off to arrange with Ratua, the chief, as to where to bury me. He pointed out a clump of trees and told them to dig my grave there. But I knew I was recovering, and with a plentiful supply of fresh milk I soon picked up, and was able to proceed with the canoes that Liwanika had sent for me.

"It is now seven months since I got news of any kind from the old country, and close on twelve months since I saw any periodical. I am quite shut in here; and, like Noah, have but the one window. The weakness resulting from the fever is lingering and depressing; but I trust soon to get over it. Excuse my shaky writing.

"I shall be the first Scotchman, and the second British subject, who has gone beyond Shesheke since Livingstone's visit; the other is Mr. Westbeech.

" This is a copy of the letter I received at Shesheke from Mr. Westbeech :

" ' LEALUI, *5th October*, 1882.

" ' DEAR SIR,—I have got permission from the chief for you to come on here, and this without much trouble. He sends you two boats, and both he and I shall anxiously await your arrival. He sends you two responsible people with them—the older one is named Monie-Ki-Umbwa, and the other Mato Kwan.

" ' You will have purchased food for the road by the time they arrive. If you have not, do so at once.

" ' Try and gain a good name amongst your boatmen, as they come from different kraals, and, of course, many questions will be asked them. If you shoot anything along the road, take as much as you will require for yourself, and from what part you like best, and give all the remainder to your headman, Monie-Ki-Umbwa, for division amongst your crews.

" ' The king must have brought about 20,000 head of cattle, taken in war, to the Barotse Valley, exclusive of what have died along the road from poverty and tsetse.

" ' Remember me to Ratua, and wishing you health and success,

" ' I am, yours faithfully,

" ' GEORGE WESTBEECH.'

" With fair prospects of a quick journey up the Zambesi, and a friendly reception from the chief Liwanika, I started from Shesheke. During the first few days the journey was very pleasant. Though still very weak, I enjoyed the varied scenes that pass before one on an African river.

" On one occasion, towards evening, going round a sharp bend in the river close to the bank, we came upon two lions that were sporting on a beautiful sandy beach. The male at once shook his shaggy head, lay down with his paws out as a cat does when watching a mouse, and kept his eye upon us. So close was my boat to the beast that I could distinctly see him closing one eye and opening the other alternately as he lay surveying us. The lioness walked up and down in a restless manner in front of a clump of reeds. The men assured me that she had cubs hidden there. At another point the boat was passing along the side of a steep bank, covered with a net-

work of roots, in the midst of which the paddler in front of me
spied a puff-adder coiled up. He immediately lifted his spear
from between his toes and threw it at the snake, which instantly
uncoiled itself and struck at its assailant, grazing my hat with
its fangs. The spear, however, had done its work, pinning the
lower part of its body to the ground, and in a short time my
men killed it.

"Shortly after leaving Shesheke I found the country entirely
deserted of people. Occasionally we came upon a few fishermen throwing their nets, or some wandering Basubia digging
for lotus roots among the lagoons and backwaters ; but when
they saw us they rushed off and hid themselves in the bush.
My men, however, assured me that there were many villages
on the hills on each side of the river ; but the poor people seem
to dread this great waterway, which no doubt has been used by
conquering tribes as a highway for their evil pursuits.

"Our difficulties began when we entered the cataract region.
Although the river was low at this time, the current was so
strong at many of the rapids that the boats had to be unloaded
and the goods carried overland, that the boats might be
dragged up the river empty. At Nyambe there is a decided
fall in the river, and we had to take both boats and goods
overland.

"After leaving Nyambe we were dependent entirely for
food on what we might kill in the bush. We were unfortunate
in this, however, and were obliged to have recourse to rather
mean ways of getting our supper. Crocodiles abound in this
great river, and they are very artful. When the larger game
come down to drink they creep up, and seizing them by the
nose, drag them under the water. By this means the crocodiles
always have their larders well supplied. It is their custom
to hide the food thus obtained well under the river's bank until
it becomes rather putrid, and to bring it to the surface for
airing before eating. I used to lie on the bank of the river
and watch these animals come up with perhaps a quarter of an
antelope, and by firing at their heads I compelled them to drop
their supper, which my men picked up from their boats, but
it afforded us anything but a dainty feast.

"On one occasion we made for the deserted camp of some
elephant hunters, hoping to pick up their scraps. My men
got a few bones to boil, and I tried to pound and boil for a

long time a piece of elephant's skin ; but, after all, it was not possible to eat it.

" As we approached the Gonye Falls the men had to carry the goods overland for three miles, and afterwards come back for the boats, so that we were delayed some days. I tried very hard to walk across the belt of sand, but failed completely, and my men had to rig up a hammock, and carry me after the boats and goods had been got over. We were entertained at the town of Silomba, a small river chief, who provided us with a little meal and maize-corn.

" From this point the banks of the river are less steep, and the country around us is more flat. A terrific hurricane from the south-west burst upon us one afternoon, lashing the river into violent waves, and compelling my boatmen to flee for shelter. No sooner had we touched the bank than my canoe, which had been gradually filling, sank. Nothing, however, floated away, as the men had taken the precaution to bind my bundles to the canoe with cords. So long as the storm lasted we could do nothing but seek to shelter ourselves under a few bushes.

" Later on, the men went down to the sunken canoe, and as the water was not deep, they succeeded in removing my goods without much difficulty. Their plan of getting the water out of the canoe was simple but ingenious. They seized the canoe by the bow, jerked it forward, and thus set the water within in motion , then they pushed the canoe back, and the water flowed out. By repeating this process the canoe was emptied of perhaps a ton of water in a few minutes.

" Heavy rains now set in. It was some days before I could get my blankets dried after their soaking in the river ; and thankful I was to reach the town of Nalolo, who is a sister of the chief Liwanika. She did her best to make us comfortable, and supplied me with food. My men built a long, low shed with reeds and grass, and kindled large fires, and, with sunshine for the next few days, I got my calico, clothes, and other things dried. The few books I had were more or less destroyed. When at last we had got things fairly comfortable again, and were hoping to start next day, heavy dark clouds arose from the south, which increased so quickly that in a short time the whole southern sky was inky-black. My men ran to the river, and drew the boats to shelter on the bank, cut a little extra grass and laid it on our shed, and as it faced the north we thought it might afford us sufficient shelter. The hurricane broke mercilessly over our little camp, and with such force as to carry all our shed and carefully made little huts, into the river, leaving me and my newly spread bed and a few precious bundles exposed to the torrents of rain that poured down for the first part of the night, and extinguished all our fires, leaving us in a more desolate and forlorn condition than before. A little sunshine, however, next day enabled me to dry things somewhat, and off we started, making our way through a flat, grassy country My boats were repeatedly chased by hippopotami. Along the banks of the river we saw large herds of cattle grazing. The population of the Barotse Valley, though considerable, is very much scattered ; but all the people are more or less, breeders of cattle.

"There is an open door for the Gospel here. I could not, in fact, with any comfort, now leave to return home. All the mass of the people along the river represent many tribes, formerly conquered by the Makololo, a Basuto tribe from the south, whose language is almost identical with that of the Bechuana. These conquered tribes, being all together, required one language, and, of course, they all learnt the Sekololo. Twelve years ago or so the Barotse, one of the conquered tribes, rose up and killed all the Makololo men (leaving only the women alive), but they retained the language of the Makololo, so that amongst these many tribes and peoples I can with comparative ease talk a little of the things of God, seeing that the Sechuana, which I have learned, is almost identical with their tongue. When last up the river large companies listened attentively to the reading of Scripture, and asked many questions. They have heard of teachers living among other tribes, and have a slight idea of one or two of the outward effects of the Gospel, but of the Gospel itself, or of God, they are thoroughly ignorant. They do speak of a god they call ' Nambi,' who lives among the stars, and they acknowledge his power over life and death ; but further than that I can say nothing. Otherwise, the depth of their heathenism seems unfathomable ; secret bloodshed, superstition and enchantments everywhere prevail. How we should rejoice and praise the Lord that even the ears of those who have for ages been in such a state should be opened to hear God's Word !

I do greatly thank the Lord for giving me such a privilege as to read and seek to make them understand it ; but the trying part of the work will not, I am sure, be forgotten in your prayers. Oh, the patience that is needed, seeing how bitter and deadly is the opposition of the medicine-men and doctors, who live by their craft ! The power of those men is very great, but ' God is stronger than His foes.' Surely I can but say, ' All my springs are in Thee ' ; for this work is too great for me.

"As for my soul's prosperity in this great country, I still ask for your prayers in a special way. I had thought that, being alone and away from all controversies, and many other evil influences, I should attain to a more spiritual and devoted state , but I have learnt that the one drag to a soul's communion with God is a thing tied to it, this old dead self, which, in the absence of Christian fellowship, is more inclined to increase in bulk in my solitude than to diminish. Yet, thinking of all, I can but magnify the grace and the wisdom of God."

E

CHAPTER VI

"*DECEMBER* 19*th*, 1882.—I arrived safely at Lealui on Nov. 20th. As the lukamba or landing place for the town was at that season some five miles distant, we had to wait for porters from the king to carry my bundles up to the capital. Night fell, so there was nothing for it but to huddle together without fires or shelter, and wait for the morning. We were cold and hungry, and my men so cross that they were ready to fight with one another over anything. Something had to be done, and the idea struck me of starting a needle-threading competition in the dark ; for in Africa the men are more interested in needles and in sewing than the women. To their great surprise I succeeded in threading the needle every time it came round to my turn ; and so hour after hour passed, but they could not do it, and had to give up from sheer exhaustion without finding out the trick of holding the eye of a needle up to a bright star.

" With morning light, porters arrived, and a horse from the king to take me to the reed and grass hut he had prepared. Liwanika came to greet me. I was much taken with his appearance—bright and smiling and alert. But, oh dear ! my hut had been built only the day before ; the ground was wet, the grass was wet through and through, and reeked , firewood was out of the question. A bush with a hollow wood stalk that grew in the plain like the castor-oil plant, was the only firewood available. Bouts of fever laid me prostrate every third or fourth day. I could neither eat nor sleep.

" To crown all my miseries I had to witness trials for witch-craft taking place daily in front of my hut. A small company gathered just in front of me, and began an animated discussion, which grew hotter and hotter, and shortly a large fire was kindled, and a pot of water set on it. The two persons charged had to wash their hands in the water, and if, after

24 hours, the skin came off, the victims were to be burnt alive. First one, then the other, dipped his hands in the fiercely boiling water, lifting some up and pouring it over the wrist. Twenty-four hours told its tale, and I saw the poor fellows march off to be burned before a howling, cursing crowd.

"One evening as I was sitting enjoying the cool evening air at my hut door, two young men came running rapidly towards me. I saw that one was bound, and that the other carried a short club in his hand. When well in front of my hut, and quite on the outskirts of the town, the man with the club gave his prisoner a sharp blow on the back of the head, killing him instantly. This was an execution, and the wild animals and vultures saw to the final disposal of the body.

"*March 2nd*, 1883. [To his mother.]—I write this short line in the hope that it may by some means reach you before the large one that is at present in process of scribation which I will send with the first certain opportunity. This letter goes to Panda-ma-tenka. From there it is possible that some men may be going to visit Lobengula, the king of the Matabele. From there it may go by occasional post or messenger to Tati, and Shoshong. I cannot write much as it may be opened many times. I am getting on fairly well, and am getting the confidence of many of the people here, and the affection of some who treat me very kindly, chief among whom is the king. To give you a running account of things : I arrived here on the 20th of November, 26 days by boat from Shesheke ; much weakness on the road, and one or two relapses of fever. Cataracts very bad ; rain, rain, all the way ; wet blankets, wet clothes ; robbed by the men the king sent to fetch me, and poor, weak Fred could only lie quietly and smile. Twenty-six days I won't forget, not so much because of any small suffering, but because of the goodness and comfort of the Lord. The king reserved me a house, and gave me an ox to kill. He provided food in abundance, and ordered one of his own servants to live with me and serve me. The king is a man about my own age, very pleasant looking, always smiling, fond of everything European ; eats always with a knife and fork ; favourite pastime making wooden spoons and drumsticks (drumming goes on in the kotla night and day). The people are fond of noise, and dance and sing continually. They come in troops to my house which is the museum of the town,

and the white man, I suppose, the living lion. They want to
feel my hair and see my feet. This I bear with, though I get
to plain words sometimes. Poor things! I fear they little
understand my mission. The fever has left my mind weak,
For some weeks I had forgotten almost everything, could
scarce speak my own language. . . . The more I think of it
the less possible it seems to me that this letter will reach you,
so that to write anything like a long one is difficult. A waggon
has arrived at Panda-ma-tenka, and goods have come up for
the king, but no letters for me except a few lines from Mr.
Westbeech. Where have all my home letters gone to? Last
letters dated 7th April, 1882, near a twelve - month ago.
Mr. Westbeech sent me up a small bag of wheat meal, a little
tea, coffee and cocoa, for which I am most thankful. At the
same time, after a long blank, the king gave me another ox to
kill so that I was able to dine on beef, bread and coffee.

"*March* 15*th*, 1883.—Sorry I have not been able to make
daily notes. It is only within the last few weeks that I have
felt my strength returning in any measure The first hut the
king gave me is now in ruins from the flood. He then gave
me another in the centre of the town, but it was dry for one
day only. One night of frightfully heavy rains flooded hut
and yard, and sadly wetted my small stock of goods. The
rain continued for days. The king could give me no dry hut,
so I just had to lie to, day after day, in that filthy round hut,
scarcely wide enough for me at full length, with my goods
rotting by my side, and a perfect swarm of rats devouring
everything, and running over me at night. There for ten long
days I sat on my stool in semi-darkness by day, or lay by
night, in perfect inactivity. At last the rains ceased a bit,
and I went out to seek a hut. I got one from a headman and
at once entered it. It was dry and comfortable, so I remained
there for ten days. The damp house, and about a month's
feeding on native porridge (without milk), morning, noon,
and night, brought on an attack of dysentery; yet I cannot
but recognise the hand of the Lord in preserving my life in
such trying circumstances.

" Towards the end of February, when the Zambesi overflows
its banks for miles on either side, the king and almost all the
people removed to their summer town, Mafula. Liwanika
invited me into his large boat (made of several canoes); and

perhaps 2,000 canoes accompanied us. This annual flitting is made the opportunity for a grand display of native African pageantry. Planks, hewn from great mahogany trees, are shaped and sewn together to make a barge capable of carrying the king's court intact. Here in the centre stand his seat of state and his drums, his flesh-pots are cooking over fires kindled on thick layers of clay ; his principal courtiers sit all around, and 40 headmen and nobles of the Valley punt and paddle with long poles, not to speak of the gang of slaves vigorously baling, and three or four ship's carpenters going about with bundles of bark-string oakum, stopping up the innumerable leaks and longing earnestly for the dry land to appear again. Hundreds of canoes, formed in battle array on either side, completed the spectacle.

" By this time I was on fairly good terms with Liwanika. He and his headmen had decided to wait for M. and Madame Coillard on the one condition that I would remain with him until they arrived. This I gladly consented to do.

" At Mafula I had much discomfort and losses by robbing. The king was taken ill, and then a lot of goods arrived from Mr. Westbeech. He asked me to receive them, and my hut was packed for days. I had nine men beside my own to provide for and look after for about 20 days. I also had a serious relapse of fever. The place was surrounded with marsh.

"*April 8th*, 1883 —My sickness is now over, and I am faring well, though food is very dear and scarce. I have had a school here for some little time. The boys learn pretty well, but it requires patience and perseverance to look after them. Hunting a young truant from house to house under a hot sun is not pleasant. The parents show little interest ; in fact, they have little influence over their children. The leather thong rules the family above a certain age.

" A short time after I began teaching, the king cross-questioned me as to what I had come to teach. I spoke to him of sin, death, and judgment, and of God's love in the gift of His Son, and he listened attentively. ' This,' I said, ' was my first and chief message, besides which I wanted to teach the children to read and write ; also all about the world they live in, and other things that white men know, which are good for all people to know.' The king then said, ' Yes, yes, that is good, to read, write, and to know numbers. But don't, don't teach them the Word of God ; it's not nice. My people are not all going to die now. No, no, you must not teach that in this country. We know quite enough about God and dying.' I kept silent till his excitement was over, and then said that we would talk again when he thought more. The school went on for two months longer, when it had to be stopped because of an affection of my eyes. After recovering I again had talks with his majesty on the above subjects. He never again got excited as before, and would occasionally express his confidence in me that I had come to teach them good things. He knew, he said, that I was one of God's men because I shewed that I loved the people and the children ; and one day without my asking he said that I could teach all his people and children the words of God. giving me perfect liberty in his country.

" For nearly six weeks I suffered severely from acute rheumatic arthritis—a common sequel to malarial fever. During that time I had to bury myself in my hut ; but those grass-covered hovels are anything but dark, and, in spite of all the bandages and skins with which I covered my head as I lay on the ground, rays of light would come through, intensifying the pain in my eyes.

" On May 10th we returned to Lealui.

" A week or so after my return to Lealui two Jesuits came to see the king. Four had left Panda-ma-tenka, but one had to return because of sickness. Another was drowned on the way up, through the upsetting of the boat in the rapids. The king and headmen had a large meeting, and told these priests they could not stay. They were friendly with me, and I bought a few small things from them The smallness of their present to the chief, in proportion to the amount of goods they had brought for their own consumption, was no doubt the cause of the ill-favour shown by Liwanika to them. He went to visit them one afternoon, expecting to get more from them, but with no better success, and he came along to my little hut in a very bad humour. Sitting down, he said, ' They are not the men for my country ; they have no sense.' Without waiting for a reply from me, he called one of his men, and sent him to the hut of the Jesuits to ask for a needle and thread. The man r turned with but one needle and a single thread, which Liwanika held up in triumph before me, saying, ' Didn't

I tell you these people had no sense? If they had they would have given me a packet of needles and a bundle of thread.'

"Having recovered somewhat I proposed to return to Panda-ma-tenka hoping to hear of someone coming to join me in the work. For some time before I left Liwanika was more friendly towards me, and I had many talks with him. He did not get so excited as before, and would occasionally express his confidence in me, saying that he believed I had come to teach them good things, assuring me also of my having perfect liberty in his country to teach the Word of God to old and young. My supplies were now completely run out, and on this account also I was compelled to make a trip down the river. As yet, with careful planning, I had been able to buy nearly all I needed. Although the king was always ready to give me presents of food, I generally refused, not wishing to afford the baser sort occasion for remark, as they watch all strangers and visitors with a jealous eye, lest they should rob them of their share of the king's bounty. I have been compelled to part with everything saleable, and am now under skins instead of blankets.

"*June 12th*, 1883.—The king sent me away in his largest river boat with good men, and with instructions that I was to be landed while the boat was shooting the rapids. Besides Khama's young man, Setobi, a little lad, named Sikinini, accompanied me. We have now been 12 days on the river, but delays have been constant. Oh, these people are slow! We stopped at Litofe two nights, and I was nearly devoured by mosquitoes and vermin. I have had two fever relapses, but not severe ones

"*Sheshehe.*—After a very tedious journey we arrived here. My principal food was buffalo meat, as I had not goods enough to buy sufficient corn for the road. The boats got through the rapids without serious damage. I preferred being wetted with the water to getting my legs cut with rocks and reeds, and did not leave the boat, but we had a narrow escape at one point.

"*Leshuma, July 3rd*, 1883. [To his father.]—I received your letter of the 9th August, 1882, only ten days ago. I assure you I was glad to see your handwriting again, and it was the first letter I read. I got 43 in all. I came out from the Barotse now with the intention of going at least as far as

Shoshong with the hope that there I might meet with someone to join me, but owing to a short line I got from Mr. Beaumont, Natal, saying that B—— had decided not to come, I could not find any proper reason for going further than Panda-ma-tenka. Besides I have had such a long journey down the river, so much time put off by the king's headmen in charge of the company, hunting and collecting ivory for trade, that now it is too late for a stranger to the country, as I am, to go out with a light ox-cart as I had planned. The water on the road is drying up so quickly, and travelling now to Shoshong I should have to be acquainted with all the extra waters off the road. Mr. Westbeech has just come in with a large stock of goods for trade so that I will be able to get from him a fair supply of stuff, although at a long price. My progress in the Barotse has been slow during the past months. In the first place the language spoken there is very much mixed up, the words of many tribes being introduced into the language of the Sekololo, which is a sister language to the Sechuana. And then the fever for a time sadly distorted my mental faculties. It is a distressing fever, and I think I have got over it easily. One thing with the fever here, it never returns, with the same acuteness as at the first. After recovering strength a bit, on my arrival at the king's town I tried to get up a small day-school for children, but the king always put it off , and of course the Barotse would not send their sons until the king gave some consent. They also seemed suspicious of my books, schools, etc. They seemed afraid that their children would become wiser than they and learn the sorceries of the white man. I had but to wait on quietly and leave the matter of a school in stronger hands, studying the language and talking quietly with the people meanwhile. Again I spoke to the king with a little better result, the third time still better, but beyond a mere expression of confidence in me he gave no decided reply. However, I made bold to set about advertising my, as yet, scholarless school. I went to the king's eldest son, and some of his other boys, and to some fathers to get their sons. In a few days three boys came, the king's son and nephew, and another lad. This was my beginning. We went on for a few days ; then I went and told the king of what was going on. He seemed pleased. I complained to him of his nephew who did not seem to care about learning any longer, and latterly was only got to school by a good deal of running after on my part The king turned to one of his servants at once and ordered him to go and tell his nephew that he must attend school at once, and regularly. From this I saw that I had got his full consent to carry on a school.

" On the 17th of July I left Leshuma for Panda-ma-tenka with the view of making purchases at Mr. Westbeech's store there. The first day's walk of 20 miles sadly blistered my feet, making one of them very sore. Next day we had hoped to reach the Gashuma Wells, but my sore feet hindered me greatly. I, however, hobbled on until nearly midnight, when we came upon smouldering fires which had been left by a company of raiding Matabele. I called to the men to lie down and rest, knowing that we should come to water after a short march next morning. Before going to sleep I commended all to God, and asked Him in prayer to lead us safely to some place where we should have a supply of water next morning. Little Sikinini, who had heard my request, and probably thought that I was suffering from want of water, could not rest with the others, but started off alone in the direction of the water. After a few hours' sleep we got up to continue our journey, as the day was breaking. To my surprise I met Sikinini coming back with a calabash of water in one hand, and a cup in the other. The little fellow had got to the water during the night, and had brought back a supply for his master.

" When within about 20 miles of Panda I met a hunter, whose horse I hired, and rode into the town, where I remained five days, and was able to buy enough barter goods to keep me going for six or nine months. The crops have nearly all failed this year at the Barotse, so that living will be very dear ; and I have to pay a heavy price here for very poor calico ; the white is the best for buying food.

" Leaving Panda-ma-tenka again on the 26th of July, I arrived at Leshuma on the fourth day. To show how quickly the water dries up here, I may mention that where, ten days before, we found quite a large piece of water, we now had to dig for it, and only got a little muddy stuff for our trouble.

"*August 7th*, 1883.—Having now a suitable opportunity I started from Leshuma this morning for the Victoria Falls. Had a pleasant day's walk to the river over desolate country.

Camped in the evening on the steep, wooded banks of the Zambesi, surrounded by most beautiful scenery.

"*August 8th.*—Walked some distance along the river, stopping opposite to Sepupwa's town to engage one or two more carriers, and buy corn, etc.

"*August 9th.*—The country was very rough and wild; no path, constant stumbling over big boulders, and ploughing through high grass and reeds. The grass in many places is like long lances, cutting one s hands and face frightfully at times. Mr. E. Selous fell into a game pit, and got hurt slightly. These pits are very cleverly covered over with sticks, grass, etc., so that they are very dangerous to strangers.

" On the morning of the sixth day after leaving Leshuma we reached the Falls I had expected something grand, but never anything so stupendous and terrific as they appear; yet they are beautiful in the extreme. The depth of the fall of water is about 400 feet. In some parts it breaks, in descending, over projecting crags, and in other parts comes over in one sheer plump. The cloud of spray, in which beautiful rainbows appear, rises a long distance into the air, falling again over the banks as it is blown by the wind, so that the vegetation close to the Falls is of the richest and most tropical character I have yet seen."

" Here I had a narrow escape from a lion. Walking along alone, a horrid growl and rustle of bushes at my very side startled me. I must have been within a few feet of the monster whose voice was unmistakable Turning back I walked slowly backward, with my eyes on the spot, and then, when well clear, I went off at a quick walk. I had not a gun with me On returning to camp I found that two large lions had come up in broad daylight to within 60 yards of the camp. They were shot at, and one, which was wounded, again came fiercely up at night, and would have done mischief had not all been awake, and kept him off with shouting, scattering fire, etc."

It was concerning this visit to the Falls that Sir Ralph Williams wrote several years later, in *How I Became a Governor*, the following testimony to Arnot:—" At the great Fall (the Victoria) we crawled to the very edge, and lying flat looked down into the chasm below. . . . While thus wondering we were amazed to see two white men coming towards us, who proved to be Mr. Edmund Selous, the brother of the famous hunter, and Mr Arnot, a Missionary amongst the Barotse and later on I think, a Gold Medallist of the R.G.S It was a strange place in which to foregather. Mr. Arnot, the Missionary, was a remarkable man I met him some weeks later, and had many talks with him. He was the simplest and most earnest of men. He lived a life of great hardship under the care of the king of the Barotse, and taught his children. I remember him telling me with some pride that his pupils had mastered the alphabet. I have seen many missionaries under varied circumstances, but such an absolutely forlorn man existing on from day to day, almost homeless, without any of the appliances that make life bearable, I have never seen. He was imbued with one desire, and that was to do God service. Whether it could be best done in that way I will not here question, but he looked neither right nor left, caring nothing for himself if he could but get one to believe ; at least so he struck me. And I have honoured the recollections of him ever since as being as near his Master as anyone I ever saw."

Arnot's story continues ·

" On the north side of the river one, Mosotan, has a large town. I had met him before, and sent word that I wanted to visit his town. He sent two of his men to greet me, with a large calabash of motoha, a native drink, and asked me to go up the river to his drift or ferry. According to promise I went next day, and he was very glad to see me, and gave me a goat for food. In the evening I crossed over and walked to his town, and spent the first part of the night surrounded by crowds of his people dancing and drumming. These Batoka are very open to conversation, more so than to be lectured to. I stayed the next day with them, and left early the following morning, travelling back again on the north bank of the river. We came upon many companies of scattered Batoka and Basubia, with whom I had short conversations in passing. Towards the evening of the second day we made for the town of Sepupwa, on an island in the river, and camped there. In the morning we hailed the people, but were told that as the headman of the town was absent they could not speak with us, nor send boats across. I waited and tried to persuade them, but they said they were all slaves, and were afraid to look at strangers. Another day brought us to Mahaha's town,

close to the Gezangula ferry by which we intended to cross.
Our way lay across low, flat country, full of marsh, which we
had to wade through, sometimes struggling for miles up to the
waist in water and rotting grass. I knew Mahaha pretty well,
having met him at Lealui. Next morning we crossed over and
walked to Leshuma, where I waited for carriers from Shesheke
to take me up the river.

"Shortly after my return to Leshuma, Ratua, from Shesheke, came down with others saying that the king had sent
the headman from the upper river with his boat to take me
up. Ratua laughed outright when he saw me, began by poking
my cheeks and saying :—' There is nothing but fat there, nothing but fat ! ' It is quite true what the old man says, but I
feel greatly ashamed to own it, that I am really getting fat ; I
hope not fat and lazy. He then turned to those around and
began describing touchingly the state I was in when I came
up to Shesheke sick. ' I came to his hut,' he said. ' I asked
Setobi where is the teacher, your master ? ' ' I don't know,'
replied Setobi, ' I don't know whether he is in this world or
not.' ' I went,' continued Ratua, ' and lifted the door. I
saw a blanket. I spoke and touched it. It moved. I said,
' Monare ! Monare ! ' and I heard, ' Eh ! Eh ! ' very small.
Next time I came back Setobi said that Monare was dead.
I looked in and saw the blanket. It moved like breathing.
I spoke out ; I called to him. He answered me with a very
weak voice. Next day I went and roused him and took him
out to wash. Then he got better.' I was much amused at
the old man's plaintive story. Had he been a physician, or
even a quack, he would have known that a long heavy sleep
after a fever is life and not death. He then began picking my
cheeks and laughing all over calling me the most youthful
names possible. (It is a compliment to a middle-aged or old
man in this country to tell him how young and boyish he is.)
In this case, of course, he was complimenting me with youth
on his side. I began gravely to show him my grey hairs, but
these had little weight with him. He only laughed the more
and declare them cheats and liars. I was a boy ! a boy ! a
boy ! I was forced at last to give in and let him have his own
mind out. I am fond of old Ratua (father of lions), a brave,
kind and honest, old man, a thorough heathen, but I believe
an enemy to the secret devil-like deeds of the magicians and

doctors. Most peculiar men those doctors are. I will write more of them when I learn more, but I hope it may not be experimental knowledge. I have had enough of their ghastly ways which are seen in every line of their ghastly demon-like faces.

"*Sheshele, Sept. 24th*, 1883.—After a very tedious journey I got here safely two days ago. One evening we were benighted on the river. It became very dark, and my men were anxiously paddling up-stream, when a hippopotamus came after the boat I was in, grunting fiercely and gnashing his teeth at us. We pulled hard to get to shallow water, but the beast followed us. I had no powder at hand for my gun. The men jumped out ; but being loth to leave the boat at the mercy of the brute, I took my steel and flint and struck fire in his face. This stopped him, and he turned back to deep water. The men would not come on further so we had to camp on the river's bank.

" On the way up I had a splendid view of two immense lions, walking up and down the white, sandy beach of the river. Although we were within 50 yards or so of them they looked at us quite undisturbed. Oh ! wasn't I sorry that my powder was in another boat. It was very grand to see them so near, the male lion with his large black mane looking at us with his deep, winking eyes, and the female pacing up and down the sand as they do in cages at home, her head lowered and swinging from side to side.

" Here I have met the Jesuits on their way home. The king has sent them back. They, however, are determined not to give in. The Pope has given them the country, therefore they must get a footing in it. They say they will come back next year and overcome every objection, by presents, I presume. I should think they have already given ten to twenty times as much to the king as I have, and yet they get nothing for it. The king is right when he says that their presents are not from a good heart. They give them to get favour.

" Yesterday afternoon a company of headmen and wives came to visit me, especially to see my photos. Their remarks were very amusing. I was amused at the comical way the men began chiding the women for their ugly looks, big lips, flat noses, etc., and that the Barotse now would go to the white people for wives, and didn t want them any longer   One poor woman got quite beside herself with rage declaring that the white women were soft and useless. They were all greatly pleased with the picture of the two wee bodies (Arnot's two little sisters). They seemed to think they were not children of this world.

"I remained at Shesheke for some time as the guest of Ratua. A happy incident occurred which was helpful to the old man. The king had commissioned Ratua to buy for him a very expensive greyhound, which Ratua had done, taking it with him to Shesheke, and intending to send it on to the king. Here the dog broke loose, and made for the road by which it had come. It would have to pass through a country infested with lions, and, worst of all, swim the Ungwesi and Zambesi, in both of which crocodiles abound, so that Ratua gave up all hope of ever seeing the dog again, and was much cast down. Shortly before, a horse in his care belonging to the king had been lost, also some goods ; and now, if this dog did not turn up, he might as well drown himself. He came into my scherm in great distress. I tried to soothe him ; but he added, ' It is no use ; I shall never see the dog again.' The thought struck me that this was an opportunity given me to prove the power of the God I had been speaking to him about two nights before. I prayed silently to the Lord about it, and felt confidence in telling Ratua that the dog would come back. ' No ! No ! ' said he ; ' No ! No ! ' and soon went away. In about an hour afterwards the dog came back. Some men cutting firewood had met it and turned it back. Poor Ratua could not find words to thank me and express his belief in the reality of my God. The news went all through the town that the teacher's God had sent back the king's dog. The dog must have been caught just about the time I asked the Lord for it. Quite a lively interest sprung up. Ratua to-night said that he and his wives wanted me to have a large meeting with all his people in the daytime ; they all wanted much to hear. ' We listen to you praying and singing at night,' said he (when alone I forget that the reed walls of my house are so thin that every word spoken is heard outside), ' but we want you to speak to us more during the day.' I felt like a horse ready for the race pawing the ground, but held in with bit and bridle. Most heartily would I not only talk with them all day, but pour out my very soul upon them, but my little knowledge of the language compels me to keep to very small companies.

"Already there is 'a rustling among the leaves.' A silent solemnity has taken the place among many at the mentioning of the things of God, instead of loud laughter and profane questioning. You will not fail, dear mother, to tell all those who are praying for Africa about the happy encouragement I have got since coming back again among the people, and stir up all to more prayer and earnestness before God so that we may get all that the gracious Lord may please to call out of this nation, not a hoof left. Praise the Lord! 'From every nation and tongue and people.' Oh! my heart goes beyond those tribes to the tribes upon tribes, nations upon nations, extending north, west, east, living to kill and be killed, unknown and knowing nothing. Millions of our fellow-beings knowing not that there is a God, a Saviour, and when told in their old age the precious gospel message of life, which was for all people, they marvel at the fact that they have lived so long without having heard it. I desire that you make this one message known to all, mother. The heathen wonder; they are surprised; they cannot understand how it is that those who have known these things, and have believed in God, and in His Son, have never come before to warn them, and to tell them of the true God. These words come from the very heart of Africa, not the words of one man only, but of many.

"When my place may be taken up here my desire would be to push on north, up by the sources of the Zambesi, up by Lake Bangweolo, and east and west and south by the River Chobe. There are tribes upon tribes open and waiting for the Gospel, though they know it not. You will perhaps say that the last part of this is a bit of Fred's spontaneous zeal. Well! I won't contradict you, but it is zeal that has been tried lately by a few practical tests, and if it burns up a bit at a time it doesn't do so in a cold grate. I know your heart is with me, mother, in all my erratic ways.

"*Oct. 1st.*—Left Shesheke this morning for the Barotse.

"*Oct 5th.*—Started early. A strong wind arose and compelled us to rest an hour or so. After I had urged Molonda to get into the boats and start again he replied sagely: 'Don't you know that the river has no ears? There are three things without ears, the river, the wind and the rain. They do not

hear, as they are in the hand of God. To-day, your own father
and mother might be sailing on the river, the wind might rise
and swallow them up, but to-morrow you would not come with
an assegai to fight the river, you would only drink its
water. So now we must sit still until the river and wind be
quiet.' (This is a specimen of their droll way of talking and
answering.)

   " *Lealui, Oct. 22nd.*—Nothing of importance occurred during
the first part of our journey up the river. My boatmen were
very diligent in hunting, so that this time we were fairly well
supplied with meat. On one occasion a troop of buffaloes were
seen near the water, and all the men started at once in pursuit,
whilst I remained by the stuff, sitting quietly reading under
my umbrella. In a short time I noticed some curious objects
on the tops of the trees, here and there an old shirt, or a little
piece of white cloth fluttering in the breeze. The secret of this
I soon discovered. My brave crew had overtaken the buffaloes,
but after firing a few shots they were attacked by an infuriated
old bull, who had compelled them all to climb the trees, and
kept them prisoners there for some hours. We were thus
obliged to sleep at this place that night, and to make the best
of our disappointment. A few days later my men organised
another hunt, with the help of a small company of natives we
met at the Nyambe Falls. They succeeded in killing a large
rhinoceros close by my camp. This gave us a supply of meat
sufficient to last for many days, and we were enabled to push
on without many delays.

   " At one point I and my crew had a very narrow escape
from total destruction. We were pulling along against a heavy
stream close to a high precipitous bank of heavy soil, when
suddenly the whole bank gave way, falling into the river just
alongside of our boat, so that some of the men were thrown
overboard, and the boat was filled with earth and water. We
instantly began baling out, and she soon righted. Had we
been a few feet nearer shore we should all have been buried
alive. The water under before the landslip was very deep,
and flowed in a steady even current. Immediately after the
landslip it was but a few feet in depth, and the current was
diverted to the middle of the river.

   " Arrived to-day at landing-place for Lealui, and sent word
to the king. Next morning ten of the king's men came down

with a horse. They shouted out many a hearty welcome, jumping about, lifting up my bundles, and running here and there. Liwanika received me very kindly, and gave me a nice snug hut in the town, but said he was going to build me a large one outside the town, on a small mound or hill, a much better site than I had had before. After two days the king sent to me by his private servant eight children to be instructed (two being his own sons), ranging in age from eight to fifteen.

" *Lealui, Oct* 30*th.*—Besides teaching the boys the alphabet and numbers, I read a little from the New Testament, and try to explain it to them. We get on famously. How different everything is this year from last ! My health could not be better ; the people, small and great, are kind and thoughtful, and do their best to make me comfortable. The king has given me a present of a cow and a calf, a parrot from the West Coast, a little slave boy (free now), and a handsome waterproof coat brought to him by a Portuguese.

" Old Mamwia, an elderly Makololo woman, was very glad to see me. She gave me some corn, and kissed my hand over and over again. This old woman came into my hut, shortly after my arrival in the Valley, and sitting down asked me to tell her of ' Jesus, the King of Galilee ' (repeating thus, as I afterwards learned, the last line of an old Sechuana hymn). I answered her by opening the Sechuana New Testament, translated by Dr. Moffat, and reading passages that I knew she must have heard before, had she been, as I supposed, in contact with the missionaries down south. Her face lit up with delight, old memories were awakened, and she crept forward and kissed my hand. Her story was that when quite a child she had lived on the Chobe River with her parents. A Mission, led by Dr. Price, brother-in-law of Dr. Livingstone, came to Linyanti, and little Mamwia was employed by one of the missionary ladies. But the missionaries all began to die, and her mistress died, and the rest returned to the south. Then the Barotse came down and killed her father and all her people, and carried her away to their distant Valley. Now 30 years had gone by and she had forgotten all that the missionaries had taught her ; but a love for the Saviour to Whom they had led her remained. And now Mamwia was among the first to welcome me on my return. It was her husband, Gumbela, who took me before the king and all the Barotse headmen, asking

F

in the name of the Barotse that I might be better cared for,
and my wants supplied. I think old mother Mamwia put him
up to this. Next morning I got a fat ox to kill "

Writing at a later date, concerning Mamwia, Arnot said :
" Her husband sent her away to his possession in the country
and I heard nothing of her until one day during these months
of famine. I had sent my faithful MaKoffee away to buy
meal, telling him not to return until he had found some. The
first day went by with no food in the hut, and no signs of my
servant ; the second day wore on without either breakfast,
dinner or tea ; but about ten o'clock, when about to go to bed,
a knock came ; then a black head ; and two baskets of food
were pushed in. Mamwia had sent her slave woman with a
little food that she had managed to secure that day quite
unexpectedly.

" I was much interested in a young man named Simboula.
My own two servants—Setobi, and a lad the king gave me
to work for me—were very troublesome, and at times, if I was
at all unwell, would be away all day. So this poor slave would
come at every opportunity, and sit beside me, always cheerful
and willing to do anything for his white ' baas.' I took a great
liking to him ; but he was sent down to his old master at
Mbova. When I was there recently he came to see me. I gave
him $2\frac{1}{2}$ yards of cloth for his help to me at Lealui when I greatly
needed it. As he looked at me I had to turn away my head,
and a big tear rolled down my cheek. Meeting the poor lad
brought to my mind many a kind act by night and by day.
These cases, with others, stand out more brightly, because of
the general feeling of utter indifference and coldness that
reigns in the hearts of most of these heathen.

" *Lealui, Dec. 9th.*—On the 18th Nov. I heard of the illness
of a Mr. Henry Bryden, who had come in from Damaraland to
trade with the king and had returned from here to his waggons
across the Chobe for more goods. On his way back to the
Barotse on foot he took very ill out on the veld, so I started
out on the 19th with a hammock and men to bring him in. I
myself rode in the hammock. We crossed the river in the morning and travelled through a wide flat with two small belts of
wood, about half-way across, where we rested. In the afternoon we reached a large sand-belt, heavily wooded, through
which our path lay. We stopped at a little town belonging to

one Mesanga on the face of the hill. This old man is the great
gunsmith and carpenter of the natives. We slept there.

" On the 20th we started early and got through the long
belt of wood. The variety of flowers, and their rich fragrant
smell were most refreshing. The grass everywhere had shot
up after the early rains, sweet and green. The trees were in
full fresh foliage. A sweet fruit, not unlike a fig, was very
plentiful. Beautiful birds gleamed and scratched about so
that in everything the wood we passed through this morning
was the perfect ideal of a forest ; but believe me, mother, I
would not have preferred a hundred walks in such parts to
a stroll in your own ' kail yard.' I find myself constantly
looking out for flowers and plants like those at home. If I can
associate anything with home it delights me.

" We reached the town of Moleni at night. At this place
were two of the king's horses, so I rode on with them another
day. I was now among the Mangetti tribe who do not understand Sekololo. I fear I will have to make an effort to learn
Serotsi so that I may be able to reach these other tribes so
close at hand all round about Here I sent the boys on before
to bring Bryden to me as the horses could not go further for
the tsetse fly. In four days he became very ill indeed. I was
able to help him with medicines, food, etc.

" Got back on the 28th to find the people collecting for a
war with a tribe to the west. They are always fighting here,
or going to fight.

" I hear from Blockley that the Jesuits are going to make
a great effort next year to settle here. Two more waggon loads
are coming for the Barotse Mission. The king told Blockley
that he is determined to have nothing to do with them on any
account. ' Monare ' (otherwise F. S. A.), he says, ' is my man,
and he is quite enough. He comes to me and is not afraid to
speak. He is young yet, but wait, that will be a man.' Perhaps
what he considers courage and manliness in me others might
take for impudence and rashness, with truth on their side.

" A great many men have been killed here lately, big men
as well as slaves, for the most absurd reasons and superstitions.
The saddest thing in connection with my school is that most
of the boys who come are under a secret sentence of death.
The poor boys themselves know it, but make as light of it as
possible. One is the son of Sepopo, a former king killed by his

people here ; two sons of Wanawana, a later king also killed ;
and two sons of the present king. It is considered by the nation
that it is not safe for these boys to live, so they will be speared
when they reach young manhood. I mean to set myself to
save the lives of these boys if I can.

"It would greatly amuse you if I told you all the tricks
and plans the people have tried here to get me married. Here
there is a law that men must marry at a certain age, and the
king and some of the headmen think it a very bad example
that I should remain unmarried, unless it was a part of my
religion like the Jesuits. I assured them, of course, that it
was no part of my religion. Well ! the conclusion, on their
part, was that I would have to marry. So the king appointed
me my wife, a daughter of his eldest sister, without ever consulting me. And I was invited to a feast where all the king's
female relations, and the friends of the damsel, were assembled,
I went in perfect ignorance of what was to happen. The king's
sister presented me with a pot of mead, and then introduced
me to her daughter as my wife. I was thunderstruck, and
began to boil with indignation, and to demand their meaning.
By acting in such a way they were making an entire mistake.
The king, I suppose, could not understand my refusing his
handsome gift of a princess, rich in cattle, slaves and gardens.
I explained to him quietly not to trouble me again with marry-
ing. When I wanted to marry I would get a wife of my own
nation who would be able to speak with and teach his women.
This pleased him. ' That will do,' he said. ' You must bring
her the next time you go home and I will be satisfied.' I
promised him in a sort of ' I'll ask Mamma ' way.

"Some of the older women here are very motherly and kind.
With them I have long talks. But with the mass of the women
and the girls it is impossible for me to reach them with the
Gospel. They are not allowed to sit with the men in a promis-
cuous audience as at home. They are very shy of strangers,
and very silly and stupid too. More silly creatures than some
of these women are I have never seen, but they seem to be
tender-hearted and impressionable. At home one hears a
great deal about the hard work the women have in savage
countries, but I do not see it here. The men in the first place
have a good deal to do. They lay out the gardens, clear the
wood, clear the grass, are regularly out hunting, tend the oxen,

milk the cows, prepare skins for themselves, their wives and their children. These latter (the skins) they have to preserve, soften (a long process), and then sew together so as to form different garments. They sew so very neatly with sinew that it takes a whole day to sew a seam a yard long. Then every year a commando of men is out fighting, and in this they all take their turn They do not do much building. They bring the poles, however, for their houses and set them, whilst the women do the reed and grass work and put the mud on the sides of the houses. The women also do the cooking, hoe and clean the gardens, and reap the crops. But the hoeing is the mere scratching of the surface of the earth ; nature is so rich they have but ' to tickle her, and she smiles into a harvest.' They have far too much time on hand for quarrelling and making rows. I for one am glad when hoeing time comes and the women clear out of town to their gardens. The attention they give to their families does not occupy one half-hour in the twenty-four. The children have simply to sleep where and as they like, most often with the dogs round the fire. Their food they get into their two outstretched hands. But in time of want the children fare badly, and fight for bones with the dogs, and dig up roots with their sticks. They are wonderfully hardy. I have seen little boys sleeping out at nights in the cold and drenching rain, without a stitch of covering, and yet without any harm, night after night.

" *Lealui, Jan. 1st*, 1884 —Had a long talk with the king this evening about the stars and the sun. He then wanted to know where God dwelt, and what He did with man when dead. I answered that God was not confined to one place, as we are ; that when man's body died, the spirit of him who was a child of God went above and dwelt for ever in the presence of God, and those whom God knew not here in this life were cast into a place of sorrow and burning. ' But why does God do so ? ' he asked. ' What reason has He for putting man from Him ? ' I explained to him something of the righteousness of God ; that He could in no wise clear the guilty. The king argued that here they did not know God's laws ; how then could God punish them for not keeping them ? I answered that God having planted His law in their hearts, they all knew what was right and what was wrong. ' You know,' said I, ' when a man lies to your face and steals from you that he injures you, and you call him bad and wicked. So when you to-morrow do the same thing, God judges you with the same judgment with which you judged your fellow-creature yesterday.' His only answer was, ' Yes ! that is true ; that I understand.' Presently he muttered something about the hardness of man's lot, and I tried to explain God's love to him in the gift of His Son ; and after listening for a little he suddenly bustled away, saying, like Felix, ' Well ! well ! I will call you again to speak about this matter.'

" *Jan. 4th.*—War is the great employment here at present. One impi has just come in with long strings of captives—poor naked women and children. The man who can show by the pieces of skin from the bodies of his victims that he has killed many is danced round by the women as a great hero.

" *9th.*—The king seems more afraid of the Word of God since our last talk, as he is little inclined to speak again on the subject.

" *14th.*—Candle making to-day, with beeswax and ox fat.

" *16th.*—Washing day.

" *20th.*—Down with severe headaches ; no sleep night or day. Silva Porto, the Portuguese traveller, arrived here a few days ago. He has come to trade with Liwanika for ivory, and has brought with him a large quantity of calico, guns and powder. He is most urgent that I should return with him to Bihé. From him I heard of the many tribes occupying West Central Africa with which he, as one of the oldest of the West Coast traders, had come in contact. This remarkable old man landed at St. Paul de Loando as the guns from the fort were booming in honour of Queen Victoria's coronation. He was the first European to visit the Barotse Valley, and letters from him were carried by his men overland to the Portuguese Governor of Mozambique. He had no compunction in telling me that in those early days he bought many slaves, but that now he was gradually giving them all their papers of freedom, and that although still a trader he was a missionary like my-self ! Telling me of a visit he paid to a cannibal tribe down the Kassai, he said he was so shocked with what he saw that he returned to them the year after with a quantity of salt blessed by a priest, and making the people come to him at every stopping place, he placed ' holy salt ' on their tongues, charging them never again to eat human flesh.

" *26th.*—Two men were tried for witchcraft in front of my yard this morning. They went through the customary ordeal, dipping their hands into the boiling water as coolly as possible ; for these brutal trials are so common that even the victims show but little concern. In the evening both were brought out of their prison hut, and being found badly scalded, were considered guilty and condemned to the flames.

" *27th.*—The two men were burnt this morning. I asked the king and his people to come to my yard and hear the Gospel, but he seemed annoyed at this public invitation, and said I must be content with the children ; nor would he allow me to speak to him there, saying that the big people did not want to learn these things.

" *29th.*—Headaches very bad. I fall into fits of stupor, probably owing to the great heat, with little rain.

" *Feb. 6th.*—Much better ; have been keeping indoors more during the day, and am getting on well with the Testament and a dictionary of Sekololo and Serotsi (the languages of the Makololo and the Barotse).

" The heat so affects everything that the people of the town are either asleep or lazily lying about, drinking thin beer. Not even a dog is seen. The oxen out in the plain try to stand or lie in each other's shadow, caring little for the rich long grass all round ; the king's horses get into the shade of some hut, and their heads hang wearily between their knees ; scarcely a bird flutters, and the smoke from the little fire at which the boys are cooking my dinner ascends slowly in an even column through the hot air. Such days are generally followed by a tremendous thunderstorm, lightning without intermission, and startling crashes of thunder, far on into the night. During a severe thunderstorm the natives do not eat, drink or work.

" *12th.*—The valley is now flooded ; one cannot go a few yards from the door without a boat.

" *20th.*—The king and the people of the town, my scholars included, have gone on a grand deer hunt, so I am left alone, with only a few women and slaves in the town. I have taken advantage of this quietness to begin chair making and sewing, and to clean my gun for some duck and goose shooting, my only hope of getting some meat during the king's absence. The slaves of the town got up a fight in their masters' absence, and two men were brought to me to have their wounds stanched

and bound up. The one had a knife stab, the other's head and
face had been laid open with an axe.

"22nd.—Last night an attempt was made to break into my
house   To-day the king's head servant sent round the town
crier, threatening with death any who should attempt to steal
from me.

"March 14th.—Have had a run of quartan ague all this
month. Hearing that Senhor Porto was laid up, I borrowed
a boat and went across the Valley, and found him very ill indeed
with ophthalmia.

"29th —News has come up the river to the effect that a
waggon has just arrived from Shoshong   M Coillard has sent
a blanket to the king with a few lines from Basutoland, dated
April, 1882, to say that he was coming on. The Father-Superior
of the Jesuits has also sent a letter and a blanket to the king.
They are very energetic and determined to succeed

"Lord's Day, March 30th.—Had very few at my house this
morning, but a large company at the afternoon meeting, which
lasted from three o'clock until sunset. Sitting in a draught I
got a chill, and spent most of the night in passing through the
three stages of ague.

"April 9th.—Found Senhor Porto better, but he has lost
the sight of one eye.

"10th.—The king returned from his hunt and held a grand
reception in the kotla, sitting in state in his chair under a big
Ashanti umbrella. The people greeted their chief by kneeling
in front of him and rolling their heads in the dust.

"17th.—There has been quite a plague of serpents here
lately. Within the last few days I and my boys killed two in
the house and three in the yard. While bathing near my house
I saw three serpents hanging from the reeds above my head,
and the same day, when landing from a boat, the boy in front
sprang back in terror as he pointed out two black cobras coiled
in the grass in front of us. One big yellow snake had been
sharing my bed for I do not know how long.

"18th.—Senhor Porto's man came to ask whether I would
go or not, but to this I really cannot say 'Yes!' or 'No!'
My eyes have been failing, and threaten as they did last year.
My goods are gone, or nearly so   Strange rumours are afloat,
and strange things have been going on since the king's return.
I fear it is the beginning of another civil war.

" A poor old woman who has always been kind to me was burnt this morning as a witch. She was suspected of putting a crocodile's tooth amongst the king's corn in order to bewitch him, and having been tried by the boiling-pot test was condemned. I believe it was a trick of some spiteful rascals who were her servants, and had prepared corn for the king, for they brought the tooth to one of the king's head servants.

" 19th.—Another old man tested by the boiling pot to-day ; he was supposed to have betwitched the king's brother, who, though a young man, is so fat that walking is a difficulty to him ; imagining that his fat was leaving him he decided that this old man must be the wizard.

" 20th —The old man has, strange to say, come out of the trial uninjured. I saw him twice dip his hands into boiling water, allowing the water to run over his wrists as he lifted his hands out, and yet to-day his skin seems quite natural. The only cause for this, that I can think of, is that he is nearly a century old, and his hands are as tough as tough can be. This was flourished before me as a great victory, achieved under my very eyes, in favour of the boiling-pot trials. The advocates for this piece of barbarism declare that if the hands of an infant who knew nothing of witchcraft were placed in boiling water not a particle of skin would come off. They delight in the practice because by it the rich can get rid of their poorer enemies without staining their own hands with the poor man's blood."

CHAPTER VII

MORE ABOUT THE BAROTSE

" THE Barotse are a very strange nation. Their country is bounded on the south by the Zambesi and the Chobe Rivers; and this line of demarcation is strictly guarded against all comers. No white man is allowed on any condition to hunt or to travel across that border. The headmen of the country expressed themselves pleased that I had come along; and several times when I spoke to the king about bringing a brother back with me the next time I went south, he objected, and said neither he nor his people wanted white men in their country. At last, however, he said of his own accord, ' Bring your brother with you when you return that I may see him.'

" Covetousness is the ruling passion of these natives, and it destroys all other natural feelings. Here a man will kill another for his coat. Seeing a defenceless party with, as they think, more of this world's goods than their share, they will try every means to distress, rob, or even kill them, for the sake of their goods. This was one cause of the failure of the L.M S. Mission, sent to the Zambesi 15 or 20 years ago at the advice of Livingstone. The things they took with them were many and good, and very tempting in the eyes of the natives; so they tried every means to dispose of the missionaries, and succeeded too well. This is one great cause of the present failure of the Jesuits. One ' father' was undoubtedly poisoned for the sake of a waggonload of goods of which he was in charge, and the party was openly robbed at different places to the amount of many hundred pounds. Now, as the people think they have obtained all they are likely to get, they are bent on getting the priests out of the country as soon as possible.

" I proved this power of avarice over other feelings to a small extent myself. When I first went to the king's town, I had, of course, a few things on hand for buying food, etc. So long as I had even a little I was very much troubled by people coming to me simply to beg for presents, headmen and their wives, even the king and his wives were not above begging and troubling me in the meanest way for a small present. At last my things were gone, and I had to live, as my boys lived, on porridge and corn; and I could only buy a meal at a time, tearing up my blankets and sheets, selling them for food, and also my spare clothes, etc. Then the begging and the pestering ceased; and those who came to my hut did not come to beg and peer into every corner to see if I had anything nice that they could ask of me. Before, when I used to try and get their attention in conversation, every now and then I would be ingeniously interrupted by the one miserable request, but when they found me as poor as themselves, if not much poorer, they came to talk, and perhaps would rather bring me a small present than ask for one, and I could get their ears and attention without distraction. This world's goods may certainly be helpful in furthering the Gospel, and may be sanctified and accepted by God for that work, but they also can be made a terrible hindrance. My plan now is to live as much from hand to mouth as possible, taking up the river only as many goods as will keep me for four or five months, sending down once or twice in the course of a year to Mr. Westbeech's station for fresh supplies, and living on native food, which I hope daily to become more accustomed to.

"It was well for the lame man sitting at the gate of the temple that Peter had neither silver nor gold; so surely it is well for these Africans that he who seeks to bring to them the one priceless treasure should not be burdened with what, in comparison, is trash and tinsel, serving but to blind their eyes to better and heavenly things. Many in South Africa urge the necessity for the missionary's going to the raw African tribes in the guise of a great man with a large retinue of servants and abundance of goods. Then, I have been told, he gets a position in the tribe, and his voice is listened to. But surely this is a fatal mistake, and far from the Divine pattern. In such a case the heathen may easily be brought to believe in the man and his goods, and, in the hope of improving his social position, may make a profession of Christianity without having seen or known anything of the meek and lowly Jesus.

"The African is loth to obey, but fond of imitating. The

sum of their own native belief is, that according to the position
a man has in this life so will his place be in the next. Goodness
or badness, righteousness or sin, are not in their creeds. If
a man dies a slave he will have a position akin to that when he
is dead ; if one dies a chief he remains a chief, and so on. Thus
the more a missionary seeks to attain and keep up a position
of power and greatness the more does he confirm those who
follow him in retaining their old heathen delusion. When I
tried to explain to King Liwanika that a man's position in this
world had nothing whatever to do with his place in the next,
that God dealt with the hearts of men and not with their skins,
that a poor ' matlanka ' (lowest slave) might be seated in the
palace of God, and a king or a chief shut out he got very excited
and forbade me ever to say such a thing again or ever to teach
such things to his people. I told him not to be angry with me
as these were not my words but God's. He didn't care ; I
might say so, but he and his fathers knew enough of God,
and of dying, and all that. ' Besides,' said he, ' we are not
all going to die just now ; why then speak about it ? ' It was
some time before he again came round to talk quietly of the
things which, though he little knows it, concern him so much.

" The native's pride of position is consummate, and for a chief
or a free man to come down to the level of a poor ' matlanka '
sinner is humanly impossible. ' Unto the poor the Gospel is
preached,' and most gladly would I give all my time among the
many poor slaves of this country ; but meanwhile I am not
allowed ' Those are not my people,' they say ; ' they are our
dogs.' So it is only by stealth that I get amongst them.

" I have great hope that blessing awaits the declaring of the
Gospel up this river ; but one thing I desire is that what may be
done may be very real and entirely of God. Let us go in for
real out-and-out conversions to God as among the Thessalon-
ians of old, who ' received the Word in much affliction,' so that
God's name may be honoured in this country as it was in
Macedonia

" My one desire is that I may please God by making His
Gospel known in all faithfulness and sincerity, so that His name
may be glorified by the gathering out from heathendom of
those whom He may please to make the subjects of His sovereign mercy. I rejoice to think that for the people we have a
full and complete salvation to carry to everyone, but Godward

we can but cast poor, sinful man upon His sovereign grace and
mercy. There has been little to try me here in the work, but
much to encourage. I am thankful to say that I have received
much of the confidence of the people; they trust me now as
they did not at first. During my stay at the king's town my
time was well occupied. Besides having a small day school and
spending time with the people in conversation on the things
of God, I was much occupied with doctoring, gun mending,
teaching them how to sew, and to make shirts, etc. In the
doctoring line I was several times very successful, even in
important cases which had been given up by the native magicians or doctors. The king Liwanika himself had been long
ill, though he had been working away with all his doctors;
he recovered slightly, only to relapse again. One of his headmen, who has the honorary title of ' The king's mat,' asked me
to go and see his majesty. I said I did not think I could do
much for him, but, if I could not, God could. I told him to go
back to the king and that I would follow, which I did, earnestly
asking for the Lord's blessing upon the remedy. The next
morning the king was able to attend a large council meeting
and to all appearance looked quite well. Several of the headmen came to congratulate me on my cure; but when I told
them it was God and not man who had restored the king's
health, they gravely shook their heads.

" Nothing of importance can be sanctified without a human
sacrifice—in most cases a child. First the fingers and toes are
cut off, and the blood is sprinkled on the boat, drum, house,
or whatever may be the object in view. The victim is then
killed, ripped up, and thrown into the river. The burning of
men for witchcraft is carried on to a fearful extent; not a day
passes but someone is tried and burnt. The details of scenes
which I have been forced to witness in this line are too horrible to put on paper; many a guiltless victim is marched off
to the horrid pile. A few hundred yards from my hut there
lies a perfect Golgotha of skulls and human bones, fearful to
look upon. Yet one gets somehow used to it and to all their
murdering ways.

" The trial for witchcraft is short and decisive. If one man
suspects another of having bewitched him—in fact, if he has a
grudge against him—he brings him before the council, and the
ordeal of the boiling pot, to which I have already referred, is

resorted to. My proposal is, that if they consider it a fair trial of whiteness or blackness of heart, as they call it, then let both the accuser and the accused put their hands into the boiling water. The king is strongly in favour of this proposal, and would try any means to stop this fearful system of murder, which is thinning out many of his best men, but the nation is so strongly in favour of the practice that he can do nothing. An old friend of mine, called Wizini, who took quite a fatherly care and interest in me for some peculiar reason of his own, was charged with witchcraft. He pleaded earnestly to be spared the terrible trial, and was reprieved because of his years, but banished from his people and country for life, for no other reason than that a neighbour had an ill-feeling against him. Had he been first to the king with his complaint he might have got his neighbour burnt or banished instead of himself. I much missed this old man.

" The manners and customs of the negro ' pure and simple ' of the interior remind one of many things mentioned in Scripture. The Barotse have such names as ' Child of Sorrow,' ' Child of Joy,' ' Born by the River,' and others, suggested by events occuring at birth. When a man of property dies, leaving no children, his nearest kinsman takes his brother's wives; and children born of them inherit the dead man's property. This custom, however, is dying out. In 2 Kings ii. 11 it is said of Elisha that it was he who poured water on the hands of Elijah. On the return of a man to his town or house a servant regularly waits with a vessel to pour water on his hands. The average negro is the reverse of cleanly, but there are many laws and customs among them as to cleansing. The better class negro washes his hands regularly before and after meals, but this is because he eats with his fingers. He may use a spoon with thin porridge or thick milk, but only to ladle the food into the palm of his hand, from which he drops it into his mouth. Houses defiled by dead bodies must be cleansed, and a woman who needs cleansing must live so many days outside the town, after which she is washed with water, anointed with oil and perfume, the inner fat of an ox is hung round her neck by her husband, and then she returns home. Circumcision is very generally practised by different tribes, and in different ways.

" The native manner of speech is very quaint, and the mere expectation of good things causes such delight that men will dance and shout all night with empty stomachs in prospect of a feast on the morrow Regard for decency in conversation is utterly unknown There is a city of refuge among the Barotse, and anyone incurring the king's wrath, or committing a crime, may find safety by fleeing to this town. The man in charge of it is expected to plead for him before the chief, and he can then return to his house in peace.

" The African native, as found in his own home, is, like ourselves, a man with all the instincts of a man, and this is shown by the conduct of the lowest slaves. A poor slave, whom I saw kicked out of a hut in which he had sought shelter, folded his arms and calmly said, 'Yes, master, I know you think me to be a dog, but, sir, I am not a dog, I am a man.' There was, for the moment, a dignity and impressiveness about the poor naked fellow, which subdued the man who was abusing him, and he was told to return to the hut.

" Many good laws as to constancy and fidelity are to be found among these people, but their innate cruelty is, I think, without comparison and makes war a terrible thing with them. On returning from raiding, the warrior exults in telling the horrible cruelties he has committed. A man will woo a woman with accounts of the devilry he has been guilty of, for the women delight in it, and the remembrance of things I have seen done to captives makes the blood run cold. Among the Mashukulumbe the women and children turn out to applaud their brave warriors, who, I am told, string up by the neck, to tall trees, the little children they have taken captive, a spectacle which gives entertainment to the whole countryside. Their punishments are very cruel. Burning alive is, among the Barotse, a common occurrence ; also tying the victim hand and foot and laying him near a nest of black ants, which in a few days pick his bones clean.

" When manners and customs are referred to the particular district must be born in mind Africa is an immense continent, and there is as much variety in the customs of the different tribes as in their languages. Certain tribes take delight in cruelty and bloodshed ; others have a religious fear of shedding human blood, and treat aged people with every kindness to secure their goodwill after death. By other tribes the aged would be cast out as mere food for wild animals.

" There is an old but waning belief that a chief is a demi-god,

and in heavy thunderstorms the Baroste flock to the chief's
yard for protection from the lightning. I have been greatly
distressed at seeing them fall on their knees before the chief,
entreating him to open the water-pots of heaven and send rain
upon their gardens. But last year the chief acknowledged to
me that he knew he was unable to do so ; yet he keeps up the
delusion for the sake of power. These ancient beliefs of the
negro in the power of chief's medicines and enchantments have,
as might be supposed, very slender props to rest on, and they
are kept up merely to fill a want in the mind, much as a drown-
ing man will catch at a straw in his need of something to bear
him up. The king's servants declare themselves to be invinc-
ible, because they are the servants of god (meaning the king) ;
but when some discontented Barotse went to King Sepopo, the
late chief, none fled faster than the king's bodyguard. Sepopo,
like the present king, would boast that he possessed medicines
and enchantments which made his body impervious to spear-
bullet ; but when he heard of the insurgents, Sepopo fled in
haste, and a bullet through the chest killed him.

" Man is a very fragile being, and he is fully conscious that
he requires supernatural or Divine aid. Apart from the distinct
revelation given by God in the first chapter of Romans there is
much to prove that the heathen African is a man to whom the
living God has aforetime revealed Himself. But he has sought
after things of his own imagination and things of darkness to
satisfy those convictions and fears which lurk in his breast, and
which have not been planted there by the evil one, but by God.
Refusing to acknowledge God they have become haters of God.
The preaching of the Gospel to them, however, is not a mere
beating of the air ; there is a peg in the wall upon which something can be hung, and remain. Often a few young men have
received the message with laughter and ridicule, but I have
afterwards heard them discuss my words amongst themselves
very gravely. I heard one man say to a neighbour, ' Monare's
words pierce the heart.' Another remarked that the story of
Christ's death was very beautiful, but that he knew it was
not meant for him ; he was a makalaka (slave), and such a
sacrifice was only for white men and princes.

" Their memories are so acute, that many days after being
spoken to, they will return in order to discuss some question
which has been weighing on their minds. I judge from their

A Picturesque Scene in Angola

A native hut is standing beneath the beetling rock ; and a man is climbing a palm-tree to cut down nuts.

actions that a few among the Barotse have consciously received
something of the truth. Molonda, who was a very kind friend
to me, repeatedly professed his belief in the things about which
we had long talks when travelling together from Sheshcke ,
but he is secretly afraid of the king ; and the putting away of
his extra wives would, in his eyes, end his career among the
Barotse. Mala, of Secumba, one of the nobles of the land,
when he came to the king's town, used to dine and sup with
me, and we would read and talk over the Scriptures for hours.
Mamwia has suffered much from her husband Gumbela, the
king's prime minister, for loving to come and hear the Scriptures read, and she professes to know the Lord. Our Lord
knows all. He who will not quench the smoking flax, nor break
the bruised reed, can nourish the little spark into a flame.

" During the time I was in the Barotse, the chief of the
Matabele, sent a powerful embassy to Liwanika, bringing
presents of spears and shields, and inviting Liwanika to become
his blood brother, and to join with the Matabele in resisting the
invading white man. I was able to persuade Liwanika that,
apart from promises and the power of respective chiefs, Khama
was a better man to make friends with than Lobengula. Lobengula's men were treated with great hospitality and sent away
with many presents, but Liwanika immediately decided to
write to Khama asking for his friendship, his daughter to be
Liwanika's queen, and a black hunting dog. I wrote the letter
for him, and my man, Setobi, was the bearer of it. He was, of
course, accompanied by several Barotse. Liwanika added a
postscript to the effect that Khama was to do all in his power
to help M. and Madame Coillard and party forward. It so
happened that this letter arrived in time to meet the Coillards,
and it is quoted by Miss Macintosh in the interesting life she has
written of her uncle and aunt, M. and Madame Coillard.

" Khama replied to Liwanika by sending a horse instead of
his daughter, giving him to understand at the same time that
he must join with him, not against the white man, but against
the white's man drink if he wished to be Khama's friend.

" When staying in the Barotse Valley I came into contact
with many interesting people.   Here was a headman bearing
the honourable title of ' the King's Mat,' and there were ' home '
and ' foreign ministers ' at Liwanika's court. Also ' the keeper
of the city of refuge,' a kind looking old man, who was also the

G

softener of the king's heart when he was angry with his people. Of all these, however, the king's head blacksmith made the most lasting impression upon me, and that chiefly for his son's sake. I think I can see him now splashing across the flooded plains that surround the Lealui, during the first rains, with his son riding astraddle over his shoulder, plying his father the while with all sorts of interesting questions. When first I saw Kakonda, and his father the blacksmith, pass my hut door, I had just recovered somewhat from a long illness and was beginning to look around for a few pupils, but it seemed difficult to make a beginning. When his father reached the shed where he usually kindled his fire, and repaired the king's guns, he set Kakonda down to play about with the village children, and soon they all came trooping along to see the standing wonder of the day, the white man Kakonda had never seen me before, not at least at close quarters. To their great delight they found that the white man was about to begin breakfast ; now they would see him ' swallow his needles.' This story of the ' bunch of needles ' I was supposed to swallow each time I took a meal, had gone far and wide, and even Liwanika asked me seriously if it was true. I had no difficulty, of course, in explaining how it all arose from my using a three-pronged steel fork instead of my fingers ; and I had the pleasure of giving this great potentate (afterwards so dainty and correct) his first lesson in the use of the knife and fork. But to return to my little crowd of visitors. They were almost too many for me that morning. So I had, with a few sticks and string, constructed a barrier beyond which none were to pass. I soon picked Kakonda out as a little stranger, and while the others were going into fits of laughter over my fork, and other little freaks and fancies peculiar to the white man, Kakonda kept his eyes gravely fixed upon me. At last I saw that his curiosity was getting the better of him, and that he had already crept under the string barrier, and was moving towards my hand as it hung by my side. Of course I pretended not to see him, although all the other little chaps were holding their breath and watching the stranger. At last I felt his cold fingers stroking my hand down from the wrist to the points of the fingers again and again. ' Well, little boy ! What do you want ? ' I asked, as I looked down and met his great, big, wondering, half-tearful eyes. He hesitated but for a moment, and then in a shrill tone of voice asked me to tell him,

' Where was the river that I washed in, for he would like to wash in that river too.' The dear little chap little knew how I loved him as I looked at him, and longed as never before to lead him and his companions to the living fountain of waters. So without delay I had the table cleared and started my first class. I explained first of all that the colour of our skins did not matter; the skin is very thin, and on a piece of paper bent over the side of my table, I was able to show how a dot of blood taken from my own white hand, and a dot taken from Kakonda's black hand, were both red, for God had ' made of one blood all the nations of men.' And then I asked them what it was that lay inside of skin, and blood and flesh, right in the middle. All knew, of course, and answered, ' the heart.' The African makes more of the heart than we do. He not only loves and hates in his heart, but he thinks in his heart; in fact his heart is his soul. But I had no needle long enough to prick the heart to see what colour it was, so I explained how God who made us, sees right through our bodies, which to Him are just like so many clear glass bottles, like the one that I held in my hand with a black stone inside; and He tells us that our hearts are not some black, some white, but all black, and made blacker each day we live, because it is sin that defiles a man, lying, stealing, etc. But God also tells us of a river that can wash our sins away, and so on.

" My little class came together for several mornings; and, between spells of fever, I was able to spell out the Gospel, line upon line. Kakonda's father was killed in a revolt against Liwanika, and his family sold into slavery, or scattered to remote parts; but one of the boys of that class, thanks to M. Coillard's training, is now Liwanika's Prime Minister, and the British Commissioner in the Barotse speaks of him as ' the one shining light among the Barotse people.'

" One day Liwanika was sitting in the public court, disposing of slaves that had been brought in from the Matotela and Bankoio as tribute. All the good looking and able bodied were soon disposed of to eager sycophants, who rushed to prostrate themselves at the king's feet in their deep gratitude. But one middle-aged woman and a little boy remained sitting alone. I felt keenly for the woman, she looked so sad, and overcome with shame at her exposed, humiliating position. I could not help her, but on learning that the boy was not her son, I asked that he might be sent along to my hut. He was so worn and emaciated with hunger that it was with difficulty I brought him through. For weeks after he could not see food without making for it. One day I set him to clean a few potatoes, and seated myself on a chair close by to keep guard over my prospective dinner, but, strange to say, the potatoes began to disappear. In a few minutes there were certainly fewer in the basin than when Sikinini set out to wash and I to watch. So I determined to unravel the mystery, and quietly watched every muscle of his body. I then observed that with the middle toe of his foot he was digging a hole in the sand, when he had dug deep enough the little thief eyed me very steadily, watching for a sudden turn of my head, or a look off in another direction, to drop a potato into the hole and instantly to smooth all over with a quiet gliding movement of the foot.

"Although 30 years have elapsed since Livingstone first visited the Zambesi and the Barotse Valley, and more than 20 years since he was last seen there, yet the remembrance of him, his ways, his words, his physique, is as fresh as yesterday. I carried a photo of him which was recognised readily by those who knew him. I being of the same nation, and no doubt having a national likeness to him, was called by the same name, Monare. This I at first resented, feeling altogether unworthy of such distinction. However, the name has stuck to me, sometimes Monare nyan (Young Monare). I am not his only namesake. At the Barotse they have named many of their children, born at the time of Livingstone's visit—now grown lads—after him. Sekilitu's mother, and one of Sibituane's sisters are still alive though very old women. I found that they were very full of his memory. One thing surprised me: nowhere was it even as much as mooted that Livingstone was in any way indebted to them, or had received from the Makololo any material help in his travels. Everyone in fact looked upon Livingstone as their great benefactor. Of course there are many absurd stories afloat as to his powers, how he flew down to the bottom of the chasm of the Victoria Falls (Livingstone let down a weighted line, with a piece of paper attached, to see the end of the line better); that he could raise the dead and make spirits to appear (the magic lantern which was indeed magic to them); that he had a dish of water into which he looked and read instructions as to the road before him (no doubt his compass).

" Many of the older men had whole sermons of his off by heart. One old blind man named Zape, who said that he was in Livingstone's service when he was young and could see, had some very vivid recollections of Livingstone. And one evening, at my request, he gave to me and to a lot of young men gathered in my yard, one of Livingstone's sermons. He got up and went through it bravely as follows : ' You people of the Makololo, you great men and warriors, I tell you you are not great men. You are bad and mean. You are not content with living in your own houses and hoeing your own gardens, but you go and attack weak people, and kill them. You see children hoeing the gardens of their mothers, and you take them prisoners. You see men hunting their own food, and herding their oxen, and you kill them. This is very bad. This is a great evil. The Evangalia has gone into all the world to teach men that to be great is to be good.' This was spoken in a high authoritative tone of voice. He dropped this, and in an uncertain fluttering way touched upon one of Livingstone's graphic pictures of the last judgment. Of the Evangalia he had confused notions, thinking that that was the name of a person, but upon my explaining to him the story of God's love, which was the Evangalia, or the Gospel, it brought many more of Livingstone's words to his mind, and, repeating them as he did to me, it has helped me greatly in explaining the Gospel story in the Sekololo to others.

" His character among them was unimpeachable. As far down as Natal I heard slander stories told about Livingstone's conduct in the far interior. But surely if there had been an atom of truth in the same I would have heard something to corroborate them in the far interior. The African keeps no such secrets   I was told, however, from some man who came from the West Coast, and had met Livingstone at the Barotse, that Monare was not like me ; he married a native woman and had a child alive near to his country. This I did not for a moment believe. I questioned him closely, and up and down, on the matter, and found that he was confusing Dr. Livingstone with an Arab trader who came to the Barotse at the same time as Livingstone, and who also went to the West Coast in company with Sen. Porto by a different road from Livingstone.

" Some Bechuana hunters came to the Barotse about this time. Their home was near Kuruman, Dr. Moffat's old station ;

but they had been hunting elephants for years in the deserts north of Lake Ngami. One of these hunters was well on in years. He told me he was one of Dr. Moffat's ' children,' and undertook to instruct me in the great missionary's methods. Moshete (his native name) would go, he said, to the chief's councils, and when the business was over he would always stand up book in hand, and preach vigorously. If any chief tried to stop him he never grew angry, but asked so earnestly to be allowed to go on that they always listened to him. So I became more courageous, and repeatedly tried to carry the war more earnestly into the enemy's camp. But for a long time Liwanika cleverly managed to head me off. ' Had he not given me his children to teach ? My words and stories were really only for children,' etc. But one day he added, ' Was there anything in my book suitable for a king to listen to ? ' This gave me a glimmer of hope of some little progress, and I assured him with emphasis, that there was more in the Bible for kings and about kings than any other class of men. ' Well,' he said, ' if that is so, I will give you a proper hearing ; come on a certain day, and I will gather all my nobles, and we will listen to the message that your book has for a king.'

" But now my troubles began ; I could not think of a suitable message. From morning till night I thumbed my Bible without a gleam of guidance. After a quiet hour of prayer, I turned again to look for my message. The story of Nebuchadnezzar now seemed to stand out before me in golden letters. On the appointed day I went to the kotla and turned to the book of Daniel, translating in short sentences the story of the great Eastern potentate. Liwanika listened intently, turning round to his nobles to see that they were listening too. At last he could not contain his delight, but burst forth with, ' That is what I am going to be. I am the great Nebuchadnezzar of Central Africa.' But when I came to the downfall of the great monarch, how, because of his pride and boastfulness, he was reduced to the level of a beast having claws and eating grass, the king's countenance fell somewhat, so I pressed the truth home on himself, telling him how wicked he was as a man, and as a king, in God's sight, but I was to proceed no further. Liwanika sprang from his chair, and left the enclosure with this strange remark : " What does the white man mean ? I am not going to die to-day.'

" For two months I was left severely alone by both chief and
counsellors. Then I heard that the chief was ill, ten oxen being
driven in in one day for the doctors to sacrifice in the process
of preparing remedies, etc. A messenger came to me from
Liwanika to say that he had had a dream that I had the
medicine that would make him better. As soon, however, as
he was assured that there was no one near to hear what we
were saying, he forgot all about his health and began to tell me
how he abhorred burning witches, selling slaves, and making
war on the poor tribes around, but he was helpless, he said ;
still, he wished to keep my ' Sunday.' As I listened it seemed
clear that he was not ill in body but in mind and conscience.
This gave me the opportunity of beginning where I had left
off in the history of Nebuchadnezzar, and of pressing home on
his acceptance the unconditional gift of God s forgiveness. The
king listened patiently, and as I left him, he said, ' Come every
morning and teach me.' Troublous times, however, were awaiting Liwanika, and the shadow of a serious revolution was
already upon him."

CHAPTER VIII

"*A PRIL* 22*nd*, 1884.—Gumbela, and some of my friends, seemed to think it was well that I should leave just now, because of the troubles brewing, so I told Senhor Porto that I would accompany him to Bihé. I had repeatedly asked Liwanika to allow me to proceed up the Zambesi to the tribes living north, but he would not grant my request These people were the dogs of the Barotse, and missionaries would not be allowed to visit them. So I decided to go West with Senhor Silva Porto.

"*May 1st.*—As the king sent word that a boat was ready for me, I packed up, sending to his house what things I was unable to take with me, and giving the key of my house to one of his servants. When I went to say good-bye he shook hands long and warmly, saying, ' You are my friend, come back very soon. But,' he added in a tone of sadness, ' you may not find me here.'

"*May 3rd.*—Alarming news as to the Barotse. Plans are laid for a revolt against Liwanika, and it is intended to set up the son of Sekuferu.

"*May 4th.*—I arranged to-day with Senhor Porto about carriers, and shall ride upon an ox instead of being carried in a hammock, as he proposed, for that would be too comfortable a way of travelling, and might make me discontented and extravagant at other times Liwanika gave me a young ox as a parting gift I broke him in, and he proved a most valuable riding animal.

"*May 8th* —I set out with Senhor Porto, not without much pain and difficulty on my part, owing to an accident which I met with last night, and which, but for the mercy of God, might have been a very serious one. I had been repairing some guns for the Barotse, and, on firing a breechloader, the hinge of the block gave way, and my face and right eye were badly

scorched by the explosion. To add to my misfortune, my
riding ox was sent off by mistake in the early morning, so I had
to be led by my little boy for ten weary miles, most of the way
wading up to the knees in water, and then through rough bush.
Reached the town of Kangete and camped there.

" *May* 10th —Started on a small ox of Senhor Porto's. Our
road lay through thick forest, and a sorry journey the ox and
and I made between us. The footpath was bad and narrow
enough, but my ox had no idea of keeping to it, and dragged
me about in all directions. After any delay, in catching sight
of Senhor Porto's oxen he would canter straight towards them,
leaving either me, or bits of my distressed clothing, detained
by the ' wait-a-bit ' thorn bushes. I managed with difficulty
to retain my hat, but the bandage I had round my eyes was
left in the thorns. At last I sent the ox about his business
and lay down quite out of breath, and, I fear, sadly out of
temper. Some of the carriers came to urge me on, but it was
of no use, till a female slave, carrying some provisions on her
head, gave me a cool drink and some coarse bread, which sent
me on my journey, moralising on the superior humanity of
women.

" *May* 12th.—My own ox was secured this morning, and I
got on much better with him Started from Kakap long before
cock-crow (Senhor Porto carries a cock with him to crow), and
early in the day we reached Osore, a lake of considerable size,
and camped there. My eyes are gradually getting better
through the constant application of poultices of ox-dung,
heated in a pan.

" *May* 13th —Crossed, on the shoulders of a stout Bihé
porter, a deep-running river, and camped by the Nyengo.

" *May* 14th —Passed through much water on the Nyengo
flat, my ox swimming bravely with me on his back. Camped
at Relva.

" *May* 15th.—A tedious journey through a dense, dark
forest. which smelt like a dank dungeon, with moss and lichen,
but no grass. Camped at Ka-kinga on the River Ninda, as
the upper part of the Nyengo is called, where the Ambuella,
a small tribe of the Bambunda race, are living.

" *May* 19th.—Travelled along the right bank of the Ninda.

" *May* 20th.—A wild-looking company of Bambunda
hunters came to the camp ; they dress their hair to imitate

the horns of wild animals, and one had a stick through his nose. In this part the Bambundu are peaceable, but further on they form robber gangs, and would be dangerous to a small party.

" *May* 21*st.*—Journeyed along the Ninda. Ever since leaving the Barotse Valley we have been constantly ascending, so that now we are travelling through hilly country, very cold at night, with sharp touches of frost, but during the day the sun is strong. I have tried to walk barefoot, my boots being worn out, but the sand was so hot after half an hour's hopping along I had to give in, with four large blisters on my feet ; this is winter here.

" *May* 22*nd*—To-day we reached the source of the Ninda, which flows from a range of hills dividing the water flow between the Zambesi and Quando rivers. Here the hills are high and thickly wooded.

" *May* 23*rd.*—Crossed the hills and reached the source of the River Shulungo, tributary to the Kumbule, which again is tributary to the Quando River. Following the Shulongo we came to the Kumbule, a large, beautiful stream, which seemed to dance along over a bed of silver sand, so bright that it was painful to look at it. Orange, green, and other bright coloured water weeds were growing in abundance, and were beautifully mixed. All the rivers and little streams have the same bright appearance in this part of the country, showing that ' Afric's sunny fountains ' is no mere poetic dream ; but the sands are silver, not ' golden,' as in Heber's hymn. It is a pity to see such a fertile, and undoubtedly healthy country, so thinly populated.

" *May* 24*th.*—Crossed hilly country, densely wooded, and reached the River Shikoloi, running south through a valley.

" *May* 25*th.*—The oxen refusing to cross the river, were sent up-stream to look for a ford.

" *May* 26*th.*—There being no sign of the oxen we started for the Kuti River, crossing four hills and three valleys.

" *May* 27*th.*—One of the carriers, who has a familiar spirit, being asked to divine why the oxen would not cross the Shikoloi, called up the spirit of an old servant of Senhor Porto's, who said that he had stopped the oxen because presents had not been given to his friends after his death. One of his friends was amongst the company of carriers. The events that followed bore out the diviner's theory only too truly. We should, however, have said that the friend of the aggrieved dead man was one of the ox herds, and not merely one of the carriers. For when the lost oxen did turn up, the slaves in charge declared that when driving the unwilling cattle across the river, one of them broke away from the rest and escaped into the forest. After days of searching they found a torn piece of ox-hide which they had brought with them that their master might look at it and see with his own eyes if this was not a part of the skin of his own ox, who had doubtless been torn by a lion. The brethren of Joseph, with his coat of many colours in their hands, could not have presented a more doleful spectacle. Senhor Porto had been suffering badly from ophthalmia and could not inspect the skin, and so let the matter drop. But I could see that the skin had been hacked around with a knife, and that the tooth of a wild animal had never touched it.

" *May 30th.*—Deciding to visit the line of small towns along this river belonging to the Bakuti, a people akin to the Baluchaze, we got a boat and pulled up the stream, stopping at all the huts and small villages. The people showed much frankness, and said how glad they were to see an ' English ' for the first time. I asked them to gather together at their chief town in two days' time, and then I would speak to them.

" *May 31st.*—All day buying food, which the people bring in abundance. I never saw food anywhere in Africa so cheap as it is here. A piece of calico, about the size of a handkerchief, will buy about 20 lbs. of meal or a calabash of honey.

" *June 1st,* 1884.—In the afternoon a goodly company had assembled to be spoken to, all men, for everywhere in Africa the women are the most conservative and the most difficult to persuade into receiving anything new, and here they had shut themselves up in their huts. These people had lived in such seclusion that they knew nothing of teachers living amongst other tribes, the limit of their knowledge being the West Coast trader, his goods, his ivory, and, in past years, his string of slaves. Speaking through my interpreter, Antonio, I told them in the simplest language of God the Creator, of man's departure from Him, of the sending forth of God's Son as a Saviour, and of His now sending messengers throughout the world to call men back to Himself. Their close attention made me feel that the Spirit of God was blessing the Word, and at the end they expressed their thanks by clapping their hands. The chief then said that they could not tell how happy they were that I had spoken in that way to them ; he had believed in a great God Who had made all things, but he wanted to know that God, that he might pray to Him at all times

" Senhor Porto says that these people are exceptionally simple and honest ; he has never known them to steal any of the goods that he has left in the charge of their chief from time to time. They live in square houses built close to the River Kuti, which forms their highway ; each person possesses a boat, and, as there is a continual traffic going on, the river presents a very lively appearance   The hair of these people receives more dressing than their bodies , the men wear a skin before and behind from the girdle, but the women use calico for their clothing.   They have blankets made of the inner bark of a large tree, beaten soft.

" *June 4th.*—Many gathered at the villages, and we had a good time this morning.   One man showed great interest, and said afterwards, ' This day I am a child of Jesus Christ : now I will pray to God alone.'   Some wished me to return to-morrow, but the chief said, ' No, we shall tire the white man by his coming so far ; we will gather together, and go to his camp.'

" *June 5th* —A goodly number came to the camp to-day.

" *June 6th.*—Had a long talk with the chief and the man who said he was a child of Jesus Christ, and told them that though I was leaving, I would, God willing, return to them. The chief replied that they would look much for my return, that they would not forget the good news brought to them, and that they would pray God to bring me back in safety.   I have hope toward God that these two men have indeed drunk of that living water, of which if a man drink he shall never thirst again. As yet I have not been able to fulfil my promise of returning, but should be indeed glad to do so.

" *June 8th.*—Started for the village of Kwawewe, but learning that the people had moved away and were living amongst the reeds some distance off, I at last found their huts, but in the chief's absence was not allowed to visit them.

" *June 9th.*—The chief came to-day, saying he was sorry he was absent yesterday, but that now he had brought his people to hear what I had to say.   I spoke to them all in my hut, and the chief, who seems to be a sensible, cautious man, thanked me repeatedly, and wanted to give me a little boy as a present.

"*June 13th* —Started early in the morning, the main body of the carriers being behind We passed several villages safely, the people only coming out to look at us, but when we reached one of their large towns they gathered round us dancing, shouting, and yelling to us to stop, and swinging their weapons over their heads. They then laid hold on some of the carriers, and drove off my ox, so I ran back and kept them off the goods until Senhor Porto came up with some more men. I was within a very small inch of getting my head split with an axe. Springing from his hammock Senhor Porto seized his gun, which made the ruffians fall back. Having recovered my ox, I started off with the boys and women carriers, while Senhor Porto and some armed men kept the Baluchaze at bay.

"*June 14th.*—Reached the town of Herero, who is headman of the Baluchaze living along the Kuti. He proved as disagreeable as his people, demanding from us an ox and some leopard skins. I sent word to Herero that I was a man of peace, who had come from far, and that I hoped to return to them shortly

"*June 15th.*—Got off without further trouble, Senhor Porto having given some leopard skins to the chief. Left the Kuti, and, crossing a very steep hill, descended to the River Kuvangui, a rapid and deep stream, which I crossed by a frail wooden bridge, the carriers going further up to a ford. Keeping by this river for four hours we passed Kankanga's, and then camped at the town of Kashima's daughter. I speak of ' towns ' ; but though the people are in considerable numbers, gathered close together under their chief, their huts are so hidden and scattered in dense wood, that to a passer-by the only signs of the presence of human beings are certain narrow and winding footpaths here and there.

" The regular camping places are generally on the border of some forest, where the porters can get sufficient poles to erect rude frameworks, the spaces of which are filled with leafy branches ; and in the rainy season a rough thatch covering is added. We were busy getting our camp into order when some Baluchaze came, evidently bent upon mischief. Getting nothing for their impudence they left us. In a short time, however, we saw the long grass on all sides of us on fire. All our men turned out, and beating down the flames as they approached our camp, they succeeded in stamping out the fire. We then called the men together and discovered that eight of our number were missing, so that our worst suspicions concerning these Baluchaze were confirmed. They had set fire to the grass around our camp to distract our attention while they carried off all the stragglers they could catch. We found that two of our men had been taken some distance, but the other six were still in the neighbourhood.

" Calling for volunteers I procured from the bottom of my trunk a pistol that Mr. Westbeech had given me, and set to cleaning and loading it We soon had 30 smart young men ready to follow up the robbers I lined them up, and as all claimed kinship with the stolen men I knew that they could be relied upon. And now what about a short prayer ? I fumbled with my pistol. Certainly to the African mind I knew I could not have it both ways. So after a struggle I hastened back to my box, replaced the pistol, and then in the midst of the men I knelt and humbly asked God, for Jesus' sake, to give us back the two stolen men. And so off we set. The light was just sufficient to enable us to find the trail ; soon darkness fell as on we sped in silence.

" After a weary ten-mile journey over the hills we came upon the robbers, and found them ready to fight, as they only thought we had come to recover by force the stolen men. I made every effort to get between my own men and the Baluchaze, and, as a sign of my peaceful intentions, I held up one of their native stools in front of the threatening crowd and then sat down upon it, urging them to sit down and talk with me. The old chief, seeing the younger men fall back, began to chide them for being afraid, and rushing forward he levelled his gun at me, ready to fire. By this time our Bihé men had their guns to their shoulders, but I called upon them not to fire. The young men, fearing that their old chief would bring mischief upon them if he shot me, laid hold of him, took his gun from him, and marched him off to a hut close by, in the most ignominious manner, with his hands behind his back. At last, one by one, they came near and sat down, and we talked the matter over. They said they were not angry with us, but with other white men who were their enemies, and they at last promised to bring down the two captives next day to camp. They kept their word, and the stolen men were brought back next day; presents were exchanged, and thus ended what had been to me a very trying ordeal.

"*June 21st.*—At the head of the Rovangwe River some men, who remained behind with a worn-out ox, were attacked by a roving company of Baluchaze, but a few carriers, observing what had happened, laid down their loads and ran back to their assistance, and the robbers decamped.

"*June 22nd.*—Left the Okovangu Valley, crossed a high range of hills, in the midst of which runs the Smsoy River, and reached the Kwando River in the afternoon. It is nearly two years since I first struck this river some distance below Linyanti, where it is broad and reedy, taking hours to cross while here it is but eight or ten feet broad.

"*June 23rd*—As we go up the Kwando the scenery becomes more expanded and grand. The hills on each side are high and wide apart, and covered on the tops with dense forest. Bright, rapid streams run down every valley. It is strange to find every stream in this part of the country full in the dry season; during the rains they are low. The hills here seem to be one mass of sand, firm though very porous. They absorb the rains as they fall, and months pass before the water reaches the bed of clay underlying these sand hills. The rivers run off this clay bed, and all through the dry season the water trickles into them from both banks and all along their courses.

"*June 24th.*—Reached the head of the Kwando, which rises very quietly out of a pool about 15 ft. in diameter. Our camp being soon crowded with people, of whom there are many here, I told one of the fathers of the tribe something of my mission, and of the God whom I served. The old man ran off excitedly to bring some other old men, who greeted me with clapping of hands, and to them he retailed with great energy what I had said to him. I told them I was only journeying to get cloth wherewith to buy food, and would return soon. But my old friend wanted to know exactly when I would come back. Would I return when the corn was so high, or so high, or so high?—lifting the hand a foot or so each time.

"*June 25th*—Crossed the Kutau and Biseque; camped at Kambuti, at the head of the latter river. The Biseque joins the Kutau, which falls into the Lungebungo, a tributary of the Zambesi. For some time back I have been travelling almost entirely on foot, as my riding ox is quite done up for want of grass, which the frost by night and the sun by day have withered to tinder. Walking 15 miles a day through deep sand and under a hot sun is not easy work, and on hearing of it Senhor Porto was quite angry, saying that I should surely be ill after it ; so between us we rigged up a hammock, and he has given me four of his own men to carry it. To-day I enjoyed my hammock ride amazingly.

" *June 26th.*—At Kambiti. This is the first place where I have seen the domestic pig in native territory.

" *June 27th* —Reached the Kansambe River, and camped at Brutwe. The Kansambe is a small river running east, not west, as Serpa Pinto has it in his map ; it joins the Kuango on its western side, which runs parallel with the Kutau into the Lungebungo. Crossed a high range of hills, and camped by the Kambimbia, flowing west ; its waters go by the Nyonga and Kuito to the Okovangu River, which flows into Lake Ngami.

" *June 29th.*—Crossed the Kuito River. The Baluchaze are not found further west ; they belong to the Ambuella race, which is the same as the Baluchaze, their language being merely a different dialect. Like all hill men, they are wild and troublesome, continually roving about. Among themselves, however, these natives are very playful and childlike, and seem very fond of one another. Many of the Bachokwe live amongst them, but do not wander much from home like the hill people. Some who had been a short distance away, and travelled in our company, seemed to be quite overcome with joy at getting home again. Their friends were not satisfied with merely embracing them, but caressed them in the most affectionate manner. It reminded me of the conduct of a poor Masaroa woman, who with her husband and baby had been captured by a company of raiding Matabele. Her little boy of ten had escaped in the fray, and remained behind ; but on the way her husband was killed, and the woman, watching her opportunity, ran away from her captors. After a wearisome journey of over 70 miles through a most dreary and desolate country, with her little babe on her back, she returned to the place where her boy was. Taking him in her arms, with all the warmth of a true mother, she burst into tears, saying, ' Ah, my boy, you have lost your father, and you do not know how near you were to losing me ! '

KUTAITU CROSSING

Carriers resting preparatory to crossing the river.

" Their attachment to one another, although a beautiful feature in their character, is embarrassing at times to strangers, for, on seeking to strike a bargain with one of them, you find you have a dozen to deal with. The same thing happens when one thinks he is injured, be he young or old. A cry is raised, and all come to the rescue. In this way I have seen the most serious disturbances arise out of the merest trifle.

" *July 2nd.*—Following the course of the Onda River, we passed through a fine open country, crossing a running stream of water every half-hour, some large, some small, but all running rapidly. During the dry season the whole country could be put under water by irrigation. Why it should be almost entirely deserted by the Kimbanda I cannot say We reached the town of Kabango, who had recently died ; the Kimbanda were very civil, and careful not to give offence.

" *July 3rd.*—Camped by the Letot River. Here a trouble that had been brewing for a long time amongst the men, broke out. We were now getting near to Bihé, and one of the men insisted that another who owed him something should pay his debt before they entered their own country. The other refused to acknowledge his indebtedness, and hot words led to blows. Seizing his gun, already loaded, the debtor pulled the trigger twice while aiming at the other's breast. but being only a flint lock it missed fire on both occasions. The creditor in self-defence rushed on his assailant with a club, and compelled him to drop his gun by breaking two of his fingers. The injured man then seized his knife from his belt. rushed at the man he had failed to shoot, and stabbed him, the knife entering rather deeply into the abdomen. By this time the men in camp had come to the rescue, and prevented further mischief by separating the antagonists.

" *July 4th.*—Spent four hours in crossing the Quanza River ; such confusion I never saw, everyone rushing into the water to get his own load into the boats. I stood up to the waist in water, with a big stick, to prevent the men from overloading the long canoes. Ultimately all got over safely, and camped at Yapepa, close by the Kukema River.

" *July 5th.*—Crossed in boats, and after a long day's journey lodged at Chikoma's town, the same who found Cameron far in the interior in very destitute circumstances, and brought him out to Bihé, whence he reached Benguella

H

" I am now in Bihé territory, and mark a decided change for the better in the outward appearance of everything Everyone is well dressed ; the men wear hats and coats and a rather long cloth kilt ; the women wrap themselves in cotton cloth from the armpits downwards , bright, grotesque patterns being the rage amongst them. Their houses are square and well built, with hinged doors and native-made iron locks ; all, of course, in imitation of the Portuguese. Their gardens are large, well tilled, and neatly furrowed, quite like our fields at home. But they are sadly given to drink and immorality, it being an undeniable fact that those tribes which live near Europeans, and imitate them, are more depraved in their manners than the tribes of the interior.

" *July 14th.*—We safely reached Belmonte, Senhor Porto's residence in Bihé, and he kindly entertained me. Bihé is the name of a district, which is thickly peopled. To-day we went to see the king of these parts, a man about 60 years of age, who looks all fat and good humour ; he is lodged in the centre of a large town, quite a city. Senhor Porto said that we were fortunate in finding him sober, as his normal condition is much the reverse.

" *July 16th.*—Bad news has come from Bailundu to the effect that the American missionaries have been robbed and turned out of house and home.

" *July 19th.*—Men who were sent to Bailundu informed us, on their return, that they found the missionaries' houses in the hands of the natives, but where the missionaries had gone, or what had become of them, they could not learn. I cannot think of sitting here when my brethren are thus in trouble, so start to-morrow to see and hear for myself.

" *July 22nd.*—Crossed the Kutato River, and reached the town of Dungenugo, the son of the reigning king of Bailundu, who said that it was entirely owing to the conduct of a European trader that the missionaries had left the country.

" *July 24th.*—Passed many towns, the people of which brought out dishes of maize beer for me and my men to drink. Two men met me at some distance from Atinda to run my hammock into the town ; they ran so fast that they broke the hammock pole, and instead of having a grand entrance into the town, I was landed rolling in the dust just before the gate.

" *July 25th.*—Reached the town of Chikulu, the chief man

in the country at present, and had a long palaver with him and a few of the headmen, through my interpreter Jumbo. They had been persuaded by an evil disposed trader and rum distiller that the little tins containing meat, etc , were full of fetish enchantments, intended by the missionaries for the destruction of the Bailundu kingdom. The missionaries had to flee, seemingly taking nothing but their wives and little children. It was distressing to see all round the destruction of valuable property. Books of all kinds, photographs, letters, clothing. tins of sugar, tea, etc., were in every native's hands. With all my energy I spoke out to these Bailundu people as to the way in which they had permitted men to be turned out of house and home who had come to them with a message of peace from the true God ; they had treated them as they would not treat their dogs.

" Chikulu sent for the trader, who tried at once to make friends with me, but being in no gentle mood I brought him to the point, and asked what charge he had against the Americans. ' Oh,' said he, ' I thought they were Jews, and not Christian missionaries ! ' He was compelled to explain matters to the natives, and I asked Chikulu if he was satisfied ; to which he replied, ' Perfectly,' adding that as the trader had only been telling lies, he himself was willing, if I would only say the word to lay hands on him then and there. I said I had come, not with any authority or intention to punish him, but to see justice done to my friends, and that Chikulu must gather the missionaries' goods together and keep them in safety until their return. My visit, I am thankful to say, ended in his sending one of his headmen and 50 carriers to bring back the missionaries

" The despotic power of the chiefs makes all mission work very uncertain in Africa at present, except where law and order are established and upheld, and therefore prayer for those ' in authority ' in Africa is especially needed. Any whim or sudden enmity of the chief, and fetish divination, or, as in this case, the evil counsel of an interested trader, may lead to the overthrow of years of work, and it may take a long time before it can be resumed. On this occasion it was my most unexpected arrival from the interior that led to an unusually speedy turn of the tide in favour of the missionaries Though Bailundu and Bihé are within the province of Benguella,

Portuguese authority has not yet very much influence there. In the far interior the perils of missionaries are of course greater, but in the Western half of Africa things are in this respect much better than in the Eastern half.

" Senhor Porto has been very kind to me. He is quite a gentleman. He has been trading in the interior for over 40 years. He is now close on 70 years old, but hale and strong, and is ever planning long trading journeys for the future. So you see Africa is not such a deadly country after all to the Europeans.

" *August 16th*, 1884.—Here at Bihé we have a civil war on foot just now. The greater part of the nation is with the king to put down the young claimant to the throne. However, everyone is in camp. Even Senhor Porto was called out, but made the excuse that he was too old. I was at Bailundu at the time, else I might have been forced to join the camp. I had left my gun at Bihe. This they took, so if I am not fighting, at least my artillery is at work   The Bailundu are also by this time all on the war-path, so I will have to remain here until the fighting is over ere I can get carriers.

" The work in which I have been most blessed, and which has been most joyous to me, and for which I seem to have most aptitude, is pioneer and out of the way work. As a teacher of children I want aptness, and am about as uneasy on the teacher's chair as on the scholar's bench at home. This, however, is not excusable and ought to be overcome. Again, with the raw savage negro I get on, I think, very well. I have any amount of patience, and though they fall out with me a dozen times in the day I never fall out with them, so there is no quarrelling. Because of this they call me many curious names, and say, ' Monare ! he wouldn't injure his greatest enemy.' As the result of this policy I had the unspeakable satisfaction of seeing the whole town turned out to flog a young man by making him run the gauntlet between two long rows of slim fellows armed with stripes of hippo hide. It was on my behalf, but not at my suggestion. He charged me with committing a shameful crime, which I know in my heart of hearts cannot be brought against me by anyone, and wanted me to pay so much cloth to shut his mouth. I was indignant beyond all expression, and drove him out of my yard   He brought the matter up before the headmen who soon found out that he was lying, and that he was a rogue and a thief. His skin soon healed after the flogging, and he had the good sense to come and beg my pardon. I never saw the young men of the town go about the matter so heartily as the flogging of that young man. All day long they danced about with their strips of hide showing how nicely they gave him a cut over the back or just across the fleshy part, and boasting of the great things they would do to the next man who would dare to injure Monare

" *Oct.* 16*th*, 1884 —I do not think there is anything so essential to real service for God in a wholly heathen country as an entire separation and devotion to the work, so that even isolation often has its advantages. I have found that one's time cannot be divided and laid out beforehand as at home. Amongst the Barotse I have risen to, say, a day of writing, but it turned out to be an all-day meeting. At festival seasons at Lealui crowds of people used to come in from all the country round ; at such times it was, from morning light until midnight, one constant stream of people passing through my house, all curious to see, some to hear, and some wanting to speak of what had been said on a former visit. Again, on making short trips amongst the villages I found the press of work almost unbearable at times, from pure lack of strength. The work is trying, but all engrossing, and it needs one to be wholly free from all temporal things. At home the earnest street preacher may gather a few little children around him after much noise and singing ; but in heathen Africa one is sometimes glad, in coming up to a village, to hide oneself. Everything is laid aside , the child toddles out to the field to call its mother , the hunters return and call in their dogs ; and the cattle are driven to their enclosures, that the herdsmen may come and listen to the white man's words. The more isolated and ignorant the people the more eager they are. Wherever I was able to make the character of my errand known, their willingness, their intelligent enquiry, their excitement even, quite wore me out.

" I expected to have been back to such precious work by this time, but the Good Shepherd knows what is best for His sheep. Meanwhile I have been getting rid of some of my fever legacies. Ague now seems to be a thing of the past. My spleen, which was so much swollen that I could not lie with comfort in any position, is now almost reduced to its proper condition. My body has in every way picked up in this fine healthy country.

"The languages, though of course perplexing to a stranger, are undoubtedly easy, both in construction and pronunciation. Speaking as they do in fidelity to the natural law of euphony, they are wonderfully accurate. When reducing the languages to a written form, missionaries find that if they can but discover any grammatical rule it has almost no exceptions. African languages are not to be learned at all correctly by direct conversation with the natives. They are more accurately acquired by constantly listening to their conversation one with another. Their manner of conversing with a European is absurd and very misleading. Not only do they distort their own language greatly, but they are constantly using outlandish sounds, which they think belong to the white man's tongue, and which they in their smartness have picked up.

"Again, if a European wishes to be intelligible to the raw native who has not been tutored to understand the sounds of strange tongues, he must remember that African languages are composed not only of sounds, but of accentuated sounds. If he does not pay the closest attention to this, though he may be able to speak fluently to the natives in a white man's store or town, he will require a person to interpret his words to a company of raw villagers. The Bushman's language goes to an extreme in this respect ; certain sounds and clicks accented differently, pitched in a higher or lower key, shrill or deep-sounding, have all their different meanings ; their language is consequently very musical. To hear the little children speaking and laughing in their play is often like listening to the tinkling of a musical box.

"*Oct. 23rd*, 1884.—Met Mr. and Mrs. Sanders, the American missionaries, to-day at Bailundu, and had a happy time with them. Their hearts are indeed in the work here, and they mean to go on in the name of the Lord. It was soul-stirring to see them, and their little caravan, wending their way across the wooded hill to their old home at Bailundu, having been robbed, plundered, forced to fly almost for life, but coming back again undaunted.

"The arrival of Mr. and Mrs. Sanders brought my study of Ovimbundu superstitions to a close. I was so glad to see

them that it did not dawn upon me for some time that my
clothes were hardly respectable. An old coat of Senhor Porto's
buttoned up to my neck betrayed the fact that I had not a
shirt to my back. Just then a young native came bouncing
along with a flowing white shirt on his back that Mrs. Sanders
recognised as part of their stolen belongings, and it was a clear
case of ' stand and deliver.' The shirt came over his head and
through a bath of soap suds, and on to my back, ere the sun
set that day.

" I thought of waiting at Bailundu until Senhor Porto
came along, but learning that he would be delayed for some
days in building a bridge, I went on. On the way I met a
company from the far interior. They were not different from
the rest of the people, but in my present state of mind they were
naturally of great interest to me. They were from the chief
Msidi, of Garenganze, and had been sent with a letter to the
king's brother-in-law, Coimbra, a half-caste, who read to me
the letter just received from Msidi. It was dated this year,
was written in a wretched sort of Portuguese, possibly by some
half-taught black, and contained an earnest appeal that white
men might come to Garenganze. I looked with amazement
on the piece of rude, well-travelled paper. Of course it was
as traders that he wanted white men, but I felt I had something
even better than good trade, which, if Msidi could only com-
prehend, he would gladly receive. The brother-in-law was
delighted to hear of my proposal to go thither, and sent for
a black, lanky slave from that part ; he knew exactly the place
where Livingstone died, at Ilala, by Lake Bangweolo. I may
yet get this man to go with me, but the guide I have already
employed knows all the country.

" Let us look up and take courage ; the Lord reigneth.
Surely he has taken many ways to show me from the first His
desire to guide me ; He comes down to our weak faith, as He
did in Gideon's case, and repeats the signs until we are filled
with shame at our blindness and tardiness. I think it is now
clear that I must seek another way to the Batoka, Liwanika's
Barotse ' dogs ' ; in this case the Lord may feed the ' dogs '
before the ' children.' I shall be at liberty, so far as I can
learn, to come as near to the Barotse as possible, and yet
remain outside their sway , and were I to go down among
them at any time, I should, humanly speaking, suffer no harm,

having so many friends amongst them. I might be able, by going between both, to unite these two great countries, and secure a way for others, through the Baiotse, to the north, which at present, through jealousy, is shut.

"I am told that Garenganze is as healthy as Bailundu; if so, there is no fever there; one might hope to live, and not merely exist. I shall make a particular request to each chief by the way to have a young man ready to run with my letters as they come from the interior or the coast, and think this plan would work in time of peace. Native news in this way flies like the wind, and why not my letters? The only question would be the amount of pay.

"The Governor of Benguella took the trouble to write to Senhor Porto to take care of me, and bring me safely to the coast. Perhaps because of the trouble the Americans had at Bailundu, the Governor feared that I, being English, might suffer from the Bailundu, and bring down an English inquisition upon him. Senhor Porto is my guardian in the meantime, and although I have been running about to my heart's content, I fear he would consider me ungrateful were I to go to Benguella before him, so I must wait here for a couple of days, as he has been detained on the road. Strange that patience towards the end of a journey is far harder than patience at the beginning. Staying a whole week here, within three days or so of the coast, seems intolerable.

"A Portuguese called to-day, and after talking for some time he remarked that at Benguella they were expecting one 'Padre Arnot' from the East Coast. He knew that I had come from the East, but could not recognise the Padre. I heard him laughing when I told him that I was the Padre.

"True and faithful service is not thrown away as the following shows: Mr. W W. Bagster, now gone home, gave three years ago a Testament to Coimbra, with whom I am staying, the reading of which touched him, and Mr. Sanders has since had long talks with him. Coimbra is anxious about his soul. Although I had not been speaking to him in a personal way, he took down his Testament this morning and turned to Mark x. 29, saying to me, 'This is my trouble.' He could not leave wives, children, houses, and all. I told him that the Lord did not ask him to leave anything, but to receive, and that when God's love filled his heart he would know by the power of love how to serve Him. He said that he was greatly relieved, and that his way seemed more clear; he did not desire any longer to live with more than one wife, but he could not turn into the fields those who were the mothers of his children, nor put away his children. The good Lord will not quench the smoking flax.

" *Nov. 9th*, 1884 —At Catumbella at last. Waiting for Senhor Porto; a sharp attack of dysentery detained me. I ate too freely of bananas. Fortunately Senhor Porto came along just then. He engaged 20 hammock carriers and packed me off to Benguella. My men carried me all that night down through a series of steep passes strewn with boulders. Leopards kept up a constant barking roar. When morning broke we reached a river into which I was glad to roll myself, and with the cold water flowing over my fevered body I went off into a sound sleep for several hours. On resuming the journey again I knew I was better, and as the sun grew round and red we came in sight of the sea."

CHAPTER IX

THE following extracts are from letters written towards the end of 1884 concerning the beliefs of the various tribes through whom Arnot had passed up till then.

" ' Nambi,' the one great spirit who made all and rules over all, the Barotse believe in, but they look upon him as an austere person, who only heaps sorrow, death, and punishment upon them. All good that comes to them they trace to the power and intercession of the spirit of some departed chief or forefather. The idea they seem to have is that those departed spirits, whom they worship, have a sympathy which ' Nambi ' has not, a sympathy with them in all the joys and sorrows connected with their journeyings, crops, hunts, cattle, wives, etc, because they, while in the body, experience the same Alas! they little know at what a cost our God has provided for us, and for them too, a Saviour and High Priest, who feels for us as no man can feel, who suffered and sorrowed as no man ever did, and who yet has verily a fellow-feeling with us. The religion of these Upper-River people is widely different from that of the other tribes. It has been known to some that they believed in one supreme God, but no more was known about them. There are many other interesting ceremonies of theirs connected with the offering of oxen, corn, beads, and cloth, concerning which I hope to get more information. They have their diviners, seers, magicians, and doctors, who work with a mass of beads, human bones, speaking horns, claws of wild animals, and a whole host of things, all of which together they call ' Lequalo,' and to read them, so as to prophesy about them, is ' Noqualo.' They give this name to the Word of God and all other books of the white man. The only difference they think, between our ' Lequalo ' and theirs is that ours is a confused mass of little black marks on paper, and theirs is surely much more sensible, as it consists of substantial things.

122

" When going to pray the Barotse make offerings to the spirits of their forefathers under a tree, bush, or grove, planted for the purpose, and they take a larger or smaller offering, according to the measure of their request. If the offering be beer, they pour it upon the ground ; if cloth, it is tied to a horn stuck in the ground ; if an ox be slaughtered, the blood is poured over this horn, which is, in fact, their altar.

" The tribes we have passed through (from the Zambesi to the Kuito) seem to have one common religion, if it can be called by that name. They say there is one Great Spirit who rules over all the other spirits ; but so far as I can learn, they worship and sacrifice to the spirits of ancestors, and have a mass of fetish medicines and enchantments. The hunter takes one kind of charm with him, and the warrior another. For divining they have a basket filled with bones, teeth, finger nails, claws, seeds, stones and such like articles which are rattled by the diviner till the spirit comes and speaks to him by the movement of these things. When the spirit is reluctant to be brought up a solemn dirge is chanted by the people. All is attention while the diviner utters a string of short sentences in different tones, which are repeated after him by the audience.

" These professional diviners are no doubt smart fellows, arch rogues though they be. The secret of their art lies in constant repetition of every possibility in connection with the disaster they are called upon to explain, until they finally hit upon that which is in the minds of their clients. As the people sit around and repeat the words of the diviner it is easy for him to detect in their tone of voice, or to read in their faces, the suspected source of the calamity. A man whom I knew had a favourite dog which was attacked one night by a leopard, but succeeded in escaping with one of its eyes torn out. To ascertain the reason of this calamity the owner sent across the Valley to call one of these diviners. When the man arrived he was told that a disaster had befallen my acquaintance, and was asked to find out by divination what it was. Beginning in the morning, he enquired respecting the man's family, without mentioning their names. All the members of the family and their connections, male and female, young and old, at home or absent, were carefully gone over Not getting any clue, he left the relatives, and came to the oxen, questioning the spirits concerning them ; but still receiving no reply through the fragments, which he

continually shook in his basket, he next enquired about the
goats. This was not satisfactory, and at last he thought of the
dog. In the faces and tone of voice of his audience it was not
difficult to discern that he had hit the mark, and after hours of
dreary waiting his oracular utterance, obtained, of course, from
the bones and claws, that something had befallen the dog,
seemed to come as a relief. He now asked if the dog was dead ,
then if it was stolen ; then if it was wounded ! Slyly reading
the response in their countenances, he said, ' Yes, it is wounded.'
Following up the trail he touched upon all possibilities that
occurred to him, his audience mechanically repeating his questions, till at last he demanded of the spirit, ' Was it a leopard ? '
All the company roused up as they echoed, ' Was it a leopard ? '
while they cast a knowing look of satisfaction at one another.
' Yes ! ' the diviner replied, ' it was a leopard.' Then all present
shouted, ' It was a leopard.' But that was not enough. The
cause of the disaster had to be traced still further back. What
demon so possessed this particular leopard that it should attack
the dog of this wealthy man ? So other questions had to be
asked, and the same process was continued. At last, towards
evening, the diviner arrived at the same conclusion that the
owner of the dog had come to early that morning on hearing
of the accident to his dog, namely, that the spirit of the father
of one of his wives had been grieved at the man's long absence
from his town and family, and employed the leopard to tear
the dog's eye as a gentle reminder that it was time he should
be going back to his own village

"I have detailed the foregoing incident at some length to
give some idea of the measure of religious enlightenment that
these poor people have. Yet among all these tribes there is an
open door for a messenger of the Gospel. Every time I have
been able to gain their ear, unhindered by any quarrel, they
have shown much interest and delight, and have acknowledged
that they are living in darkness, and in ignorance of the great
Spirit who rules over all.

"In Chikulu's yard (Chikulu is the chief of the Bailundu)
there is a small, roughly cut image, which, I believe, represents
the spirit of a forefather of his. One day a man and woman came
in and rushed up to this image, dancing, howling, and foaming
at the mouth, apparently mad. A group gathered round and
and declared that the spirit of Chikulu's forefather had taken

possession of this man and woman, and was about to speak
through them.   At last the ' demon ' began to grunt and groan
out to poor Chikulu, who was down on his knees, that he must
hold a hunt, the proceeds of which were to be given to the
people of his town , must kill an ox, provide so many large
pots of beer, and proclaim a grand feast and dance.   Further-
more all this was to be done quickly.   The poor old man
was thoroughly taken in, and in two days' time the hunt was
organised.

"Thus I find, as amongst the Barotse, that divining and
prophesying, with other religious and superstitious means are
resorted to, in order to secure private ends, and to offer sacrifice
to the one common god, the belly.   The more I see of them, the
more I am persuaded that they have no other god, and this I
tell them continually.

" At another time a man came to Senhor Porto's to buy an ox.
He said that some time ago he had killed a relation by witchcraft to possess himself of some of his riches, and that now he
must sacrifice an ox to the dead man's spirit, which was
troubling him.   This killing by witchcraft is a thing most
sincerely believed in ; and on hearing this man's cold blooded
confession of what was at least the intent of his heart, it made
me understand why the Barotse put such demons into the fire.

" Among the Ovimbundu, old and renowned witches are
thrown into some river, though almost every man will confess
that he practises witchcraft to avenge himself of wrong done,
and to punish his enemies.   One common process is to boil
together certain fruits and roots, with which the wizard daubs
his body, in order to enlist the aid of the demons, and the decoction is then thrown in the direction of the victim, or laid in his
path, that he may be brought under the bewitching spell.

" These West Africans have not that attachment to other
members of their own tribe which is seen among the Zulu,
the Bechuana, and even the Zambesi tribes, where each man
is his neighbour's brother   Here they live to bite and devour
one another.   The most trival mistake or breach of etiquette
is a crime, and has to be paid for dearly.   A man who acci-
dentally knocked over a small pot of fat was fined thirty shillings' worth of beeswax.   A stranger passing through the
country is liable to be entrapped into paying heavy fines.   If
a slave steals, say a few ears of corn out of a garden, he is

seized, and if not redeemed by his master s paying a large compensation, he is at once sold.

" Death is surrounded by many strange and absurb superstitions. It is considered essential that a man should die in his own country, if not in his own town. On the way to Bailundu, shortly after leaving Bihé territory, I met some men running at great speed, carrying a sick man tied to a pole, in order that he might die in his own country. I tried to stop them, but they were running as fast as their burden would allow them down a steep rocky hill. By the sick man's convulsive movements I could see that he was in great pain, perhaps in his death throes, hence the great haste. If a Bailundu dies in Bihé, the Bihé people have to pay the Bailundu heavily for the shameful conduct of the Bihé demons in killing a stranger, and vice versa.

" When a man dies at home his body is placed on a rude table, and his friends meet for days around the corpse, drinking, eating, shouting, and singing, until the body begins actually to fall to pieces. Then the body is tied in a faggot of poles and carried on men's shoulders up and down some open space, followed by doctors and drummers. The doctors demand of the dead man the cause of his death, whether by poison or witchcraft, and if by the latter, who was the witch ? Most of the deaths I have known of in negro-land were from pulmonary diseases, but all were set down to witchcraft. The jerking of the bier to and fro, causing the men bearing it to stumble hither and thither, is taken as the dead man's answer ; thus, as in the case of spirit rapping at home, the reply is spelled out. The result of this enquiry is implicitly believed in, and, if the case demands it, the witch is drowned   There might be some reason for their superstition if the dead body were laid upon the ground and allowed to jerk itself ; but to put the corpse on the shoulders of six drunken men, and to say that the jerking and stumbling are caused by the inanimate body is so thoroughly ridiculous that one cannot imagine how it ever entered the minds of men to judge and condemn their fellow creatures by such a process as this. Compared with it the Barotse boiling water ordeal is reasonable.

" After all these knotty points are settled the poor man gets a decent burial, but chiefs and great men do not get to rest so soon. Their bodies have been kept above ground two years after death. When a chief dies they at first say that he is sick or asleep, and all the business of the state is conducted by a man who sits in a hut beside the dead body.

" The people have a great fear of death, which they do not seem to look upon as a certainty, and as the natural end of life. At least to say so in conversation gives offence. They would fain believe that death is a mishap, an evil brought about by fetish agencies; but for which, man would be immortal. Consequently, all their so-called religious observances and charms are meant to counteract the influence of these evil fetishes by other fetishes. Before starting on a journey a man will spend always a fortnight in preparing charms to overcome evils by the way, and to enable him to destroy his enemies. If he be a trader, he desires to find favour in the eyes of chiefs, and a liberal price for his goods. As there is no limit to a man's fears, superstitions, avarice, or hatred of his enemies, so there is no limit to the number of his charms; and at the end of his journey he finds himself loaded with such things, sown into belts and hung in little horns around his neck.

" As to the articles used in the composition of charms, I may say that everything under the sun is used. I have been told here that they can turn the hills into water with some of them, can make an ox impervious to bullet or spear, can create a living lion out of the skin of a dead one, and can bring death or sickness upon anyone.

" Many half-castes and Portuguese believe strongly in the charms of the Ovimbundu tribes; but on questioning them closely as to certain of the mysterious things alleged to be done, I always find that the thing has happened in the night time, and that the fetish doctors will not cast their charms or work miracles at any other times. How close the connection between spiritual and literal darkness.

" In conversation with the people of Bihé about the one true God I find that they profess to believe in His existence, and say that there is and must be a great Spirit over and above all, whom they call Suku, but that they do not know him. They do not appear in any way to connect Suku with the things which are daily occurring around them. I cannot even say that they truly believe him to be a universal God, for they always speak of the white man as being under a separate set of gods and spirits from themselves.

" Judging according to human judgment, I should say that the missionary of the Gospel would find the ground here very hard indeed. Besides the mass of superstition, which surpasses anything I ever heard of in Africa, there have been for nearly two centuries many evil and brutalising influences working upon the people, and few humanising ones. During all this time rum and the slave trade have had full scope. For the greater part of the seventeenth and eighteenth centuries there were many Roman Catholic missionaries at work all along the West Coast, and for some little way into the interior; but the only remaining trace of them or their work are a few Christian ' relics ' added to the heap of native charms, and here and there a wooden cross standing at the head of some pagan's grave, sharing the ground with fantastic heathen images and symbols. Many thoughts come into one's mind on looking upon such a scene of confusion. Only the one confident assurance that there is a God who liveth could strengthen the heart of any servant of the Lord coming to this part."

CHAPTER X

AT AND AROUND BENGUELLA

"*BENGUELLA, Nov. 11th.*—Arrived here early this morning in the company of Senhor Porto. Nothing could have been more hearty than the reception I received from Mr. and Mrs. Walter, of the American Board of Missions, and nothing more delightful to me than meeting with these earnest Christian friends after my long exile

"*Nov. 12th.*—Called on the Governor of Benguella. He was very pleasant, inquiring about Africa Central, and has promised me letters to Bihé and Bailundu, guaranteeing my protection. This he did because of the cool way I was robbed by the Bihé chief.

"*Nov. 15th.*—Sent off to Bailundu for fifty carriers to be here on or about the 10th of January. Mr. Walter has asked me to return inland as soon as possible so as to give the missionaries at Bailundu as much help as I can before I start for the interior.

"*Nov. 16th.*—Had a meeting on the American barque *Horace Scow* this forenoon. About eighteen present in all. It was a great privilege to have the opportunity of preaching Christ once more in my own tongue. It was nearly too much for me. I don't know—it seems strange to say it—but to me it seems one of the hard things by going off to the dark, heathen parts of the country, to give up the preaching of the Gospel in all its fullness, as one can do to an intelligent audience. But that I fear is one of the many fancied 'hard things' that we are too apt to fill our thoughts with, for surely it is a higher privilege to be able to speak of Him in places where His name has never been mentioned.

"*Dec. 5th*, 1884.—Welcome letters from home to-day. German man-of-war came into the Bay with Prof. Nachtigall on board. He called and asked many questions. Home friends seem to be all in favour of the Garenganze project. This is good. They are even reconciled to my going alone.

I   129

"*Dec. 9th.*—Benguella is a very quiet, unbusiness-like place. The Custom House duties are very heavy; they average 25 per cent on everything, and this on the value of goods here, not on invoice value, so that all goods imported are of necessity expensive. I should say that the place is unhealthy; the Portuguese, at least, consider it so, as the most of their convicts are sent here, and all government officials, while in office here, are reckoned as serving double time. It is not so at Loanda.

"It seems as if the sea had thrown up a sand dyke, forming the present shore; much of the country inside appears to be at a level lower than the sea; consequently it has no drainage. Fortunately, little rain falls; even now, though it is the rainy season, green spots are only to be seen in a few hollows. The heat is very great, but every afternoon a fresh breeze comes off the sea, which makes the evenings pleasant. I am in the best of health.

"May the Lord be pleased to look upon my work for His name's sake, and may I be in His hands like soft clay, impressionable. Surely the one thing needful for perfect service is that we be susceptible to His sympathies and to the guidings of His Spirit. God will not guide and lead us into His work unless we first have hearts in sympathy with Him as to that work So let us hang and wait upon God, that we may go forth as men ' driven of the Spirit '

"I had now to consider seriously the advisability of returning to the interior alone, in case of no one coming forward to join me. On that subject I then wrote my impressions: I have a growing conviction that some one or two are being prepared for the work here, but any will not do; excuse my saying so. Africa is a very trying country in every sense of the word. It is not always the bright, smart, active man who does for Africa; for such a man to find himself in the hands of some miserable creatures, and actually made a plaything of by them, would often be utterly unbearable. To find that when he is planning to make a few days' quicker march, his men are planning a few days' extra slow march; to have to deal with men who, directly they think they have become indispensable, delight to exercise the most cruel tyranny; to find oneself surrounded by lip-friends only, whose hearts are like drawn swords, as a general rule—these are discoveries so utterly foreign to first impressions of the negro races that the hearts of many sink under them. The white man who comes to Africa thinks, as a rule, that the negro looks up to him as an essentially superior being ; but let him hear them discussing round their camp fires, as I have often done when supposed by them to be lying asleep, and he will think differently   Is there a race under the sun which does not in its heart of hearts believe, ' We are the people ' ?

" In thinking of journeying alone, friends at home interested in this pioneer work will see that it is not an undue hastening on my part. I must get my goods up to Bihé in time for a final start this dry season, so as to reach and cross the Lovale flats near the sources of the Zambesi, before they are flooded. Otherwise the journey would be much more difficult. I shall, God willing, first make for those high ranges of mountains which are marked in some maps just above the Barotse country, and shall engage carriers—some I have already partly engaged —for Msidi's town, which is among the hills in the country called, in the interior, Garenganze. From the first I was very desirous of going at least in that direction, but was prevented, no doubt for a wise purpose, from going beyond the immediate neighbourhood of the Zambesi River, as the Barotse do not want any ' good things ' to go to the tribes under their sway. I have seen large companies of natives from that part, and have many times conversed with them. From native sources in the interior, I learn that the Garenganze is one of the most densely populated districts of Central Africa. The people there are famed for the abundance of their corn, rice, sugar-cane, etc., and they work large copper mines, cleansing and smelting the copper out of the ore in a very perfect way, of which I have seen many samples. The question, whether I should merely go on a visit to the chief asking his permission to return, or whether I should go prepared to settle, should the way be open, is one difficult to decide. If the simple invitation of the chief of the country were the only thing desired, that might be obtained by sending a messenger; but nothing counts like a personal visit. I therefore propose to go to the Garenganze, hoping, with God's help, to get the permission, not only of the chief and headmen, but also of the people, to remain among them. It is more and more evident to me that much Christian diplomacy is required for the establishment and carrying on of African mission work. The people are not so many poor, intelligent monkeys; and this I have learned, that, fond as they are of presents, they are not to be bought by money. It may, however, be different with those on the coast.

"Going merely as a visitor will not prevent my remaining for one or two years. It requires all that time in Africa ere the people will venture to say that they know you. If friends at home could just get one glimpse of the burning need here, the open sore, and the willingness withal to hear, they would sympathise with me a little in my desire to remain as long as possible and at all cost, providing at the same time all things honestly, and receiving 'nothing from the Gentiles'; for the moment one begins to do so, he is branded by his enemies as 'an eater-up of the people.' The work of carrying the gospel to Africa's millions is going on, for it is the Lord's work, and it will go on in spite of any of us; but time is passing, and I would say to myself and to others, 'Let us in all our service be prompt. Let us ever have our loins girt for the ready, speedy carrying out of the will of our Lord.'

"*Dec. 25th, Christmas*—(To his mother.) 'This day must not pass without a letter to you. I know how happy you will be with all your big boys at home, and all off to Aunty's in the afternoon. I don't doubt but that you will be consoling yourself by thinking, "Well! Fred is a little nearer this Christmas than last, and that he will have the company of someone," etc. But this is not so, mother of mine. I am, as far as company goes, as much alone this Christmas as I have been in the last three spent in Africa. An English man-of-war, H.M.S. *Forward*, came down from Loanda, wanted me and the Walters to return with them to spend the "festive season" with the Governor-General and the British Consul at Loanda, promising at the same time to bring us back in a fortnight's time. The officer-in-charge, Lieut. Furlonger, had heard of my journey across (it seems to be a great feat in the eyes of these men), and wanted to be "at my service," took me on board, said "here's my carpenter, my sailmaker, blacksmith, etc., just say if you want anything done; could he make a tent for me, etc., etc. Did I want ammunition? Could give me some. Anything from Loanda? It's a British vessel, and we are quite at your service." If I had thought he really meant what he said, I would have politely asked him to turn that big gun upon that Customs House, and then in a playful way clear off a few of the Portuguese vile institutions, whisky mills and millers (the Custom dues are awful, 20 per cent, the lowest, on value of common things such as potatoes, 40 per cent and 50 per cent on ordinary things. The dues on cloth are more than the price at home). Well! I did not accept of his invitation to go to Loanda. So here I am with Dick cooking up a bit of soup. I have just been oiling a canvas coat to make it waterproof, and writing " rush away " letters promiscuously. Not a single Portuguese looks in here unless it be from across the street. I hear the distant jingling of a kirk bell, the spasmodic howlings of some drunk, having his " merry Christmas " out , the children's voices are shriller , the women passing up and down speak in a more light and laughing way. These, and such like tokens of " This is Christmas Day " reach my ears and eyes, but nothing more. My heart is with the dear home gathering.

" ' I am sure you will have many anxious thoughts as to my future journey. This time I go with my eyes more open to all that is before me. If there was anything of a boyish tone of adventure—and constant exhilaration arising from hearing and seeing many new and strange things—when I left Natal three years ago, I must confess that has gone now, and there is nothing new or novel to me in seeing on every hand constant exhibitions of a depraved and superstitious humanity; instead of being exhilarating it is beyond all expression, depressing. And yet I can say from the depth of my heart at no time have I felt more enthusiastic about any journey than now. I am sure you do acknowledge and thank the Lord with me for the truly gracious way in which He has been pleased to display His good will towards me in this country.

" ' It is a long time since I thought of this country, and some-times, even yet, I wonder if it is not a dream. Is the long, long desire of heart accomplished ? I scarcely ever, as far back as my memory takes me, opened a book, or watched a tradesman at his work, without the thought ever being in my mind, " Will this be of use for Africa ? I must remember that for Africa." So that I find all those old things turning up continuously.

" ' True I am labouring under a disadvantage in being alone, but it may be to the advantage of the work that I go forward alone, and make proper search and arrangements for a station. As Mr. G. says I would not have been altogether justified in starting out from home without a companion, but since I lost him I can only wait patiently on the Lord's time.

" ' I have an impression that it would be good for the work, and for the success of the Gospel, in the heart of one of these faraway African tribes, that such a one should be married to a devoted Christian woman. I am persuaded more and more that it requires gentlest things to overcome roughest things. The African's mode of living is purely and intensely pastoral, the people are at the best scattered. They are shepherds and cattle herds. They are hunters, and cultivators of the ground. Markets or places of public meeting, unless it be a king s court, are not native to them. They love to be scattered up and down in clumps of little villages. Now imagine one or two young men in the centre of, or close by, one of these clumps of family villages, surrounded by native family life in a way one would never dream of at home, the only steady residents being a few old men, women and children, and boys under ten. All the rest go and come; they go off on a hunt, a raid or a trading excursion. Now a single man remaining behind, if he wants to behave himself discreetly, according to native law, will keep rigidly within his own yard on such an occasion, and only converse with the old men ; to do ought else would be a breach of etiquette. When the husbands are at home of course he can speak freely to all. If, on the contrary, he were a married man, he, as well as his wife, would have access at all times to every one. Because of this, with many other things of a more serious nature, I have been persuaded that it would be a mistake for another to come out single as I am. Not that I can say I feel I have made a mistake in doing so ; on the contrary, so long as I am engaged in the present department of the work, that is prospecting, I could not be better than the way I am. But I see clearly two sides or two divisions in the work : first, the prospecting and travelling part; secondly, the " doing of the work of the evangelist." In the meantime I am bound to the first, and for some time at least would have to remain in that capacity more or less, bringing in supplies, and, as the Lord of the harvest sends forth labourers, from time to time. For the second division I could not think of any more fit than a married couple. The members of this American Mission have, I understand, sent home word to their Society, " not to send out any more missionaries un-

married." An African can understand an unmarried man travelling among them, but not living among them   It is in many
places against native law. Some of my enemies at the Barotse
(magicians and doctors) brought this up against me, and the
question was put to the king in open court, and had not the
king waived the law and decided in my favour, I could have
been legally driven out of the country. He, however, first of
all tried all he could to persuade me to marry among them, with
offers of rich presents of land and cattle and slaves and a
princess. I thought then that I would have to lift my luggage
and go, but the matter was overruled in my favour.'

" *Jan. 1st*, 1885 —The first day of the so-called New Year
receives notice generally and I suppose ought to be honoured
by at least a few lines in all well-conducted journals The word
has passed men's mouths, ' The old year is dead ! ' Only in
point of time, however. The deeds of last year, as seeds, will
order the harvest of this year's reaping for most men. The old
year is not dead. It has yet to live.

" *Jan. 4th.*—Just heard from Mr. Sanders that 50 carriers
are about to start for me and will be here in 10 days or so. I
have only 11 loads ready for them. My hope is in God. He
hath said those that put their trust in Him shall not be put to
shame.

" *Jan. 17th.*—News has just come in of an outbreak at
Caconda (12 days W.S.W. from here) against Portuguese
authority. About 200 coloured Portuguese soldiers are there
at present, or on the road, with two small field pieces.

" *Jan. 20th.*—In this country one learns to wait. In fact
this whole country, when one compares it with what one hears
of the busy outside world, seems to be, and has been, in a
waiting condition from the beginning of time, like a high sand-
bank, the last to be carried by the waters of a rushing, swelling
stream. Europe has been a sort of human volcano, every now
and then bursting out and sending off streams of human lava
to cover the earth. North and South America are well occupied,
and it seems to me that it will only be a question of a few years
ere the tide be turned towards Central Africa. I am persuaded
that a richer country in minerals, woods and water, is not to
be found. And the great mass of the interior country is
healthy.

" *Jan. 22nd.*—This afternoon carriers arrived for me. Mr.

Sanders had only got them with difficulty. When one considers how some 80 loads belonging to Sen Porto lie at Bailundu for want of carriers, and how trade here has suffered so much because the people of the interior are afraid to come down because of the war with Caconda, it is quite a surprise that I should get men now

" *Feb. 3rd,*1885.—I started on Jan. 27th, on my return journey to Bihé, with twenty-five porters. They are all in good spirits, and seem to be quite a respectable lot. I slept one night at Catumbella with the agent of a Dutch house, and after crossing about 20 miles of rough country, reached the foot of the Esupwa Pass. The road winds through very rugged places, between large boulders with high mountains on either side. We reached the top of this rugged ascent yesterday and camped by the Olombingo Hill, the double top of which is quite a landmark for many miles east and west. I put up my tent, which I had made during my stay at Benguella, to-day for the first time. It looked much trimmer, and was more easily put up than I expected. The plan of it is a simple ridged tent, the roof shed comes to 18 inches from the ground, then a short wall falls. The ridge pole which I carry with me is a tepoia pole which I can use in the daytime for my hammock if I require to be carried. At night, when setting up the tent, all that is wanted is two forked sticks, 7 feet long, stuck in the ground outside of the tent measurements. The ridge is placed on these, and the tent is thrown over and pegged down on each side.

" *Feb 4th.*—We reached Chivulu, where there is an independent native ruler. As I had to communicate with this town, I sent him a present of fifteen yards of calico, which was accepted as toll money. At Chivanda, a little further on, another independent ruler also accepted a similar present.

" *Feb. 8th.*—Arrived at Ohumbe, on the borders of the Bailundu country. Most of my men belonged to this district, so I had to remain here as their guest for some days. They took me to their village, on the top of a high hill overlooking an immense stretch of country, and entertained me to the best of their ability with fowls, goats, and meal. Too much of such kindness, however, was rather embarrassing, as I was anxious to proceed on my journey to Bihé ; so on the 10th I succeeded with much difficulty in arousing my porters out of their houses, and managed to make a short march in the afternoon. Two days brought me to Chilume, where I found Mr. and Mrs. Sanders in good spirits. Here I paid off my Ohumbe men, intending to collect a fresh company of porters to take me on to Bihé.

"*Feb 26th.*—Sent on letter to Bihé asking for men to come down for me.

"*March 6th*, 1885.—Started from Bailundu with 30 carriers. These have been sent by the chief of Bihé. I travel with a hammock and four men. These men have lots of news as to the Barotse. The details they tell me about the troubles in that country are very sad. It seems that at least four or five of my scholars have been killed because of their relationship to the king.

"*March 10th.*—Arrived at Belmonte. The journey has been so far a pleasant one, though many of the rivers were much swollen. On one occasion, on crossing one of them on the shoulders of one of my men, I looked down into the clear water, when about half-way across, and saw to my surprise that the man was balancing himself on a fallen tree, about the thickness of a person's arm, which appeared to form part of a submerged bridge over the river. My position was so ridiculous, and I so shook with laughter, that the man began to sway about, and finally losing his balance, we were both plunged into the river, with the sunken tree between us. He stupidly held on to my foot so tenaciously that, but for a kick from my other, he might have drowned me. By swimming I was able to reach the other side safely

"*March 12th.*—Having stored my goods in Senhor Porto's house, I invited a few headmen in Bihé to visit me at Belmonte, where I told them of my desire to proceed to the interior. There is every prospect of getting plenty of men.

"*March 13th.*—Walked over to see Chipongi, the chief of Bihé. He at first professed to be very cross at my coming to him without rum. This, he said, was an open act of rebellion on my part. Had he not ordered that every one coming into his country should bring him tribute in rum. The present (6 pieces of cloth and a chair) which I had brought him was slighted. 'Take it away! Go!' he said. I only answered softly, and thanked him for returning my cloth. I said I was sorry that he was so disappointed, but I had thought of giving him something better than fire-water. The cloud soon passed off. He did not like to lose his cloth altogether, and as the matter could not be remedied he passed it over with a few bitter grunts when I had promised him an additional 50 yards and a jacket. The letters that I had with me were then read. The letter from the Governor-General of Loanda caused quite a sensation. The chief showed me an official letter from the Governor of Benguella which showed that Edwardo Braza was sent by the Portuguese Governor of Benguella to expel and plunder the American missionaries. This letter closes with a prayer that ' God would protect and keep the chief of Bihé in His holy guard.' This same letter also accounts for the plundering of the two loads which were sent on to me.

" *March* 14*th.*—Returned from visiting the chief to Porto's house The chief sent a man with me for another piece of cloth, and sent me at the same time a good-sized pig, an excellent representative of himself. It seems that no justice or anything else can be got out of him but for money. Mr. Sanders wanted from him a medical book worth about 4s. He declared that although the book indeed belonged to Mr. Sanders, and that, although Mr. Sanders had committed no offence against him, nevertheless he would not give up that book for less than a bale of cloth and a gun. He also declared that if Mr. Sanders wanted to build again at Bihé he must pay 1,000,000 reis for the land. This was opposed stoutly by some of the headmen who declared that the chief could not sell the land, and that to ask such a price for a book was ridiculous The chief promised to send a letter to the Governor-General in reply to his. We shall see then a little more of what is in his heart. But in truth, though he makes great professions as to his loyalty to the Portuguese, etc., and asks for a Portuguese chief to come to Bihé, yet he has no other thought than to get rum and cloth. Two priests are expected in Bihé in April and it seems that the chief has *allotted* to them the site that Mr. Sanders had to build on. They (the priests) have already sent on a jar of whisky.

" *March* 17*th* —As I hoped to receive letters from home, and then to purchase goods for the inland journey, I again started for the coast. The men I had engaged for my tepoia demanded prepayment, so rather than break the rule I preferred to walk. I had not gone far, however, when I saw the tepoia and five men come trotting after me. I shall let them have the privilege of carrying me all the way.

" *March 24th.*—Arrived on the 20th at Ohumbe, where Mr. Sanders was delighted with the letters I brought from Bihé. Made an early start this morning for the coast, travelled seven and a half hours and crossed the Keve River. After all ' the road ' is my allotted sphere seemingly in this life. I had planned at least to have 20 days' rest in the company of Brother Sanders and his wife at Bailundu, hoping that we might at least become acquainted with each other.

" *March 27th.*—Met the mail box on the road to-day. Opened it and found an abundant home mail and was much cheered by all the good reports of friends at home. There seems to be a unanimous consent to my returning to the Garenganze. Mr. Groves and Dr. McLean both write. They warn me against forgetting the true aim and object of all my travelling to make known Christ, doing above all things ' the work of an evangelist.'

" *April 2nd,* 1885.—Arrived in Benguella this forenoon. Found that Mr. Walter had taken everything that had come from Scotland for me out of the Customs House. A huge printing press is altogether useless for me. I never could take such a heavy thing into the interior with me. Seventy or 80 men could not begin to carry it away. Two Westley-Richard carbines, a magic-lantern, a Bible, some clothing, cotton cloth, and a few books were very acceptable.

" *April 7th*—The Lord graciously delivered me of the care of the printing press. I was in a dilemma this morning to know what to do with it, intending to find storage for it somewhere in town, when a most unexpected offer of purchase came from a man who did not even know Mr. Walter or I had a press for sale, but thought the former would get him one from America. After a little bargaining he bought it for £15, and the type for £17. With this money I will be able to buy a much more satisfactory thing.

" I shall be most eager for a copy of the Revised Bible. If you send it through the mail it will reach me at Bihé—a small print edition. It will be a great pleasure to me looking over every passage during the weary months of travelling. I shall wait an extra month at Bihé so as to get it.

" *April 8th.*—I write to a friend at home as follows :

" ' In yours of January 30th, you speak of two points, about which you are exercised, in connection with my work in Africa.

I could not think of starting on such a journey as is before me, planning to return within a certain time, or intending to move about in an aimless manner. My earnest hope and prayer to God is, that He will lead me among a people for whom He has a present message. To a great extent my work may only be preparing for others to enter in. Three years ago, while at the Zambesi, I had no other desire than to remain there. My ways, however, are in God's hands. I am still ready to go back again to the Barotse if I get the slightest indication that the field is open there, but it seems as if it were not. This Garenganze route appears to be the one for my return into the interior, and I start on it with joy and gladness, not knowing that I shall ever reach that place, nor what may be found for me to do by the way   I can say honestly that I have no plan to follow out, but am fully persuaded that it is necessary to remain in some place, so that one's message may be rightly known and understood. Whether that place be the Garenganze, or somewhere short of it, God knoweth. I trust He will guide me, and I earnestly entreat special prayer for this.

" ' Ere you receive this letter I hope to have left Benguella. I have enough, according to human foresight, to provide all things honestly, and all things necessary, for two years to come. For this I heartily thank our God. May I hold all as His, seeking grace to spend every yard of calico to profit, and to His glory. I purpose starting from Bihé with about forty loads —a very small caravan for Africa, as the usual number of carriers is about 200 or 300.'

" *May 6th*, 1885.—In writing to Dr. McLean to-day I refer to my letter of Jan. 2nd, inserted in the April *Echoes of Service* and add . ' In the present frame of my mind I have a horror of doing anything in the future calculated to bring upon me the world's easily deluded gaze. I have an instinctive feeling that the moment I pass from the ranks of the humble unknown and little-heard-of missionary band, who are known only to the spiritual and the godly, and whose prayers are better than gold to me—the moment I say I pass from among these—and enter among the known and recognised by journalist and pamphleteers, I shall feel as a child removed from the warm hearth of a cottage home to the richer but colder boards of a charity house. My full persuasion is that if work, real work for God, is to be carried on at all in this country it must be done more and more

in the spirit of quietness and prayer. Anything approaching
to ostentatiousness in me or in my letters I trust will be carefully watched for and rebuked by those who receive them; and
that all who may seek to join in this blessed, blessed work be
exhorted much to avoid the very appearance of presuming to
be anything, or of being numbered among the numbers of
missionaries.'

" *May* 10th —Mr. Sanders writes from Bailundu that the
Balunda have returned from their three years' campaign. The
result of the final raid was disaster, seemingly, and in a fit of
disappointment the chief picked a quarrel with a friendly
village and took about 20 captives and a handful of cattle
away. Twenty-five men will be down for me in a few days,
so I shall get a start soon on the long journey.

" *May* 19th.—The need that I feel of God's very help in this
journey seems to press upon me as a heavy load   I cannot pray,
nor read, nor receive strength from the Word as at other times.
Still I feel a calm peace, as in the presence of a covenant sealed
by the immutable, unchangeable One , the presence of Him who
only is. The material part of the journey gives me little concern
It is returning again into the midst of the dark heathen country
as a bearer for the first time in many parts of the name of
Christ. And believing that the Lord willingly makes use of
the least of things and services for the spreading abroad of the
knowledge of His name, my prayer and burden is, that the
least impression made upon those people, the faintest remembrance that anyone may retain of me as I pass along, by means
of a look, a kind touch, a word, a something, though they know
it not, may savour of Christ.

" *May* 23rd.—No word of my carriers yet, making me somewhat impatient these last few days. But why should I feel so ?
The only way to explain the impatience of one professedly set
out to do the Lord's work is that he hath in his heart some selfish
end in view, some plan which is purely his own, which causes
him to be impatient. For the time for the accomplishment of
our own plan ' is always ready,' but the Lord's time is definite
and perfect. For He who ' hath appointed the day in which He
will judge the world,' He who knew of ' that hour,' the culmin-
ating point, ' the fulness of time,' worketh by no other rule in
the little and seemingly insignificant ordering of our daily lives.
At times I have great and strong convictions of this. At other

times my carnal impatience of delay, and restlessness, show me how much there is of selfish aim and interest in all I do.

" *May* 28*th*.—Twice within these few days the Lord has been pleased to answer special prayer. On Monday I asked Him to persuade a man to pay me 17,000 reis he owed me as balance of price of press. I was indeed in sheer need of the money to meet my running expenses. The answer came in six hours' time and after a delay of two months since the former part payment. He brought the money without my having reminded him of the debt for some time. Again, last night I gave vent to long waiting, and expecting the arrival of my carriers, in prayer asking the Lord to consider my weakness and send them speedily. This morning the tailor close by called me into his shop to tell me that the men I was waiting for had arrived at Catumbella, nine miles off. Is there anything too small for our bringing to Him ? Does He not by His ' gentleness ' tempt us to trust Him wholly.

" *May* 31*st* —My carriers came down to-day."

CHAPTER XI

A START FROM BENGUELLA

"*BENGUELLA, June 2nd,* 1885.—In taking farewell of the coast once more, many thoughts of all across the ocean occupy me, and I feel as if I were leaving you all again But with God's help I can say, these things do not move me. Indeed, never have I felt such a strong desire to be back again to my happy life and work in the distant parts of this country. Until the last Liverpool steamer came in, two weeks ago, I had a silent hope that someone might yet come to join me in this journey. Loath as I am to invite, or even to encourage anyone to do so, I firmly believe that the right person will come in the right time. The longer I wait, and the more I cast the matter entirely upon God, the more assurance I get of His perfect ordering, and the more strength and joy He gives me in my position here "

Arnot left Benguella on June 3rd and arrived at Bailundu on the 16th. The journey from the coast was uneventful. He was delayed, however, at Bailundu until August 24th, but the time was not lost. He profited not a little by the company of Mr. and Mrs. Sanders who assisted him in the study of the Umbundu language. The journal and letters continue :

"*August 20th,* 1885.—A long day's walking brought me to Dungeunga's town where I shall have to wait a day or two. The time between the day I first met Mr. Sanders at Chilume (Bailundu) and my taking leave of him at the same place looks like a last night's dream. The happy fellowship of believers, the monthly communications with home, are all past and I am back again to my normal condition with my face turned toward the lonely far-off interior. I rejoice that it is for Christ's sake I go. Surely our Lord's service, the privilege of running even the least of His errands, is worthy to be preferred as our chief joy. And will He not, in His boundless

143

compassion, give us daily and hourly the needed strength and heart comfort.

"*Aug.* 22*nd.*—I feel very comfortable and easy now when travelling. Before, when I was green to the ways and customs of travelling, each man I had was so much wiser than I, and all tried to boss me ; but now the tables are turned. In fact, I know much more about it than most of them A single word from me as to time of camping, time of starting, pay, or anything of that sort, is decisive, and obeyed without objection. And being better able to understand the nature of their quarrels, and their own laws for settling their disputes, I can generally settle ' the matter ' in a satisfactory way when it is referred to me and thus keep peace in the camp In fact I am so exacting in the matter of peace and quietness that my little camp is a perfect heaven compared to Porto's, who never interferes with his men and won't hear their disputes until they come to raising clubs and guns and knives, and then it is a case of putting some in irons, heavy fining, and all that sort of thing. It is marvellous the effect my growing beard has upon them. I had always been in the habit of shaving until six or eight months ago. Now they address me generally as ' Sekulu '— old man—and sometimes remark : ' Before he deceived us by shaving ! but we were not deceived ; his eyes are old,' etc. The natives never have any beard to speak of until they are 40.

"*Aug.* 27*th.*—Arrived at Belmonte, Bihé. I had scarce paid off my Balunda men when I booked 20 for the Garenganze. The trader to whom I gave medicine for dysentery with good effect gave me a present to-day of three bottles of claret and five of port wine. Seeing I had not any wine with me I thought perhaps I had better take it ; it may be of service. He (the trader) will not leave here for two months or so, so I will get off before him, greatly to my satisfaction.

"*Aug.* 29*th* —Went over to visit the chief to-day ; had, on the whole, a pleasant visit. I gave him nine pieces of cloth.

"*Aug.* 30*th.*—This morning a letter came from Chipongi, the chief, wanting more presents. I sent him a shawl and a shirt. In his letter he says I can proceed on my journey after he returns from an antelope hunt The begging of these chiefs causes a most uncomfortable strain on one It is the bane of travelling in Africa ; still I must get on, and I must also have something with me.

ON THE ZAMBESI

Natives pushing their canoes through the reeds.

"*Sept. 1st*, 1885.—Hitherto I find I have been making a sad mistake in putting off the needful hours of prayerful study of the Word until the evening. The weakness of my eyes has compelled me to give up night reading, and so, when not travelling, I have set apart the morning and early forenoon hours to this study, and feel marvellously refreshed and strengthened thereby. The days seem to fly from me. Is there not something in the sound of His voice that constrains us to follow Him? 'Draw me; we will *run* after Thee'; 'My sheep hear My voice and they follow Me.' If we do not acquaint ourselves *early* with His drawing love, and with His voice, how shall we *run* and *follow*.

"*Sept. 13th.*—My carriers are coming in one by one : first to talk and bargain about the journey, then, after a certain amount of time simmering over the matter at their own villages, return to get booked, and to tie up ; then back again they go to their villages to sit on their little wooden stools, and snuff, and consult the village divine, with promises of large rewards on their return, as to the road, prospects of food, etc., and having by this time worked themselves up to the ' plunging in ' pitch—just as we boys used to do in the bathing boxes on the Portobello Sands—will return to seal and bargain by carrying off their loads to their own villages. When all have been lifted I go out to camp, a few hours off, towards the villages of my carriers, and, at the silent signal of the British Union Jack hoisted up a tree, the carriers will know to take their last snuff out of the village cane, and start off for a year's toil at least. And indeed they have a hard job of it, a 60 lb. load, a blistering sun, and heavy sand under their bare feet, hot enough to bake bread in ; and this for 12 to 15 miles a day is no joke. I, with my fat sleek ox and comfortable helmet, in comparison, travel luxuriously.

" By the by I told you in my last how I had refused to get wine at Benguella for the interior, and how my first fee in Bihé was eight bottles of better wine than I would have thought to buy. Well ! there was another little thing I needed, and that was a saddle for my ox. The canvas-padded thing I used was a hot and sweaty thing and very uncomfortable. I tried to get one at Benguella, but none there ! The other day I was turning out all my material to make a new one, straps of goat skin, yes, a canvas bag, a piece of leather about the size of my

K

two hands. I could make little out of it, so laid all aside, and sat down, ruminating, when a man arrives with a letter, written in good Portuguese, to the effect that a young man, named Quilernee, had a saddle to sell; would the white man buy it for thirty yards of cloth ? ' Of course ! Where is it ? ' ' The boy is just behind with it.' And sure enough in a few minutes here comes saddle, stirrups, and belly-band, all complete and in fair condition. Its history I suppose to be as follows : Some Dutch hunter's horse had died down by the Kavungu ; the saddle had been given to some natives who sold it to this Bihé trader on his journey down there. At least he brought the saddle from that direction somewhere. So I am supplied with a snug seat for the journey, all ordered and found by Him ' Whose I am and Whom I (seek to) serve.'

" The probabilities of my visiting Lake Bangweolo are, in the meantime, out of the question. I should certainly like to see where my noble countryman fell, and all that, but until I have learned the language of the country I shall consider any unnecessary travelling a waste of time and money. But I shall likely send to Chitambo (as I am told he is now at the Garenganze) and get his news, as his side of the story. It may be that he who left such decided impressions upon many who met him while in life, did not fail to make a lasting impression upon the hearts of those he died among. Noble, brave old Livingstone ! What an honour it would be to take up even some of the threads of his life work. From continually hearing him spoken of by the natives I have formed opinions of him independently altogether of what's written or has been said at home about him.

" I have received lately a fresh impulse in studying the Scriptures, and try to give the first four hours of the day entirely to that, part of which time is taken up with analysing each sentence carefully with the help of Bengel's Gnomon (index) and the Greek grammar, and marvel continually at the Divine beauty and explicitness of the text.

" *Sept. 15th.*—Quite a lot of Bachokwe arrived here (Belmonte) to-day from Kasembe, near to the Uleva River, with rubber for sale. Their leader had been up to the Congo River and had met ' Buli ' (Stanley) and seemed distressed about the possible loss of trade which the occupation of that country by the whites would mean to them.

" *Sept.* 16*th.*—My carriers give me nothing but disappointment. A few who have offered their services are so utterly unreasonable in their demands that it is evident they have no intention of going with me. Nothing is lost by these delays ; all is conscious gain. I think labourers, or intending labourers in Africa, ought to take much heed to these words, ' Ye have need of patience.' It seems at times as if everything was at a deadlock, and every one around in a sound slumber. At last a little rustling is heard, and after a while a move is made ; but so surely as a halt occurs, all relax into profound inaction. I have been busy negotiating with carriers all this month ; hundreds say they are willing to go. I only want 30, and yet it takes weeks and even months to get them up to the carrying point ; still, they do come, and I got my fifteenth load tied up to-day.

" The chief here, in a favourable interview, has given me, according to native custom, ' the road ' to the Garenganze, and I got off very cheaply in only having to pay, as tribute, about 100 yards of cotton cloth ; but my stock was small, and I claimed a special privilege as having come from the interior, as the natives do. A young Portuguese trader, for the same privilege, gave three four-gallon kegs of rum, a case of gin, 600 yards of cloth, 50 lb. of powder, and one or two guns. A Portuguese priest told me he had to give one four-gallon keg of rum, 200 yards of cloth, two blankets, six shirts, his own silver watch, and some other small things. Senhor Porto never returns from the coast without bringing as tribute far more than this.

" *Sept.* 21*st.*—Sent on seven loads to Kapoko with 24 yards to the chief. He writes me very kindly assuring me of a speedy crossing of the Kwanza. News has come in that the Matabele have come up to the Barotse raiding.

" *Sept.* 26*th.*—A few days ago I noticed a little boy, about eight or nine years of age, who belongs to a town close by, going about with both hands in a sad condition. The left one was completely distorted, and three of the fingers were joined together in one suppurating mass. The right hand was completely skinned, and the arms were more or less badly scalded. Upon inquiry I learned that the boy had been visiting, with some of his village mates, the town of one of Chipongi's sisters. When playing about he had stolen some beans belonging to this woman, who, to punish the child, put both his hands into a pot of water then boiling on the fire. The left hand was so much injured that she must have left it in the water for a few seconds. I understand that this creature in human shape has not even been called in question for her cruelty. The child was a slave.

" *Oct. 2nd*, 1885.—It seems that by accident the yard and huts of the chief of Bihé have been burned down. He coolly sends to the Portuguese trader and myself for five pieces of cloth. I send him three 12-yard pieces, at the same time apprising him of my intended departure. Indeed, I must be out of this at once. There is no end to this chief's begging.

" *Oct. 5th* —I have been advised not to think of starting until the chief's return from his hunt. I have spent indeed a restless week, part of my goods already gone some time. Am I kept here waiting seemingly for an indefinite length of time ? In this frame of mind I had been until this evening, but I have been humbled by a sight of the worthlessness of all my works. Were I able to arrange for a start to-morrow in my own strength what would it amount to ? It certainly would not give pleasure to God, neither would it honour His Spirit. I was enabled to confess my foolish and sinful impatience to God, and, feeling the inward strength of His Spirit, my willingness to wait His pleasure. While still on my knees, I was startled by four shots close by. It was the men returning from the king's hunt. Having killed a male antelope the farce was over and the king reinstated in his capital once more. I cannot look upon this incident without feelings of gratitude to my most tender and patient Lord. Why should He thus so mercifully lead me into that state of mind in which I could but profit by the coming news ? Or was it that He knew beforehand at what time I would learn my lesson and submit myself to Him that He ordered the end of the hunt ?

" *Oct. 9th.*—Sent most of my goods out to camp with a feeling of intense satisfaction that at last another stage was reached in the slow business of ' getting a start.' At no time I think does a traveller in this country stand more in need of dogged patience.

" *Oct. 10th.*—Into first camp at Mokumba by the Longwali River. Shot at a large buck and wounded him, had a long hunt with my dog on the wounded animal's spoor, but had to return as the rain was threatening and I had not yet set up my tent. A few hours every day now will have to be taken up with hunting for game. A head of game keeps the men in good spirits, supplies food, and smooths the way wonderfully.

" *Oct.* 11*th*.—In camp to-day. I hear that nearly all the carriers I had engaged have, for different reasons, withdrawn. So I have to do a good deal of last month's work over again. Sent off messengers in all directions to call for carriers. Was willing to accept offers for one day's journey, if they would come

" *Oct.* 12*th*.—In camp, arranging with men to take me on as far as Kapoko at least.

" *Oct.* 13*th*.—Had prospect of getting another start this morning. After a hasty cup of coffee, by way of breakfast, I took down my tent and bundled it up. Those who had promised to come for loads were very dilatory, and it was towards midday before we began to get the loads out of camp. Sending some on ahead in charge of Kasoma, I told him to camp at a place called Nyani, some four miles off, and I remained behind, as there were still a few loads for which there were no carriers. In the evening I was able to overtake Kasoma and the others, and in the dark paid off all the day-workers, got my loads together, and threw a sheet of waterproof canvas over them. I had, however, barely got under cover myself when a heavy storm came on, threatening to drive everything before it. The carriers had gone off to their villages close by for shelter, and I was left alone in the damp and darkness, holding on grimly to the flapping canvas of my tent. At last the storm abated somewhat, and I got a few hours' undisturbed sleep before morning.

" *Oct.* 14*th*.—Marched a few miles in the same hand-to-mouth fashion. Camped by Kangango's by the Shambundwe. Kangango is quite a big man in his way. I gave him eight yards of material for which he returned me two fowls and some beer for the men, and conducted himself civilly. I counted 14 villages here.

" *Oct.* 15*th*.—Early this morning crossed the Uyowe River, on the east side of which I counted 12 villages known as Kakomo. The thickly wooded hill between these two districts would be a splendid place for a mission station, being within easy walk from both.

" Reached Kapoko's about midday. In going over the hill,

before reaching this place, I was delighted with the magnificent view. Before me stretched the Kukema Valley running into the Kwanza Valley, and there, far away beyond, like an ocean horizon, lay the great interior flat—flat in comparison to the country between here and the coast. The extent of the view one gets here is most impressive, and has awakened in me a thousand thoughts concerning the silent interior—my past experience there, past preservation and blessing, present joy, and hope for the future. All seemed to get full expression in ' My Lord and my God ! '

" In the evening I visited Kapoko. His town is large and very clean. The chief sent me word that he was mourning the death of a child, and that I was to return to-morrow, meanwhile I was to leave my present, which I did, viz 32 yards of calico. A little later in the evening three of his headmen came to me with a story of great dissatisfaction, said to be from Kapoko, to the effect that my present was too small. ' I surely thought,' they said, ' that Kapoko was a very small man, seeing I had sent him so small a present.' I listened to their story with much attention. And then in the most serious manner began to assure them of the great respect I had for Kapoko, that I knew that he was a very great man, and asked the royal messengers to go back and assure his majesty that the smallness of the present spoke only of my smallness, but not at all of his, and that if I was only so much bigger I would think nothing of giving Kapoko bales of cloth. The poor old men dropped their frowning visages and looked at each other in a stupified way. Some of the young men, however, behind could not hold themselves in but burst out laughing, which was the sign for a general burst of laughter. We all parted a short time after the best of friends ; the king's prime minister, who was the leading one of the group, leaving me the assurance of a good fat pig on the morrow.

" Oct. 16th.—My last night s visitors came back this morning saying that Kapoko would give me nothing less than an ox, and that he had sent to the Kwanza to procure one for me from one of his villages, and it would arrive on the morrow. I told them that I was very hungry, and that a sheep would be worth more to me to-day than an ox to-morrow. In the end a fat sheep was sent to my camp.

" Oct. 17th.—Kapoko came himself to visit me to-day. They

carried him in a palanquin. He is a very old and frail man. I must confess I am most favourably impressed with him. He is very kindly both in his look and manner. He wanted to know if I could hunt and proposed that I should go down to the river to-morrow to shoot a hippopotamus I readily consented provided his men found the hippo. My man tells me, though, that he gave instructions to his servants to take me to one of his cattle posts to shoot an ox. ' Handsome is who handsome does.' To say the least it was neatly done.

" Here I again made what proved to be almost a futile effort to collect carriers.

" *Oct. 23rd.*—Left Kapoko's capital to-day for Cisamba, six miles N.E. towards the Kwanza. This is another step forward. Three Garenganze men came to my camp. They said they had decided to return with me. They had been sent by their chief to look for traders. They had found in me a *real* white man, so could not do better than return home with me. The chief one of the three had on large ivory wristlets about 6 in. wide as a sign that he was sent by the chief. Their language seems clearly to be of the Bantu family.

" *Oct. 24th.*—Here at Cisamba it is very hot and the vegetation by the river has a tropical look. This is the last of the Ovimbundu villages. The people seem to be devoted to the interior trade.

" *Oct. 26th.*—Preparing for a start to-morrow, God willing. It has been a long trying business getting together out of the crowd the few who are willing to start on so long a journey with no more tempting offer of pay than I am able to give, viz. equal to 15 yards of cloth to each contractor for each load, paid here ; and 20 yards to each porter at the end of the journey (60 travelling days) with 2 yards and salt to each man every 10 camps as rations. The contractors have the responsibility of building the camps, seeing the loads housed for the night, and arranging about guides, etc.

" My own man, Kasoma, who has been with me for six months as interpreter, etc., has got together five men as porters. His wife also goes with him. He will remain with us at the Garenganze and promises to be as useful as he has been.

" Lokumba, my head ' sekulu,' seems to be a very worthy man, reasonable and active—two most valuable accomplishments.

" My carriers represent the variety common to all peoples.

" Chipooka stammers as he speaks, but is lively under all circumstances. He has a bad festering toe which, however, does not prevent him carrying his 60 lb. load. Though limping badly, his only response to expressions of sympathy is a broad grin. He seems to think it a very ridiculous toe.

" Saombo is another representative man, perfectly hideous in his looks, but vanity has made his ugliness look comical. All who come to the camp, he seems to think, have come to see him. When the usual semicircle of aboriginal strangers gather in front of my tent he is fit no more for camp building, but must come and sit down in front of all, clapping his thighs with delight, trying to crack jokes, the very existence of which in our minds, even for a moment, is rendered impossible by volumes of hoarse laughter from his tremendous mouth

" Then we have the sulky grumbler amongst us. He has always something to complain of. Now his load is not right, next his rations, then his pay, or a thorn pricks his foot and he can carry no longer that day. The work has to be done but certainly not by him. Only one or two of such in a company can reasonably be borne with.

" I spend each evening sitting round the camp fire with my men, trying in a thousand ways to convey to them intelligent thoughts as to my mission. It is of the first importance that they should understand me, and be able to give an answer to the thousands in the interior who will ask them what this white man has come for.

" In reviewing the occupants of my camp I must not overlook my faithful dog and a parrot. The latter I bought for a trifle for the sake of my boys. Really he is a most ridiculous bird. Generally in the evening, or towards the end of a march, when everyone is going along quietly, Polly breaks out into an old man's laugh, or goes through the sounds heard at a native dog hunt : ' Kwata ! Kwata ! ' (Catch it ! Catch it !) ; then a shouting of men ; ' to-to ! ' for guns going off ; finishing up with the pitiful crying of a wounded animal. He also sings some native airs, the whole caravan shouting out the chorus ; then another turn from Polly, until every one breaks down with laughter ; it is so ridiculous

" I have been teaching my dog a lesson or two in grace.

He is so lively and fond of stealing that I have had to punish him severely, and drive him to lie down beside my chair. Now whenever he is in fault, and I shout to him, he makes straight for my chair or his bed beside the goods. There he knows he is safe. I suppose he argues that was always the end of his punishments, so it is better at the first sign of wrath to go straight to the *end* of the punishment, and thus miss the punishment.

"A contractor and five men have given up their loads because I would not pay them beforehand—a ruse to get to their homes again. Two or three days will mend the breach I hope. Have sent back to hunt for some more. Once I get across the Kwanza all will go smoothly I hope.

"*Oct. 27th.*—I have managed to make up the number of my men again, at least in my book, but it is hard to say how many will turn up to-morrow. Kasoma, my mainstay, has met someone here who got the loan of a gun from him some long time ago, and here the fellow leaves everything and goes off after his trashy gun. We were to start to-morrow but I fear we will make another mess. Patience, however, and its end, are surely linked. The perfect end is patience perfected. I know it is no mere treadmill I am set to, but that each day, each hour, of obedient waiting, is a day, and an hour, of positive gain.

"*Oct. 28th.*—Nearly all the carriers I had engaged from the villages around Kapoko have been ordered to leave me. This is the second time my carriers have been driven from me here. Also the first batch who left me did so by the orders of a small chief. In my simplicity I did not then fully understand the situation, but now I see that not a few influentials, in this country of interior traders, are set against my going to the Garenganze. My man, Kasoma, assures me of the truth of this and says they are all very jealous about a white man going into the interior, especially an 'English,' of whose power in swallowing trade they have a superstitious fear. As I cannot imagine any worse motive in the minds of my opposers than this, their own interest, I fully forgive them for all the trouble they are giving me. They do not understand my errand. How could they! Meanwhile I send off 13 loads post haste. I also send off messengers, here and there, to pick up carriers. It is doubling my expenses, but my only chance now of succeeding

at all (with God's blessing) is, at all cost, to make a rapid move
for the east bank of the Kwanza.

" About four o'clock in the afternoon Lekomba came in
with two men and the prospect of more to-morrow. So I
started off for camp 10 miles distant, leaving Kasoma to come
on with what men turn up to-morrow, and what loads he
cannot fetch to store in the house of one who, I am told, is a
trusty man.

" I got into camp late, and very tired and almost starved
out. We have left all Bihé villages behind to my great joy.
I have goods enough here to take me on   The Garenganze men,
who return to their country with me, are indignant at the
conduct of these Bihéans, and declare that Msidi, their king,
when he hears of the way they have tried to hinder a white
man from coming to him will be very angry. They also say
that if I want 100 carriers to return with me to the coast their
chief will give them to me. So that I see clearly that this may
be the plan for opening up that country, first to *get there*, and
then to employ the bone and muscle of the country to bring
others there.

" I have been comforted this morning with these words and
promise, ' Because thou hast kept the word of my patience,
I also will keep thee from the hour of trial.' ' He that openeth
and *no man* shutteth,' said this.

" *Oct. 29th.*—Kasoma came on to-day with four loads,
leaving 10 behind without carriers.

" *Oct. 30th.*—Had a long day's march. Passed a caravan
of traders just come from the Lunda country. They had many
slaves. I counted about 30 mere infants   Some of these were
trotting along whilst others were being carried. One little
thing seemed to be hanging over a young man's shoulder, dead
or nearly so. Many of the slaves looked terribly afraid of me
and my ox. I suppose they thought they had now arrived at
the long-talked-of land of monsters   The traders said they had
bought them from an army returning from pillaging.

" *Oct. 31st.*—Travelled seven hours and camped close by
the Kwanza (a little below where the Kuiba flows in on the
east bank). I have thus gone down the Kwanza a long way
to avoid crossing three large rivers instead of one (the Kukema,
the Cuanja and the Kuiba).

" We passed a caravan from the Luba country, They had

been attacked by people living on the Lualaba and robbed, some of their number being killed. One of the Garenganze natives travelling with me was a long way behind. The travellers attacked him, threatening to kill him in revenge for the death of their fellows in the interior, but beyond stealing his hat and something of mine which he was carrying they did no harm.

" *Nov. 1st*, 1885.—After paying other eight yards to the chief of Tolonoka we started to cross the Kwanza. We employed five boats, to the owners of which I paid four yards each and two yards to each paddler. I turned out my finest cloth and everything went along with comparative smoothness. The heat to-day has been most unbearable. After standing about the river for several hours, directing the crossing of my goods and my ox, I was half stupid with the heat and could scarce sit on my ox after starting for the camp.

" Two of my carriers have run off, so I had to pack their loads on my ox and push along.

" The appearance now of the country is of an immense flat, hills taking the form of low sand-belts with scrubby bush on their tops. The natives have the wild look of the interior inhabitants and are much more sparely clad. The villages are very small and far between.

" *Nov. 2nd.*—Rain coming down in torrents, as it used to do at the Barotse, the result of yesterday's intense heat. Of course we remain in camp, thankful indeed to have got on so far. I find that every one of my men speaks of the heat of yesterday as being exceptional, so I am satisfied that it was not any special weakness on my part when I felt overcome and knocked up.

" I am secretly informed that some of my carriers are wholly untrustworthy and intend forsaking me in the Lovale country. To be forewarned is not to be exactly forearmed in this case, for what can I do ? I know that not one man with me is free from the bondage of the enemy. They are his to do his bidding. So with the best of my men I would depend only upon the power of God to keep them faithful to me in this journey. No tact or precaution on my part can do this.

" This evening a man tying up his load threw off one of my valuable tins of biscuits, saying he could not carry that, his load was already too heavy. I had no option but to open it

and divide some of the biscuits through some other loads, and
to give the rest away.

" *Nov. 3rd* —Got a good start this morning. I packed my
ox, and it proved a perfect success every way, requiring no
attention on the road. He kept up with the men. The road
passed many old and ruined villages, ruined by raiding parties
from Bihé. The few villages inhabited were very wretched and
half-built looking. The people turned out in full force to see
the ox carrying a load of salt, the first time I suppose anything
of the sort has been seen in this part of the country. The people
seem to be all in a bad way—no food, villages out of repair,
badly clothed, indeed some are on the verge of nakedness.
I sent the chief 20 yards of cloth. He sent back saying he was
delighted to see me in his country and wanted to give me a
present, but how could he on top of so little cloth. After some
palaver I consented to give 16 yards more. His present to me
was a good fat sheep and a basket of meal. He also sent his
brother to guide me on to some villages further up the Kuiba
where I can get food to buy.

" *Nov. 4th.*—Keeping to the S.E. for five hours this morning
we came to the Kuiba River again. From the point where I
am camped I can see the hills at Kapoko across the Kuiba,
Kwanza and Kukema valleys. I have got back to the regular
caravan route which crosses these three rivers, and which I
have wisely avoided I am so well pleased with my walking
that I have made up my mind to stick to it and to turn the
ox into a porter for food for the road. Camped at Mosibe's
town.

" *Nov. 5th.*—The 12 yards I sent to Mosibe yesterday has not
pleased, but he says he will teach me a thing to-day in the way
of giving. About midday he came along dressed out in his
best. Behind him was a whole herd of oxen, out of which
I was asked to kill one, which I did, a good fat ox and no
mistake. Of course I added to my present : a blanket, coat
and 24 yards of cloth—not by any means a dear ox.

" The way these people trouble me for rum is beyond description. They believe every glass bottle they see, or kettle, or
vessel of any kind belonging to me, is full of rum. If I drink
coffee they declare I drink rum. ' Rum ! Rum ! ' rings in
my head from morning until night. I have with me one unfortunate bottle, unknown to anyone with me, and the terror

of that bottle being discovered is beyond my power to endure, so to-day I opened the box it was in and buried the bottle at night. This leaves me only a little in my medicine box.

" *Nov. 8th.*—Waiting still for Cinyama who stayed behind to try and get carriers for the loads I left with him. My men have been showing every sign of discontent and impatience, demanding their payment in advance. When I remember that nearly all my regular carriers were recalled or otherwise hindered from leaving Bihé with me, and that most of them I have with me are ' free lances ' picked up here and there and going for the sake of spoil, I am enabled to understand and excuse much. How blessed also to know that I am but a subaltern ; the Lord is commander.

" Cinyama came along to-day with the last of my loads. So I go on fairly well set up with every comfort Am rather short, however, of cloth for paying my men as their demands are greater than they would have been had I retained the carriers engaged at first.

" *Nov. 9th.*—A general grumbling and discontent all over the camp this morning. ' Pay ' was evidently the subject under consideration. On the whole the men were reasonable in their demands. One or two, however, I noticed were un-reasonable, and I marked them. They were all naturally afraid that I would not keep to my promise and give them the amount agreed upon at the journey s end. So many Portuguese traders have taken advantage of them that way. I managed to hold out quietly until Cinyama and three other ' sekulus ' guaranteed to stand security for the good faith of the men if I would pay them. So I paid them each 24 yards of fine cloth, leaving but a small balance to be paid at the end of the journey in the form of beads. I managed, however, to use up in paying, the loads of those men who were most unreasonable. I also gave them all a much better quality of cloth than they expected to get. Then came a busy afternoon tying, sewing up, repacking, etc., for a final start. All were in first-rate spirits. There was no more word of returning. To add to the general satisfaction reigning both in me and in the men a messenger came across the river from Kapoko with a letter to me containing a message for my men in which he declared that he, Kapoko, was my sworn friend and that the men who went with me must treat me well, for to injure ' Monare ' was to injure Kapoko. A very good and kind letter. The only fault it had was it was behind time. For some reason or other Kapoko declined his gracious help when I was in his country, and did not prevent his headmen from molesting me. Now he sends after me, a six days' journey, his declaration of friendship."

CHAPTER XII

"*MOSIBE, Nov. 10th*, 1885.—Rain all the morning, so remain here another day and thankful I am for the rest. Everything seems ready and the men are all quiet and contented.

" Have begun to transcribe the language of the Garenganze in one of Max Muller's outline dictionaries and according to his principles of using the English alphabet. My object is to get an exact photograph of each word, and not in any way to decide as to the alphabet proper for that language. First, I write the words as I hear them from the natives of Garenganze who are with me, in a pocket-book, and, after hearing them several times, I carefully transfer them to the outline dictionary.

" In the evening I took an affectionate farewell of my friend Mosibe. He gave me another ox to eat on my return journey.

" My men have made a general demand for a ' bundera,' so I have unrolled the British ensign which a lad will carry. To travel without a ' bundera ' means bad luck to them.

" Three companies of native traders have joined me. I feel a thousand miles nearer to my destination than I did a few weeks ago, showing, of course, how much I am a creature of circumstances.

"*Nov. 11th.*—Got an early start this morning   Reached Kazombo, a clump of villages, the last of the Valumbe. The population seems to be very scarce, and food only of the poorest sort is to be had. There are many fine-looking people amongst these Valumbe, but they have been spoiled so by their wretched Bihé neighbours that a line of sadness seems to have been woven through them.   Lofty foreheads, long serious-looking faces, fantastically cut heads of hair, and sparse clothing are points noticeable.

"*Nov. 12th.*—Pouring wet day and very cold, quite overpowering after yesterday's heat. I was quite feverish all night.

The reaction from strain of work during these last few days, and the long walk under yesterday's glaring sun, have proved a little too much for me. I remain here at Kazombo buying food, as the report is that food is very scarce for 10 days ahead.

" I have just heard a report, which I have reason to believe to be true, that the Matabele have arrived at the Barotse, killing off the people by hundreds and that they have cleared the country of cattle.

" *Nov. 13th.*—A very long day's journey to-day. Crossed the Kulabe and Undumba rivers, and passed through a large tract of deserted country with here and there the ruins of villages. Much of the land had the appearance of having been cultivated but a few years ago. My men tell me that the Chibokwe, who used to live here, have all moved south to virgin country.

" It is refreshing to meet with a case of hearty gratitude from even one of those for whom one seeks to labour. A young man travelling with my company has been lame for a long time from a broken toe which would not heal. I have been dressing it and doctoring it for three weeks every day, and at last it shows signs of healing. He came to me to-day with his face beaming with joy saying that at last he could walk, ' I have nothing but myself to pay you with,' he said, with tears in his eyes.

" *Nov. 14th.*—A long seven hours' journey. Crossed three good-sized rivers unknown to map makers. Camped near the head of the Yalowa. The country is well wooded and has abundance of water, but uninhabited by either man or beast. How the greed of other nations has scourged and stripped Africa, as those silent hills declare !

" *Nov. 16th.*—Passed through an interesting country in regard to the river systems of Africa. In the early morning passed the head of the Kutia flowing N.W. to the Kwanza. An hour and a half later we reached the head of the Monyangwe flowing N.E. to the Kassai and on to the Congo. Another hour and a half and we reached the feeders of the Elume flowing E. and S.E. to the Zambesi. We also encountered tremendous showers of rain at this point, drenching everyone and nearly everything. We trudged on for an hour in the storm. I shall not soon forget this ' fountain of waters.'

" *Nov. 18th.*—Marched for eight hours through a country

bearing all the signs of having been at one time inhabited, but now deserted. Was compelled to press on for want of food.

" *Nov. 19th.*—It was a pleasant sight to-day to see even a few women in a field hoeing, and to hear their cry of welcome. I managed to buy some bird-seed from some natives by the roadside. In the evening we reached the Lumese River, all very tired. I felt an unspeakable sense of thankfulness at getting over this part of the journey. It has been so hungry and so ghastly, for human bones and skulls were met with every few hours' journey.

" *Nov. 20th.*—A short journey brought us to Peho. On the map this place is marked with a dot and a circle round it. It might be mistaken for a walled city, but on getting over the hill I could find no trace of either town or village. There was not even a garden or cultivated field to be seen. Could this really be Peho ? My men proposed that we go up the valley and camp close by the ' capital.' I went on confidently expecting to see something. We camped, however, in thick bush. About an hour after the chief, Soma Kalenge, came down through the bushes. He is a young fellow about two-and-twenty. He was drunk with honey beer. His followers were all most disappointing in their appearance.

" I gave him 30 yards of cloth, and had to add to it a jacket, a pair of trousers, a hat, a pair of shoes, and a lot of smaller things. It was a case of give and get on, or refuse and remain to starve, for scarce a bite of food could be got at any price. Indeed the fellow made me quite nervous by his constant begging, then demanding. He would pry into everything, sit on my chair, take off my hat, feel my skin, let off my gun, and a host of things.

" In the evening, hoping to find the chief sober, I went to visit him. The ' capital ' I found to be a few scattered huts in a wood. I do not suppose there were 20 people—men, women and children—in the whole place. The chief got a rickety old chair out of a grass hut for me to sit on It did not look as if it had been sat on for many years. He gave me a goat, and wanted to know to a day how long it would take him to learn to read and write. He said that I must not think of leaving to-morrow. I must give the blood of the goat, which he had given me to slaughter, time to sink under the surface before I could leave my camp, according to the custom of the Chibokwe.

L

The only thing the chief had to show me in his town was his 'three mothers.' He wanted me to show these my white arm. The solemn way in which he declared that he was born of three mothers completely upset me and I laughed out, at which he looked quite downcast and said, 'Did I think he was an ordinary person ? '

" *Nov. 21st.*—The chief came to visit me again this morning, and sat a weary two hours in my tent looking at everything. Then began the begging. I managed to put him off until the afternoon. He wants a box with lock and key, a suit of clothes like mine, hat, boots, shirt, plates, a knife and fork, etc. etc. We shall see !

" In the evening he returned ; then began a long game of try and pull—begging this, demanding that, exchanging this, refusing some other thing, opening loads in perfect desperation that I had never thought to open until my journey's end— until I was completely used up. I felt every bit of patience and good humour had entirely gone. Never did I meet with such a miserable and trying crew. It seemed at times that they would be pleased with nothing but all I had. Darkness, how- ever, put an end to the fight. He professed to be satisfied after getting 60 yards of cloth out of me, one of my jackets and trousers, shirt, candles, tin fruit, and some powder from one of my men, etc. He left, giving me abundant assurances of his intention to return to-morrow. I had intended going by the Luena road, but he would not permit me, saying I must keep on Cameron's road. My men are uproarious about this, saying ' No food there. We will never reach our destination.' However, I have no alternative. I am no fighting man. I am instructed to be subject to the powers that be. And these Peho folk robbed a caravan a few weeks ago for some trivial reason, and took over 60 teeth of ivory. I might take the Luena road in spite of those here, and get clear off but I know I could not return to Peho again in peace. I thank the Lord for bringing me through this day in such quietness, in spite of myself I may say. And I know that He will keep me all the days.

" *Nov. 22nd.*—Very wet looking this morning. A shower of rain fell as we were getting ready to start. It cleared a little, and I felt justified in ordering a start. We had not gone far, however, when the rain came down in sheets and continued for about two hours. There was no help for it but to push on to the head of the Luena River, where we camped. There are a few scattered huts here occupied by retainers of Peho, but no food for sale save a few mushrooms and some manioc. After all, rain and mud are better things to the traveller than hunger and never-to-be-contented chiefs.

"*Nov. 23rd.*—Constant rain this morning so remain in camp. My men are pretty nearly at their wits' end with hunger and bad weather.

"*Nov. 24th.*—A dark wet morning. I had hoped to remain to-day again in camp, but the men would not hear of it, so off we started and marched for more than three hours in a drenching rain, and with a cold east wind, down the Luena River. 'Cold and rain will not kill us,' the men said, 'but hunger will. We must get to some place where there is food.' Our course lay along the north bank of the Luena. The rain cleared off towards midday when we had two hours of fair weather which gave us time to cross the river and camp on its east bank.

"*Nov. 25th.*—A long seven hours' steady march through a virgin forest, i.e. one not annually swept by grass fires like other parts of the country. It was most tortuous work, it being impossible to step out of the deep, narrow path, as the whole forest seemed to be covered by layer upon layer of fallen trees and branches, all of which were woven together into one woody mass by a long dense ferny moss. Camped at the head of the Shemoi River where there is quite a number of people. Mosiko, the chief, came to visit me. I gave him eight yards of cloth, some salt and ten cartridges. In the evening a crowd came along to the camp with drums and singing. They have all the wild ways of my old interior friends. They are fond of night dancing.

"*Nov. 26th.*—These people have danced and drummed and sung all night until I have been nearly demented, yet to have turned them off would have been a great incivility. This morning I had to pay them four yards of cloth and 2 lb. of salt for their pains in afflicting me. They gave me, however, two pigs, a goat and some fowls.

"*Nov. 27th.*—A short but hot journey along the Shemoi River brought us to camp at Boma's. During the first two hours the road was lined with people. Nothing was to be seen but trees and footpaths, but there were the people in crowds.

So I had to suppose that their towns were close by and that they had expected my coming. They were very civil and evidently delighted by the shouting they made. They said that a white man had never passed this way before, and that I was the first they had ever seen. They had heard, however, of Cameron passing to the north. As my face and hands are something nearer brown than white I had to show them my arms. When I did so they all gave a shout ' Culungu ! ' (it is God) and whooped and whooped. It was so deafening that I was glad to whip on my ox and get off.

" In return for my eight yards, Boma sent me a good pig (the third pork within three days) and his people threatened me with another night's serenading. I confess a cold sweat broke over me at the very thought of it Travelling all day under such a sun (it is now at its hottest) gives one a splitting headache relieved only by a night's sleep. But to have sun by day and drums and singing all night would, I fear, put an end to my earthly career. I sent a present of meat to the town beseeching them not to come to the camp.

" Nov. 28th.—The musicians of Boma have shown them-selves to be a worthy people. They contented themselves with coming only half-way to my camp, and there they danced and sang until morning. Extraordinary people ! They have no capacity to contain a little extra excitement, but must dance and drum it out.

" This morning I was escorted a long way on the road by a band of children—laughing, singing, merry little ones ! No sight so reminds me of home, and none is so touching.

" Crossed a wooded hill and camped by the Dala Cavala, a large river which flows into the Luena. Here also there are many people. They are more scattered and come from all directions. Food is abundant and cheap : a young pig for ½ yard of limbo and a fowl for two to three spoonfuls of salt. The people are poorly clad but healthy-looking.

" Nov. 29th, Sunday.—Remained in camp Four of my men, who were buying wax yesterday, say they will remain here and will lay down their loads. I simply told them that if they would return they would have to go as they were with only their clothes around them, and that I had no intention of paying them for carrying my goods into the forest and leaving them there. I also threatened to take their wax and all they had from them, which I certainly had a right to do and would have done. I further told them that on my return to Bihé I would bring a charge against them. In this nearly all the rest of the men supported me, and by evening they had decided to take their loads and to go on quietly.

" I spent most of the afternoon reading and explaining, as best I could, passages of Scripture in Portuguese to the two mulattoes who are with me. They in turn explained to my carriers, who told all over again to the crowd of aboriginals around.

" *Nov. 30th.*—Early this morning we again reached the Luena River, now quite a large stream, and had much trouble in getting the goods across by a roughly-made bridge, half sunk in the river. I took my ox further up to clear water, and drove him across, and then rolling my clothes, like a great turban, round my head, I swam after him.

" We had not gone far on the other side when a company met us with drums and a goat tied, asking me to camp by their town. I gave Sumbula, the chief, eight yards, a little salt and ten cartridges. In the evening he came along to my camp with some meal and entreated me to remain to-morrow and eat an ox with him. I tried all I could to avoid this as it would mean my giving more cloth, but he was not to be beaten off. He used every argument he could, saying were I but to eat his ox all the people round would know him to be a liberal and a great chief, and a friend of the white man. He urged me not to think of what I would have to pay him, upon which he lifted a twig and broke it throwing a part over each shoulder, their mode of giving a receipt for debt, implying that the ox he gave me was bought and paid for. To refuse after this would be far from wise, so I agreed to eat the ox. Sumbula spent the afternoon with me, and was very pleased to talk as long as I liked. I gave him a hat and a dress of print-cloth as a token of our friendship, and he gave a guide to take us, by a shorter route, to the next camp.

" I sat up until late writing out my diary for mother, as sleep was impossible on account of five drums and 30 lusty voices serenading.

" *Dec. 1st,* 1885.—Feeling far from fresh this morning, and certainly very unequal to my task of eating an ox. The sound of drums is in every chamber of my brain.

"*Dec. 2nd.*—Arrived at the head of the Chonga River. Here there were many villages, and a perfect crowd of people came to the camp. The pressing and crowding until late at night to get a look at the white man was somewhat trying; they meant well, so I had no option but to take it patiently and all in good part. These people have been away in the Lunda country raiding, and have been completely beaten. They are coming back in twos and threes with nothing but sticks in their hands. Many have been killed. All about they are much downcast and fear more evil awaits them, as with an African one evil leads to another. I took the opportunity of pointing out to a circle of natives around my tent the miserable lives they lived because they had so many things to trust in and so many things to fear. I told them of the perfect contentment and peace I enjoyed because I trusted only in God, and counted all other things as nothing. The exclamation came in reply from every lip : ' But how can we do so when we do not know God ? '

"*Dec. 3rd.*—Reached the capital of the Kangombe to-day. The Chibokwe country is passed, and I am now in the Lovale, i.e. ' The Flats.' The Balovale (people of the flats) are in many respects superior to the Bachokwe, in the sense that they make better inhabitants of a country, being less given to wandering. I am amused to see how fond they are of singing-birds; these have a regular current value among them, and their neatly-made cages are to be seen hanging about all their villages. I notice here, close by my camp, that they have made a large fish dam. I have never before seen natives, untaught by whites, dam a river for any purpose. Kangombe is quite a powerful man. His fame has spread far.

"*Dec. 4th.*—Remained in camp. Kangombe came to see me; a very small-looking man indeed, who seemed quite afraid to come into my tent, and wanted to sit down on the ground. I gave him my chair, but that was another difficulty for him. How was he to sit on it ? At last he ventured sideways on the furthest corner of it, looking suspiciously at the back of the chair. He never asked for anything, but kept looking about him, and then at me, with a pair of eyes like needles for sharpness. He was sorry I could only remain with him one day, and gave me a goat as a present.

"*Dec. 6th.*—There is a company of Garenganze, I am told,

camped a few days from here. They are in distress. Some Bihé traders have been stirring up the Balovale to rob them in payment for goods of theirs lost in the interior.

"*Dec. 7th.*—The man in charge of the Garenganze caravan has come on to me in great distress saying that he and his companions are beset by Bihéans, who threaten to rob them if not to kill them. The camp of Bihéans we passed yesterday are active in this affair. Some six teeth have already been paid by the Garenganze. This man in charge is only too anxious to get rid of his ivory and to return with me. They are at a loss to know what to do. I cannot advise them. I say if they want to return they can go with me, but that if they want to go on I can say nothing. I know that the chief of Bihé will not rob them, whatever his people may do outside of his country enraged with losses in the interior.

"*Dec. 8th.*—At the request of the leader of the Garenganze caravan I remain in camp again to-day. They have, however, decided to go on to Bihé, as to return to their country would mark them as cowards. The leader, a son of Msidi, the Garenganze chief, asked me to sell him some cloth to buy provisions with on the road. He said his father would most surely pay me. I gave him some cloth, a little powder, and a gun which one of my men was carrying.

"*Dec. 9th.*—Was not much surprised to find this morning that four of my men had run off during the night. At first I thought there was no help for it but to leave the loads here. However, after a little delay men were found willing to carry the loads on to the border of the Lunda country.

"We camped by the Lumese River. My men are crying 'hunger' and want me to dispense rations here six days short of the regular place for receiving the same. I do not feel at liberty to pay them. It is not a case of getting along at any cost. After much talking and loud threatening, a little too loud to be fulfilled, 10 more carriers packed up and started for the road by which they had come. I made no compromise whatever with them and was fully prepared to remain here, and began looking about to see what sort of building material the country possessed. My men, however, have thought better of it as they have returned by another road to camp, all except the four who left last night

"*Dec. 10th.*—Crossed the Lumese River this morning on

a wooden bridge and entered upon a flat, thinly wooded land. We are now nearly at the end of the Lovale country proper although many of the Balovale will be met with in the Lunda country on ahead. Women chiefs are very plentiful among these people. Every little district has its male and female chief living in different villages, often brother and sister or mother and son. There is not much difference seemingly between the sexes among the Lovale as to liberty, work, etc. Men, working in the fields, are as common a sight as women. Women also come about camp on business of their own, such as selling wax, etc., without appearing to be in subjection to anyone. Indeed they are rather too free and too much at liberty, I think, considering the low moral condition of themselves and of the tribes around.

" The Lovale people seem to be much given to music and night dancing. Every day my camp is beset more or less with musicians, fiddlers, singers and comic dancers. Singing-birds are to be seen in all their villages.

" The appearance of their villages seems to be quite in keeping with their light-headed ways. A few grass huts (often neatly built and ornamented) scattered round a large tree in the bush. Little is done in the way of clearing, and often the grass and weeds of the forest nearly overtop the houses so that they appear to one approaching like so many beehives.

" The custom of selling their own children (a practice, the traders tell me, peculiar to the Balovale) is now nearly extinct, but is quite in keeping with the temperament of the people.

" The Balovale are faithful practisers of circumcision, and the rite, I am told, is gone through with much ceremony.

" *Dec.* 11*th.*—A short journey brought us to the border of the Kifumadshe Flat (there is no lake as marked in the map). The river of this name rises in the centre of a flat, flooded and impassable from January to April or May , it could not even be called a marsh, as the ground here is sandy and firm, with grass and trees growing upon a host of mounds made by ants. I went out in the afternoon to try and get some meat for my men, and shot an antelope. My men look on this as a good omen for the journey on ahead, as every day now game increases.

" *Dec.* 12*th.*—Rain this morning ; remain in camp. Every day now lost will tell on us crossing this flat as it is rapidly filling with water, and in a very short time will be quite impassable.

" *Dec. 13th.*—Another wet, threatening morning. After a little palaver and delay, however, I decided to start. To get away from the habitable parts of the earth was, I confess, a strong inducement, as I am exhausted with the begging of the people. Every few miles, and there is a little chieftain to be pacified with a gift. It is most amusing to see the airs of greatness they choose to put on. One man may have under him a few villages containing in all perhaps 100 souls, and a few pigs, and he calls himself a king and will not listen to any reasonable talk, and will keep my men trotting backwards and forwards between my camp and his capital (?) a whole day with bits of presents and talk. No matter how much or how little I choose to give at the first the dignity of such kings is not satisfied with less than a ' three times giving.'

" The first few hours in the flat were most fatiguing, wading in water up to the knees. Further on the ground was firmer. About midday we camped, choosing a clump of mounds formed by colonies of termites, each mound being large enough to contain three small grass huts, or rather shelters. I pitched my tent on one. Thus my tent was scattered over something like a square mile of marsh Though the water around me is knee deep, I feel quite snug in my tent on this dry spot.

" *Dec. 14th.*—Six long hours of one continual wade brought us again to camp in the midst of water. I managed to pitch my tent on a clump of small tufts or clods. And by a skilful placing of my chair and cot bed in such a way so that each foot got a clod to rest on, I managed to keep above water.

" *Dec. 16th.*—Crossed the Kifumadshe River and camped quite late. Here my men began to misbehave to the best of their ability, laying down their loads, demanding more rations, then meat : ' Meat, Monare, give us meat ; why don't you hunt ? you are starving us.' I lifted my gun to go. I was, I must confess, sadly out of temper, and kept scolding them while I was tugging the cover off my gun, when it suddenly went off, shattering the point of my left forefinger. There was no one who could dress a wound, so I thought the cleanest and safest way would be to cut off the top joint of the finger. I got a lancet out of my case, and my man, Kasoma, cut according to my directions. This effectually cooled my anger ; indeed,

I was compelled to rejoice at the mercy of God. Two verses came forcibly to my mind : ' You only have I known of all the families of the earth : therefore I will punish you for all your iniquities ' ; and ' the Lord loveth judgment, and forsaketh not His saints.' I have given way time after time lately to fits of temper, with no one by to rebuke me. I acknowledge His great goodness and pity towards me in thus rebuking me. My men cannot understand my joy.

" *Dec. 17th.*—Slept nearly all night. Arose once or twice to bathe my hand. Started early this morning. My finger shows signs of healing up rapidly. No swelling or pain beyond the injured part. This accident has effectually calmed down my men, for the present at least. Not a word about more rations, heavy loads, etc., but all are doing their best to please me, bringing wild fruit to me and standing round with long faces. Happily they acknowledge that it was chiefly because of their troubling yesterday that I got ' mad ' and shot off my finger.

" *Dec. 18th.*—Remained here so that my men might lay in a stock of fish.

" *Dec. 19th.*—A short journey along the Lutembwa brought us to another small chief. Being a relative of Katema's, he would have me remain next day, which I did to my sorrow. All forenoon was spent in holding out against his demands. I had given him eight yards of cloth, for which he gave me a goat, and then wanted more cloth, a jacket, etc. After four or five hours of this work I began to doze in my chair, and the chief rose and left, he sent his man in the morning, however, to ask for more. I could but refuse and tell the man to go home.

" *Dec. 20th.*—Delayed this morning waiting on a guide as the chief did not turn up according to his promise. We marched a few hours along the Lutembwa and camped at Kapwita. In the afternoon chief No. 1 turned up, with his little stool, retinue, etc. He had brought a goat and some meal. I paid him six yards. A little later chief No. 2 came along. He was a ' big man,' and every one who had come to the camp declared that he was their chief. I gave him the usual tribute, regretting only my liberality to the former ' pretender.' Towards evening, however, another lot came along from Kapwita, the ' true chief,' the ' great chief ' At this my indignation began to come out ' Three chiefs for the one camp ! ' Never ! I would not hear of it. After much discussion and quarrelling between my men and the people, I had to fork out again eight yards to No. 3, whom I have no doubt is the real chief of the place, if chief there be. But the whole thing was cleverly planned. No device is forgotten or opportunity lost to delay and fleece me.

" In spite of their troublesome ways there is much about these Balunda I like. Their villages are kept clean and they have good gardens, and the men work in the fields as well as the women. They seem to be more ' religious ' than their neighbours. One sees continually in the forests small clearings about the trunk of some immense tree, with a double rail round, and some ' fetish thing ' in front, in the shape of a horn or image, and there the people come to offer to their forefathers. Many fetish huts are also to be seen in their villages.

" *Dec.* 21*st.*—Kapwita came along this morning very early with a whole crowd. He was not pleased with his tribute and came to return it. I refused to take it back and after a little talk I gave him two yards more and got off out of camp. Our road lay at once across the Lutembwa valley. Nearly all the way the water was waist deep. A beautiful mangrove-like forest lay midway, also submerged in water. Each immense tree had a fern-covered clump at its roots, and in some places the branches and forest creepers were festooned with long lichen-like moss of a pale transparent colour, streaming down in icicle-like prongs touching the glistening water, and contrasting beautifully with the deep emerald-green moss in the water. When we came to one open spot like a lagoon, thus decked all round, I thought, in the clear morning light, it was a place of the most delicate and delightful scenery I had yet seen.

" Reached old Katema early in the day. I am glad to say there is a ' chief ' here.

" *Dec.* 22*nd.*—This morning Katema sent me a present of a woman slave with infant in arms—a pitiful sight. The chief's messengers said that food was to follow, but that Katema could not give to a white man a present of food only. I asked them as a favour to take the woman back ; and if they would only send her to her own village and among her own people, and never think of giving her away again to strangers, I should be more than pleased. The chief, however, did not quite understand my message, and thought I had refused the slave

because she was full grown, and so he sent back word that
to-morrow he would send me a young boy or girl. Though
suffering a good deal from my finger, which was ulcerating, I
determined to go to his village and explain the matter. I
found he was a good-looking man. He knew Livingstone and
was sorry to hear of his death. He was quite satisfied with
my explanation about the slave. We parted the best of friends.
I call him a coloured gentleman. I am sorry I cannot spend
more time with him, but I am hastening to Nana Kandundu,
where I hope to get a little rest, and where many of my
men, I hear, intend to leave me. I have some most troublesome men in my camp, who are never, never satisfied. Still
I rejoice in the opportunity of learning to bear patiently
even with such. They compel me daily to walk by the river of
my God.

" *Dec. 24th.*—The grumbling of yesterday has broken out
in quite a storm this morning. 'More rations!' 'Starvation!' 'We cannot carry further.' I know some of my men
are rather short of food. But certainly it is their own fault.
Nearly all the cloth I divided amongst them at the Lumese
has been spent for vicious purposes A band this morning
have gone through the camp, threatening to belabour with
leather thongs the first to lift his load. I left the matter
entirely in the Master's hands, being assured that if Matema
was the place to which He had sent me, He would not allow
me to go further. So I withdrew from the camp, never dreaming
that a march could be made to-day. While sitting on a log
I suddenly saw a general move among the men; they came
out, one after another, and went off, scarcely saying a word.
The truth was, the camp was literally alive with 'army ants,'
which came rushing in from all directions; and anyone who
knows anything about the African ant will at once understand
why my carriers turned out so speedily.

" We made a good day's journey, crossing two flooded rivers.
The first one I crossed on the back of my ox and he swam
bravely. At the second a boat was waiting. I got in and
crossed, and had scarce got on the other side when my ox of
his own accord sprang in and swam after me. We camped by
a few fishermen's huts, basking under the sublime name of
Kalilangumbu. Neither I nor my men seemed to understand
very well how we managed to get here, yesterday and this

morning having been spent in giving and hearing loud declarations that we never should. My men have gone about their hut building without a word, and seem to be rather bashful. They will break out, however, as evening falls. The light of the sun is not in keeping with their meanness. And all this fighting and troubling is simply to prepare me for a general desertion at Nana Kandundu (now known as Kavungu).

" Some Bihé traders have been murdered by the natives of the Lualaba (not without reason) and this has softened the hearts of most of my men.

" In the evening I called my men together, intending to give them rations. They, however, could not agree together and kept scolding each other. At last I packed up my cloth and all went to their huts again.

" *Dec. 25th.*—Started this morning without any delay. Passed through a beautiful piece of country. The path was lined with branching palms and tropical plants. The road, however, suddenly turned and led through a series of black slime-holes. The contrast was worthy of a description from the pen of a Bunyan. We camped at Nambanja.

" I paid my men one yard each to keep their pots going until Nana Kandundu. They discussed the matter a while, and seeing I was determined to give no more took the cloth. I hope that this will be the last of this troubling. At Nana Kandundu it will be a case either of go or leave me. My goods I can leave with the chief there and go on to the Garenganze with few men and send back for my loads.

" *Dec. 26th.*—A long day's journey brought us to Katonge. Here the hills on the east side of the Zambesi are in sight. My brave men, having ceased for the time to quarrel with me, have been letting out their spleen one against another. On the road they had two free fights with sticks. Then they fell on the Garenganze men who are with me, and took a gun from them.

" *Dec. 27th.*—Remained in camp this morning to settle the dispute. My men say that their fellows were robbed some time ago by men from the interior, that the Garenganze came from the interior, and therefore they must now pay them for their fellows' loss. I paid 12 yards of calico to get back the gun, seeing it was useless to dispute with people bent on robbery.

" *Dec. 28th.*—Another quarrel this morning between my men and the people of the country. A little dog in the camp was ill and vomited, and a native, who had come to sell meal, sat down beside the dog, and some of the vomit came on his arm. We all declared it was his own fault, and would not pay for this offence ; so he and his friends waylaid us on the road, caught a straggler, and took his gun from him.

" We camped on the east bank of the Luvua, a large river flowing into the Zambesi.

" *Dec. 30th.*—A long march to-day brought us to Nana Kandundu's town. Towards the end of the journey I began to stoop as usual, and when I got into camp I was down ; liver giving me great pain, being much swollen.

" *Dec. 31st.*—Was unable to get up to-day, and could not pay off the few men. How many, or rather how few, will go on with me is very uncertain. Nana Kandundu came to visit me. She is a smart-looking, elderly woman, and seemingly quite equal to her position.

" *Jan. 1st*, 1886.—This morning I called my men together to give them rations, and to know who would journey further and who would not. I discovered that eight were willing to go on ; the rest wished to return from here. I said, ' All right ! ' and gave them their rations.

" *Jan. 2nd.*—Busy packing and making ready, as the few men I have left may change their minds if I delay long here.

" *Jan. 3rd.*—Three more carriers have withdrawn to-day.

" Paid a visit to the chieftainess, and arranged with her about leaving some of my loads. She promised to take every care of them.

" On returning to camp in the evening I was distressed to find my men negotiating with some wild Balunda for a woman slave and child (a little boy of five or six years). The woman had been bargained for, but the price of the child was disputed. At last the Balunda said they would not sell the child, and were pulling him out of the arms of his mother, who was clutching him frantically. At this I interfered, and stopped the proceedings. They took the hint ; for before I had time to look round me, they snatched up their cloth, including the price offered for the child, and cleared away from the camp. This slave buying is a wretched business. I am utterly powerless to interfere in the matter. It is seldom, however, that they purchase in camp ; they usually go off to the villages to do this. Many of the Bihé traders say that they would rather have slaves than ivory. Every caravan we pass has strings of slaves.

" *Jan. 5th.*—Ill this morning with swollen spleen. In bed nearly all day.

" *Jan. 6th.*—Much better. Have sent 15 loads to Nana's village, and am preparing to start to-morrow.

" *Jan. 8th.*—Started this morning in fair style with eight brave carriers for the 15 days' long march to the Lualaba—a risky journey to undertake, as we shall meet with no food by the way except that which I may procure with my gun. For my part I am glad to be off, as I have been suffering the whole time at Nana Kandundu from my old Zambesi remittent fever, which shows me clearly that anywhere near the Zambesi is not the place for me. Marched for six hours ; camped at Kamisambu by the Loungashi.

" *Jan. 10th.*—Marched for eight hours through beautiful country, more tropical-looking than any other part of Africa I have been in. Small rivers without number. During the day we were overtaken by several tremendous showers of rain, soaking everyone and everything thoroughly. I got into camp at Maringa, feeling so cold that I was sure an attack of fever awaited me ; but a big fire, a dose of quinine, and a cup of hot tea brought me round.

" *Jan. 11th.*—Made a late start this morning. Had some trouble in arranging my carriers' loads. They were all over-laden with meal, and blamed my loads for breaking their backs. Crossed the Luake River, a large and rapid stream, but with much trouble, as there was a cataract at this point.

" *Jan. 12th*—Reached Sacindonga early this morning. Here I met with a few wandering Balunda, but the country is practically desolate. Remains of former towns and large cultivated fields, now all weeds, exist on all sides. War parties from the Lovale, led chiefly by Kangombe, have wrought these devastations.

" *Jan. 13th.*—Remain in camp this morning, as one of my carriers is ill, and the rest go off foraging for food in villages some distance away.

" *Jan. 14th.*—Marched this morning until midday. Camped at a place called Tambwe. No signs of inhabitants anywhere.

"*Jan.* 15*th.*—A toilsome day's journey. We lost our way, and wandered for some hours before getting back to the path again. Reached camp about four in the afternoon.

"*Jan.* 16*th.*—Pushed on and made two ordinary days' journey in one, reaching a camp very late, but only to find it occupied by a company of Bihé traders from the Garenganze. They say I am now within sixteen days' journey of my destination—most welcome news.

"*Jan.* 17*th.*—In camp to-day. Men have gone off to the Zambesi River, which is quite near, to buy food. We are all very tired and glad of the rest.

"*Jan.* 19*th.*—This morning I gave up my ox to a lad in the company, who had been bought by one of my men at Nana Kandundu, and could not walk further. The carriers could not well understand my doing so, as the white men to whom they are accustomed generally advocate in such cases leaving the poor wretches to perish by the roadside. Reached the ill-famed camping place of ' Olohosi ' in the afternoon. The name means ' The Lions.' There are many stories about natives camping here and being seized while asleep and carried off by lions. An extra barricade was built round the camp with great pains. A house had to be made for my ox, and every precaution was taken by my credulous crew, so that the lions had little prospect of supping at our expense that night, though many of the more ' daring ' of our number thought they heard the monsters roaring at a distance during the night. I think that they have long since taken their departure from Olohosi, as, judging from the number of barricades, other passing travellers seem to have been as much on their guard against affording the lions a meal as we were.

"*Jan.* 20*th.*—My men were longer getting astir this morning than usual. We generally start about the time of the ' cooing of the pigeons,' but we did not this morning until ' the dew was dry.' Crossed the Lokoshe River, about 20 yards wide here. It flows into the Luburi, which empties itself into the Lualaba, so that I am now within the lines of the Congo Free State, and am doubtless the first white man to cross its southern frontier.

"*Jan.* 21*st.*—We have now been 12 days in this hungry country. The few beans we were able to bring from Sacindonga did not last long, and our sacks of cassava meal, bought at Nana Kandundu, are almost finished. I had hoped to have

shot some game, but nothing is to be seen, not even the spoor of any. We were therefore forced to press on without losing any time. The bodies of two natives by the roadside, who had evidently died of hunger, certainly did not encourage us, though it was a warning for my men to take longer marches.

"*Jan. 22nd.*—Crossed the Luburi this morning—a heavy stream, 35 feet wide—upon a fairly good bridge. Camped at Kapa. Our food being now used up, all the carriers started off, as soon as we got into camp, for some Samba villages reported to be further down the Luburi.

"*Jan. 23rd.*—Men returned with only a few cassava roots. We crossed the Lufupa River about midday, and camped at dusk. We had scarcely made a shelter for the goods when the rain came down in sheets. The night was pitch dark; there was nothing but forest all round; everyone was tired out, and we had no shelter. We managed, however, to go to sleep, and to forget our hunger and destitution.

"Just as I was dropping off, I heard a prolonged ominous rustle among the dank grass and leaves that made my litter. I suspected that a snake, roused by the warmth of my body, was drawing closer. As soon as I awoke in the morning, I remembered my bedmate, and with one spring, cleared both bed and bedding. Then with the help of my boys I fished my rugs away, and after beating around with long sticks, out wriggled a deadly black mamba, some six feet long, which we quickly despatched.

"*Jan. 24th.*—Men all gone off in search of Samba villages. I started on ahead with one to look for game, following a long while on the track of a zebra, encouraged by its fresh footprints; but as they led across a marsh I gave up, and went towards our next camping place. When crossing a small flat I saw four pigs in the distance. Creeping up on all fours I managed to get within 120 yards of them, when they saw me and prepared to clear off. As one young hog turned to take another look at me, I took aim and fired. The lead entered his breast and traversed the whole body. The old hog turned back in a great rage to look after his fellow, when another bullet from my gun pierced his two shoulders, and he lay down with his head resting on the other. They were both of the wart-hog species; the old one, a splendid animal weighing over 200 lb., and having tusks a foot in length. Thus the Lord

M

delivered me and my men from sinking from sheer hunger; for we had nothing to eat. When my men came along I had the greatest difficulty in keeping them off the meat; some were tearing it and eating it raw like wolves.

"The country here is very beautiful, the forest not so dense, and the hills high and richly clad to the tops. Though this is the hottest time of the year the nights are quite cold. I never sleep without a fire in my hut, though I have blankets enough. During the day a cool breeze is always blowing. I presume the altitude is considerable.

"*Jan. 25th.*—Marched but a short way. I shall not soon forget the hearty expressions the men threw out one to the other as they marched along in Indian file this morning. ' Don't you remember what things we said of the white man and his God ? What names we called them ! But the white man's God has not only been with us, but has filled our bellies with pig meat.' And so their eyes were not closed ; they were willing to acknowledge that God had fed them. Kasoma's wife is taken seriously ill. How she is to be got along I know not.

"*Jan. 26th.*—Made another short march to the Muilo coppei mines Some of the men have gone back to carry Kasoma's wife in a hammock.

"*Jan. 27th.*—Remained in camp. Men gone off in search of food.

"*Jan. 28th.*—Started this morning early with two of my men to look for game ; had gone but a short way when I saw that, up a valley, some animals were moving about in the long grass. Taking a round through the bush with one of my men I got up, by dint of careful stalking, close to the animals, when, to my surprise, I found myself in front of five full-grown leopards. I refrained from shooting, as their flesh could not have been of use, and I have no licence to fight with wild animals. Four of the leopards cantered off at first sight of me ; the old one remained, and seemed as if he would attack me, swinging his tail about and crouching. I kept my ground calmly, about 20 yards from him, with my rifle cocked. As soon, however, as he saw his four relatives off at a safe distance, he trotted slowly after them, then broke into a canter. Got into camp, late and tired. Kasoma's wife is riding on my ox to-day ; it is the ambulance animal of the company."

CHAPTER XIII

" *JAN*. 29*th*, 1886—Crossing a hill this morning we came in full sight of the valley of the Lualaba—a beautiful view indeed. An hour's journey along the bank of the river brought us to the ferry. We were all taken over without delay, and at length I set foot on Garenganze soil. Mangala, the chief of the ferry, received me well, cooking some food for me, and showing real hospitality. The appearance of this man, and of his village, favourably impress me in view of my future stay in this country.

" *Jan*. 30*th*.—Rested to-day. A hunter brought in the meat of a buffalo, so we have food enough. A relative of Msidi sent a large basket of beans, and having also bought some onions, I managed with the help of Dick to prepare quite a sumptuous feast.

" This afternoon we were saddened by the death of Kasoma's wife. News has also come in of the killing of Kazembe, of Lake Mweru, a chief who has long been a sworn enemy of Msidi, and who till lately was wandering at large with a few followers, and hunted by the Garenganze.

" Kasoma's wife was buried. My men went through the usual ceremony of questioning the corpse as to the cause of death. The answer was that a female slave, long since dead, had come to take her, because at the slave's death no drums were beaten. This reply was made out from the varied jerkings of the pole to which the corpse was tied, and which was borne on the shoulders of two men.

" *Feb*. 2*nd*, 1886.—Reached Moelo's town. All were delighted when we came to fields of corn and abundance of food ; a very pleasant sight after so many days of hunger while passing through a deserted country.

" *Feb*. 3*rd*.—Remained in camp, my men eating to their

179

hearts' content. Moelo sent me three baskets of corn and half a wild hog.

" *Feb. 4th* —Marched to-day through beautifully hilly country. Camped in a hollow surrounded by steep hills, within two hours' march of Molenga's old town. I had sent a man on ahead yesterday to advise Molenga of my coming, as is the custom. To my surprise I had not been in camp more than ten minutes when people came to meet me, carrying loads of food : maize corn, pumpkins, fresh beans, all cooked, and a load of corn besides.

" *Feb. 5th.*—Arrived at Molenga's old town , he has built another, an hour's journey further on He sent a headman to greet me, and in the evening his three drummers came to escort us on our visit to him on the morrow. Molenga is the second man in the Garenganze kingdom, captain of the forces, etc.

" *Feb. 6th.*— Scarcely had we reached Molenga's this morning and built our camp when the chief's present arrived : a tooth of ivory (about 30 lb.), a good fat goat, and 29 loads of corn— enough to disconcert me ; for I had only given him as yet eight yards of calico. My first thought was to return the ivory, but all protested loudly against my doing so, saying I could not offer Molenga a greater insult. I went to greet the chief with nothing in my hand, and was welcomed most warmly. He rose and gave me his seat, saying again and again how glad he was to see me and how welcome I was to the Garenganze country.

" *Feb 7th.*—Sent Molenga this morning a present of a small keg of powder, some cloth and a blanket, nothing like the value of the ivory and food he gave me. Still he seems to be quite satisfied, saying it is I, and not my goods, that they welcome.

" *Feb. 8th.*—Upon going up to the chief's house this morning I was surprised to find none but women about the place. The natural conclusion was that the men were all away hunting ; but no, they were all off in the fields with Molenga. Taking the paths to the fields I found Molenga in the midst of a considerable clearing, directing 25 stalwart men, with long-handled hoes, which they were using in fine style, hoeing to the beat of a drum. It was what might be called a healthy sight. I sat down and talked awhile with the chief. In a short time women came with baskets of roasted corn for the hoers' breakfast. They tell me that it is the regular custom in this country for the men to do all the heavy work of tilling, and the women to do the after work of clearing, etc., with light, short-handled hoes.

" *Feb. 9th.*—Marched again this morning, and camped at Kalasa's town, on the east bank of the Lukuruwe River. Some messengers came into camp, sent by Msidi to overtake a company of his men, bound for Bihé, whom we met yesterday. It seems that one of the company, while stealing food in a field, killed a man who was attempting to defend his corn. On hearing of this Msidi sent to stop the men ; not so much that the murderer might be punished as that certain rites might be performed to remove the stain of innocent blood. Otherwise some disaster might have befallen the party.

" *Feb. 10th.*— A toilsome march through beautiful hills. To the south lay the Sombwe Hill and others beyond, in which are the inhabited caves which Livingstone was on his way to visit when death overtook him on the south of Lake Bangweolo.

" *Feb. 11th.*—A long tramp over very rough mountain country brought us to Uleya, only one day's journey from our destination.

" *Feb. 12th.*—Remain here and send on Kasoma with letter to Msidi and 24 yards of cloth. And now as I draw near to the capital of the great chief, and hear from the villages along the route of the extra tall, well-sharpened stake that Msidi has in the middle of his courtyard on which to place the head of the first white man who comes into the country to spy out his storehouses of ivory and mountains of copper, I confess to many anxious days and nights of prayer.

" *Feb. 13th.*—Marched to Kungofo. Towards the end of the journey the road lay through well-tilled gardens for three miles. A frightful storm came down shortly after we had camped and threatened to swamp everything. The cooking business was paralysed ; we had to go to bed with what supper could otherwise be provided My man, Kasoma, returned from Msidi with a small tooth of *very white* ivory to indicate how white the king's heart was towards me, and with many messages of satisfaction.

" *Feb. 14th.*—A short journey brought us close to the capital. I was shown a hill close by where I might build. On getting to the spot it pleased me every way. It was in the midst of villages, on high ground, commanding a view of the whole country, but not difficult of approach. I named it Mount Rehoboth.

"*Feb.* 15*th.*—Late this evening the chief's messenger, who had come in the morning with promises of food, came to say that the food the chief had sent for had not yet come so in place he sent me a small tooth of ivory, to keep my heart up.

" I expected to have had an early interview with the king, but discovered that it was not the custom to receive entire strangers at once, so I was placed in a sort of quarantine. During this time they were deciding, to their own wisdom and skill, whether my intentions in coming to the country were good or bad, and whether my heart was as white as my skin. Diviners and doctors from far and near were employed for this purpose.

" Some of their tests were certainly rather childish, though they had a grim humour about them. One was the placing of a little piece of bark at night in a certain decoction of some carefully compounded native medicines. Next morning, if this piece of bark appeared quite sound, it would show that my heart was sound, and that I had come to the Garenganze country without evil intentions. If, however, this little fragment of bark turned out to be unsound, or in any way decomposed, it would have proved that my heart was rotten, and that I was not to be trusted.

" Another test was on this wise : They cut off the head of a live fowl, which was then thrown into the middle of the yard, and the diviner, watching its dying struggles, judged as to my designs from the position in which it lay when dead. If the neck had pointed in the direction of my camp, danger from that quarter would have been indicated ; but, if not, then I and my companions were clear. All things turned out in my favour. They had nothing against me, and so were willing to obey their king's command and unite in giving me a hearty welcome to their country.

" *Feb.* 16*th.*—A large basket of rice and a goat to-day. In the evening corn and beer for the men in abundance, and a message for all of us to come to the chief to-morrow, and to come in style, as he was going to give a grand reception. We must fire off volleys, etc.

" *Feb.* 17*th.*—Went with my eight men, this morning, all dressed in our finest, I on my ox, to the chief's town. The town has not much of an appearance as the chief has newly come to this part. Mukurru can scarcely be called a town or village, but an immense inhabited place bordering on a range of hills, the houses of the chief's wives forming centres all over. He is said to have five hundred.

" We reached the yard where Msidi was awaiting me. I found him an old-looking man, with rather a pleasant, smooth face, and a short beard, quite white. As I approached he rose from his chair and came forward to meet me, folding his arms round me in a most fatherly way , indeed his reception was quite affecting. Behind and on either side of him were large companies of women , these he introduced to me as his wives. After the ceremony of shaking hands with wives, brothers, cousins and other relatives was over, he sent for the nurse of one of his children, who brought a child about 18 months old. This little boy was placed by Msidi upon my knee before all the company as his present, and he assured me that he was my child henceforth. Yota is the child's name.

" *Feb* 18*th* —Had a visit from two sons of the chief. Kalasa, the eldest, is a fine-looking fellow. They conducted themselves very mannerly. Indeed, all the chief's family and people are wonderfully well behaved for Africans. Immorality is, of course, very great ; but respectful, courteous behaviour towards one another is insisted upon by the king. He opposes all hashish smoking, and is not favourable to the use of tobacco in any form. He insists upon his sons acquiring a knowledge of useful employments. Kalasa is quite a skilful worker in horn, making, out of the horns of large animals, powder flasks, neatly mounted with copper and brass Another of Msidi's sons is a proficient blacksmith. Their livelihood does not depend upon these trades, but they are followed as accomplishments.

" *Feb.* 19*th*.—Had a long interview with the king, who asked many questions about the Barotse. He told me that my old friend, Liwanika, had come up close to his country and intended coming on to the Garenganze.

" *March* 1*st*, 1886.—Each day brings something with it to do I have had several interviews with the chief and am getting on well with him. He is very kind in his way. Indeed he is a strange mixture. He is fierce and cruel as a soldier and in his ambition for power and gain, but kind and generous as a father over his people. Hearing him talk of his wars, and seeing all round his yard human skulls, brought in baskets as a proof of his soldiers' valour, the sensation creeps over one of being in a

monster's den, but this is immediately expelled when trays of
food are brought in, and the old chief comes down from his
stool and himself deals out food for his people, giving special
attention to a group of aged and decrepit, a leper and a silly
woman, and then mixing up in a separate dish some porridge
and broth for my dog, which is standing by. He has the name
of being very kind among his people, but at the same time very
strict. He does not stop at taking their heads off. One young
man who returned with me to his own country, instead of going
on to Benguella with his companions, saved his head by starting
at once for Loanda with a company bound for that place.

" During one of my first interviews with the king I was introduced to several traders, of Arab descent, from Zanzibar. The
Arabs have been long in communication with the Garenganze
country, which is known to them as Katanga, famous all over
Eastern Africa for its copper and salt   Arab caravans come
from Lake Tanganyika in the north for copper to supply the
markets of Uganda. I found that these Arabs made good use
of their time at Katanga in promulgating infamous stories about
the English. They were, I was told, most assiduous in their
efforts to poison the mind of Msidi against me in particular,
when they heard of my coming. After listening to a long
harangue from them, however, he quickly replied : ' I am sure
I cannot answer your words   I do not know these English
people. I certainly do not know this man who is now coming ;
but one thing I know—*I know you Arabs.*' So he was prepared
to suspend judgment concerning me from his knowledge of the
men who were seeking to prejudice him against me.

" A few sick folk have been coming to my camp. But on the
whole my camp is exceptionally quiet and free from visiting,
owing no doubt to the fact that I have been giving no presents.
Food is not very plentiful, but sufficient. Have got two milking
goats. From these I get about a cupful of very refreshing milk
which helps over my breakfast of rice and maize porridge.

" I have been able by degrees to make known to the king my
object in coming to his country. He had heard of Livingstone's
approach from the east, and of his death at Ilala, and was much
interested when I told him that I was a man of peace like
Livingstone, and hailed from the same country and town. I
also told him that I was willing to remain among his people,
and to send back Cinyana, with the few men who had come with

me, to Bihé, to bring on others who might think of joining me in this country.

"It was difficult, of course, in a few interviews fully to disclose to a mind so dark my true object in coming to the country. And I sought for special wisdom to explain to him the nature of my message, waiting for a suitable opportunity to present itself. I feared that were I to keep back from his ears the more bitter and pungent things in connection with the story of man's ruin and God's love until afterwards, he would conclude that I had knowingly deceived him. One day he asked me to breakfast at his house, and our conversation went on, as at other times, respecting the nature and reality of God's existence. I then spoke to him in words like these · ' Great and mighty chief as you are in the eyes of men, in the sight of God there is no difference between you and the poorest, vilest slave in your country, and you need God's mercy just as he does.' My words impressed him, and I was uncertain for a few moments as to the result. At last, with an effort, he leaned forward thoughtfully, and said: 'It must be so, if God is as great as you say ; and if He is so high above us all, then we must be all the same in His sight.' Instead of alienating me from him, we were, through this plain speaking, drawn closer together, and our conversations became more frequent and interesting.

"*March 3rd.*—Went to visit the chief this morning. He took me to see some of his towns On the way we passed a house, in the course of construction, which had no less than 15 compartments, all on the ground floor, and all covered by one immense roof, a tremendous undertaking for natives. We went on to the town of his chief wife, who lives in a two-storied house with an inside staircase. She, however, was sick and unable to entertain us, so we went to the house of another wife, who had also a good square house with four compartments. She at once set her servants to work to prepare food for us. A goat was killed, and rice was dealt out to be ground for bread. True primitive hospitality, but quite unsuited to the patience of ' civilised ' folk, for before the animal was skinned, cut up and cooked, the sun was getting low. It was pitch dark when I reached camp in the evening.

"The chief, as usual, had much to say. At one time he called me aside to tell me that he had a gold mine in his country,

and that he wanted me to inspect it for him. I told him that
if he had a mine of gold he had better keep it to himself and
show it to no one, as we whites were not people when we smelt
gold, that if he showed the mine to white people they would
come in and take it by force. At this he said he would show it
to me if I promised not to tell my friends. I assured him it
would not be safe for him even to do that as my friends would
be sure to ask me and I could not tell them a lie.

"*March 7th*—The chief held a grand reception to-day to
receive a company of Bachikumbi who have come from Lake
Bangweolo with a present. Msidi turned out in a litter carried
by about 20 men, and with his immense head-dress of red
parrot feathers, and flaming coloured clothes hanging all round
him, he made an imposing appearance.

"*March 12th.*—Called on the chief again to-day and found
I had been successful in curing a favourite wife who had been
sick. The chief sent a hunter off to kill and bring in the flesh
of a buffalo as my pay. A leprous woman has also been greatly
relieved by me with crystal caustic. The chief is quite taken
up about my house and wants to build me a big one with six
compartments.

"*March 13th.*—Called out in haste this evening to see
another sick wife some two miles off.

"*March 14th.*—Received this morning a basket of rice and
a goat as fees for medicine. Was pleased with the intelligent
way some of my men connected what I said to them on
former occasions with verses which I read to them to-day
in Luke xv.

"*March 29th.*—Returned from a trip to the Lufira River ;
passed through the many villages of the place forming Msidi's
Mukurru. I had quite a ' progress,' the people everywhere glad
to see me. The Lufira flows through a great grassy plain, more
or less flooded during the rainy season, but dry in the summer
and abounding with large herds of game. On the east side of
the river there is a majestic range of mountains, rising abruptly
from the plain to a height of about 3,000 feet. There are many
villages along the Lufira, small and poorly built, and occupied
chiefly by Lamba fishermen. I shot six animals for my men and
returned with some meat for my own supplies. The amount of
wild geese and golden crested cranes, and other water fowl
quite astonished me. Like Nehemiah, however, I had the

secret of my work in my heart, and unable to tell it, but I viewed a part of the wall.

"*April 5th,* 1886.—Began clearing the ground for my cottage. Though Msidi promises me every help from his people, they are not so accustomed to build as the Ovimbundu. While some of the men who have come with me return to Nana Kandundu, with extra porters provided by Msidi, others will remain here to help in building. After measuring out a piece of ground, 30 ft by 15 ft , I began to dig a deep trench for the foundation. The lads found nothing but rock under the surface, so that it was laborious work picking and digging a trench deep enough to well embed the poles, which were to form the walls of the house. Whilst a few of us busied ourselues in digging out this trench others went to the bush to cut the poles, and for each one brought in I paid them 20 beads.

" *April 22nd.*—Alarming news reached me to-day about the little company I sent off to Nana Kandundu. One of their number came running into camp in a great state of excitement, saying he had travelled from the Lualaba River in four days, and that the lives of my Bihé men were in danger. News had also come that three Garenganze caravans had been plundered and many men killed, one at Bihé, another in the Lovale country, and the third in the Lunda country, but all at the instigation of Bihé chiefs and traders, who thought that they had been unjustly dealt with in certain transactions they had with Msidi. I went down to confer on the matter with the king, but he had little to say, so there is not much prospect of getting the few loads I left at Nana Kandundu brought on at present

" *April 26th* —Two of the men I had sent to Nana Kandundu returned to-day , the rest have crossed the Lualaba and have gone on to Bihé The chief proposes that I start back at once to Nana Kandundu for the things I left there, sending my men on to Bihé. It appears that the news that came here was brought by a runaway who belonged to the caravan of Garenganze sacked at Bihé. This man was disposed with the rest as slaves. All excepting the two sons of Msidi and the leader of the expedition were sold. The latter is said to have committed suicide If this be true, it is the first case I have heard of by a native African. Kovingevinge, the leader of the caravan sacked in the Lunda country, met, on his return, a small company of Bihé traders, and is reported to have murdered them all. This will only increase the trouble between the two countries.

" *May 4th*, 1886.—The chief has held a general council, and the general decision, as to the Bihé question, is that the road must not be closed and that Msidi should send one of his sons with a large caravan to settle this matter.

" *May 6th* —Have been asked to go and visit a sick man two days' journey from here.

" *May 8th*.—Was well received by Kagoma, the sick man I was called to see. I found him suffering from a sort of leprous sores which had afflicted him for eight years. Five witches had been killed meanwhile but without any effect on his sores. I began at once to treat him with silver caustic.

" *May 15th*.—Started for my camp this morning. Kagoma, of course, is not cured, but greatly relieved. Nearly all his sores have dried up under the caustic treatment, though they may break out again. I left him some of the medicine. He loaded me up with corn and rice, and seeing I had already ' eaten ' a goat in his village, and have had abundance of food daily, I am, according to native ideas, paid well. They cannot understand what it costs me to travel those hard, dry, hot roads. They doubtless see nothing in me of the disinterestedness of my Master.

" *May 17th*.—Called on the chief. Found him head over ears in arranging a large caravan for Nana Kandundu, there to intercept Bihé traders with his ivory. He said he was just waiting my return to ask me to take charge of this company, and to arrange for him with the chief there a site where his people might build a market and remain there trading. Should Nana Kandundu be occupied in this friendly way by Msidi it will mean regular communications between there and here. It will also greatly help my labours in the Garenganze as I shall then be able to communicate with the coast. Indeed should labourers come forward I should hope to see Nana Kandundu occupied as a station.

" *May 23rd* —Have been in bed nearly all this week with fever. Am feeling somewhat better this morning.

" *May 24th* —Kagoma has sent me a further present of rice and corn.

" *June 5th*, 1886.—All last month I was feeding on corn

mush and beans, with a chicken for Sunday's dinner, and am beginning to feel what the natives call ' meat hunger,' so have decided to start off to the country again to look for meat.

" *June 7th.*—Made an early start. Reached Kalolo, the town of Monkobe. The people here had evidently not seen a white man before for they seemed very uncertain about me, and stood a long way off, gazing in groups. The young men who were with me spent their strength in vain efforts to assure them that no danger was to be anticipated from my presence. A large hut was provided for me, and plenty of raw food laid down, and Monkobe came in towards evening. He seemed to be much more reasonable than the others, and told his wife to cook me food, which she did ; and to their astonishment I partook of it Few were willing, nevertheless, to sleep in their town that night. It was enough to have seen my footprint on the path. ' His feet are not like men's feet ; they are like those of the zebra,' they said. In the evening I kindled a large fire in front of my hut, knowing something of the attraction this is to these poor naked people, and after sitting some time I saw it had an effect. A little group gathered on the other side of the fire, and through the smoke and flames I with difficulty distinguished their eyes from their mouths, as all were wide open. The numbers gradually increased, until they were no longer able to hide themselves behind the fire ; and watching my opportunity, I began a conversation with them through a young man I had with me as interpreter, but a sorry helper he was. His debauchery became so abominable that I had literally to drive him off.

" *June 15th.*—Before returning to my camp I visited a few other villages, and met from time to time with strange receptions. One man, who had heard the night before of the coming of this ' son of the great spirit,' appeared with a pot of small beer, hastily prepared, and after politely requesting us to refresh ourselves with his gift, told me that some of his children had gone along the road upon which we were travelling some days before, and as there was a possibility of our meeting them as they returned, he hoped I would not capture or rob them. He remarked aside, to one of my men, that doubtless I had cloth in my basket to buy slaves with at the Lufira.

" At Kaunga Kasare I went out in the evening and shot a wild hog and a zebra. These kept us all next day cutting up and drying. I took another round in the bush the day after without success. On the day following, however, I encountered a troop of hartebeeste and shot only two cows as these are large antelopes. By the way, I also shot another wild hog. After remaining at Kaunga drying the meat, I started for my camp with three good loads, a month's provision at least. Slept twice by the way. On reaching camp found that Msidi had been mindful to send me a basket of meal and some corn in my absence.

" *June 27th* —Have just got out of bed after some days of bilious fever. The chief has just returned from the town of one of his wives, and he is all in haste to get his caravans started for Nana Kandundu and Bihé. On hearing of my illness he sent me four young pigeons with the message that I must not on any account take medicines from native doctors ; they would only kill me.

" *June 30th.*—Having recovered somewhat, I was able to go out in my hammock to visit the village of Chipenza, a few hours' journey north of my camp. Here I spent a couple of days and suffered severely from headaches. During a long afternoon's talk in the yard the two ways of Scripture was the subject I tried to make plain to them. I pointed out the crookedness of their ways—deception, lying, stealing, murdering, etc., with their trust in idols and fetish things to deliver them from the penalty of their deeds ; and in contrast I showed the straightness and evenness of God's ways. At the end of each sentence the headman turned to explain all I had said to the villagers One bright-looking young man, on hearing the description of God's ways, replied with much animation, ' A road to run on ! ' How often it is that those we seek to teach, teach us.

" *July 7th,* 1886.—The recovery mentioned under the above date was of short duration, my sickness returning with much pain and with the entire loss of the strength of my limbs. I am able to sit up to-day, but cannot move out of my hut yet. Msidi sent me a kind message and says that he will not hear of my going to Nana Kandundu, that I must remain and his men will bring all my things in perfect safety. I can look to him for that. He has decided to send a wife of his, who is also a niece of the chief of Bihé, to Bihé, to negotiate on his behalf about the opening again of the road for trade. So the

Garenganze porters who go for my things will go in her company as far as Nana Kandundu and will not again be afraid of the Bihé traders. They will not therefore turn back as they did the last time they set not.

" I wrote home as follows : ' The fact that my health during this dry season has been very uncertain, and has broken down several times, must not give you the impression that this country is unhealthy ; on the contrary, I consider it to be as healthy as any part of Central Africa I have been in. There are no malarial swamps anywhere near. During the hot rainy season I enjoyed the best of health, and that is considered the most unhealthy period for Europeans, but my constitution, already impaired from my stay in the Barotse, evidently cannot stand the dry and, at times, cold winds of this season. I do not think that a new-comer, with healthy blood in his veins, will be at all affected by these winds ; neither do I think that I shall suffer so much when my house is finished and plastered. In the meantime I am living in a grass hut.

" ' My journal up to this point will at least serve to show that the country is open and the people accessible. My progress in the languages has been, contrary to my expectations, slow and difficult The people are shy, and do not come readily to me, but I am ever welcome among them , in the meantime, however, poor health prevents me from visiting them as often as I would wish. I much more enjoy visiting among the villages than in the capital, which is almost wholly under the sway of the king's wives, who are given to vicious and dissolute habits. Indeed, I am compelled, from reasons of propriety, to abstain from visiting their compounds, even when invited, unless accompanied by a messenger from Msidi.'

" *July 12th.*—My poverty, I may say, is complete. My bed sheets and tablecloth, in fact everything saleable has gone for food. I am now living on the fag end of a garden of sweet potatoes which I bought some months ago, on a basket of rice I got as medical fee, and on a bag of native corn one of the chief's head wives gave me as she was gathering in her harvest. I had given her a dress when I came. So I get along. The other morning I was lying in bed distressing myself on my scanty fare, having no sauce to sweeten my meal or my rice, the goats having dried up some months ago, and wondering when I was to get any, when, to my surprise, here comes a leg of beef from the chief. He had killed one of his six or eight small oxen, the last thing one would have dreamed of as he thinks everything of his few cattle. This bit of fresh meat brought me round wonderfully. I went in for two meals a day, and lived high for three or four days. I am down again to herbs, however. In all things we have the privilege of being thankful to God and content with the things we have.

" Shortly after my recovery, Dick was taken seriously ill. I was not able to attend to him as I would have wished, but the other children did all they could for him. His illness was, however, the death-blow to my stock of fowls. These are very plentiful in Garenganze, and I bought a large number of them on my arrival, hoping by careful breeding to raise a good stock. During my illness quite a number had been cooked, and now when Dick was laid down, all that remained were used in preparing chicken soup for him.

" My other little boy, Johnny, was bought by Kasoma in the Lunda country without my knowledge. I saw he was a bright little fellow and took him from Kasoma. Though young, he does a wonderful amount of work, and is very intelligent ; says he is going to learn to write. Besides being very active, he is about the prettiest black boy I have seen.

" The third, Segunda, is a mere infant. When brought to my camp here for sale, no one would have him, so at last they brought him on to my hut which was outside the rest. I turned the man away as usual, saying I did not buy people, but back he came, beseeching me to relieve him of this little burden. He had been taken in war, and his captor was going off on another errand and wished to be rid of him. I would not believe that the boy was captured without his mother ; he, however, insisted that it was so. I sent Kasoma to find out, and he reported that there was no appearance of the child's mother ; so I bought him for four yards of calico. He has ever since been ailing, can seldom be made to smile, and only looks up half tearfully with his large dark eyes. By his language I judge that he belongs to some far-off tribe. We have not been able by any amount of compromise to come to an understanding with each other yet.

" Chinze, the fourth little one, was bought by a Bihé trader, had been suffering for long from very sore feet, and was quite unable to go with the rest to Bihé. The man asked me to

take care of her until his return, a year or so hence, but I would
not consent to do so unless he made the child over to me, as
I could not think of giving her up again after a year. We
finally agreed on the matter, so the little girl Chinze is now
mine. Were I to give her up, she would just be sold at the
coast. I think I shall manage to cure the feet within a month
or two. At this rate, in this centre of the slave traffic, there is
no saying what the limits of my family will be. These last two
little things, Segunda and Chinze, have been, I may say,
forced upon me, I cannot but acknowledge the hand of God
in the matter. It will hinder me from going round among the
villages as I might otherwise do. Still, the training of these
is of the utmost importance, and will tell directly on the work
in the years to come.

" The Bihé men who are still with me are anxious to be off
to their own country, and I shall be glad to see them away.
Keeping them all these months has been a great expense and
trial to me. When we arrived here in February I gave each of
them so many beads, besides cloth, promising that I would try
and procure for each one a small tooth of ivory before they left,
provided they did not spend the beads and cloth in buying
slaves, but kept them for food. You can imagine, then, how
disappointed I was, when I saw them, without exception,
selling all they had—even stripping themselves, and putting on
sackcloth—to find the wherewithal to buy slaves. Thus, the
number of mouths in my camp has been trebled, while the
means to provide for them has been reduced. The camp has
ever since been a regular slave pen. I have put my hut outside
of it, and given the people of the country to understand that
I have nothing to do with this slave buying and tying up
business. I have done what I can to keep my men supplied,
though it has cost me all that I had, even to my bedsheets and
spare clothing, and my own food has been like theirs all the
while.

"*August 2nd*, 1886.—Five of the loads I left at Nana Kandundu were brought on to-day. Cinyama's men, who had
escaped at the time of the scare that took place six weeks
previously at the Lualaba River, had gone on to Nana Kandundu, not thinking to return. But changing their minds they
proposed to the old lady that she should deliver up to them
some of my loads, and they would return to Garenganze in

N

search of their relatives. She not only complied with their request, but sent one or two of her own people with them.

" I heard of the robbery of a small bale of cloth which I had left at Nana Kandundu. It appears that a half-caste Portuguese had presented a letter to the chieftainess, purporting to be from me, and upon this false representation he got her to deliver up to him a valuable bale of cloth. Beads are, however, very valuable in this country, and a fair supply of them has just been brought to me. These will enable me to push forward with the building of my house.

"*Aug 22nd.*—I have been able successfully to refuse a present of ivory from Msidi. He was anxious to give me some large teeth to go out with my man Cinyama, but I refused. These African chiefs think so much of their ivory, and they always expect more in return. Besides it is of the utmost importance that I keep free of all obligations to anyone in this country.

"*Aug. 23rd.*—Sent off Cinyama and Kasoma with letters for home, and careful instructions to look out for any white man in Bihé or at the coast who might be enquiring for me. Msidi sent by Cinyama a verbal message to bring in, with all speed, any brother of mine that he might find.

" I arrived here with only one pair of boots, intending to manufacture some kind of shoe, but I have found no suitable bark here. The dry season is now almost past. The boots I have are through in the soles, out at the toes and sides, and all the sewing of the uppers rotten. Yesterday morning when going down to visit the chief, I said to Kasoma that I thought of asking him if he had any spare boots about him, but changed my mind and did not mention the matter to anyone. This morning a young man came along with a pair of boots to sell, the first time boots were ever brought to me for sale in this country. They were almost quite new, of fine leather, and on trying them on they fitted me perfectly, the best-fitting boots I have ever had ' How much for them ? ' ' Four yards.' I had just four yards on hand. I could not have believed five minutes before that such a pair of boots were in the country, for even in Benguella I could not get boots to fit me. It seems that they were brought by a native trader some time ago to Mohenge, the chief whose village I passed on my way here. One of Moshide's sons had gone to visit him, when

Mohenge gave him the boots as a present. He seems to have worn them but for a few days, then sent them for sale to me this morning. So I thank God for the boots.

"*Sept. 27th*, 1886 —You ask if the tribes around are willing to let the Garenganze alone without raiding upon them ? The tribes around, I am sorry to say, are very much weaker than the Garenganze, and instead of attempting to raid on the Garenganze they suffer immensely at their hands. Msidi —who on the one hand can take into his care some poor useless stranger with a body deformed with disease and sin, and provide for him, giving him a wife and house with a small barn full of corn, on the simple plea that the man was poor, as he said to me on my asking a reason for his conduct—does not hesitate on the other hand to form and send out, with the greatest gusto and evident delight, his war parties, who go and devastate whole districts, bringing in slaves (women and children), ivory, etc., with the heads of the slain, the flesh of which has been cut off by the women and children, relatives of the slain. Such ghastliness delights this strangely inconsistent man greatly. I can only account for it by repeating an old remark of mine, that avarice eats up all other passions and feelings in the African once that passion is roused. Poor Msidi ! a man with a noble mind as his lofty benevolent-looking head shows—he has a very grandly shaped head—and a high appreciation of that which is good and noble. For instance, when I spoke to him some time ago in Umbundu things that might have highly irritated the Barotse chief, this man only declared as to the excellence of my words. He knew also how noble a people the English were, for it was their delight to watch for slavers, and capture them, and liberate the slaves. How strangely incongruous to hear such words coming from so great a man-stealer.

"Msidi, professedly in sympathy with me, took a notion into his head that I had better move nearer to him, so that he could visit me when sick, and sent me word to that effect by his brother. This is the third or fourth time he has urged me to come near him, though now it only takes me 15 minutes to walk to his chief capital. I, however, laid the matter before the Lord, and thought perhaps that it might be His will that I should so be actually in the midst of the people. As soon as I was able, two days ago, I went to visit him. I was not prepared to contend the matter, but simply to hear Msidi's proposals.   He, however, had nothing to say further than if I thought of it he would build me a house at his town, though it would have to be a small one, as the rains were upon us.   I stated my objections · the heat, the drumming (which goes on all night at times), the gun-firing, etc. The heat and close-ness of the place, however, were my chief objection. I always feel oppressed when down visiting him, but whenever one rounds the point of my hill, ' it is like entering another country,' as Honjos' men said yesterday when carrying me on my tepoia, and when the short climb is made to my house, it is as cool and fresh as possible. I also feel that I am nearest here to the best water in the whole neighbourhood. So I feel that the Lord has had to do with my choosing this site, and that it is His will that I remain here. Msidi finally closed the conversation by saying that it was of little consequence, the matter was entirely at my own disposing.

" *Oct. 1st*, 1886.—No sooner had Cinyama left, than I had a very severe attack of fever, which laid me quite low for nearly a month   It was during the dry season, and the nearest water was some three miles distant. Turning my book box into a bath, I managed to keep down the temperature by taking hot baths.

" A young man named Susi, who had just come from Bihé, was of great service in helping my lad Dick to carry water for me. In one night these two lads went three times to the watering place. giving me as many hot baths during the night, Next morning my temperature was much lowered, and, though very weak, I was evidently recovering. I proved at this time the value of a simple food made of Indian corn meal, boiled into a thick gruel, to which was added the juice from a root, extracted by pounding. In a few hours the juice had the effect of converting the gruel into a thick, sweet, milk-like fluid, the hard part of the grain being deposited in the form of gritty, unpalatable dregs. Msidi was very kind to me during this time, and repeatedly sent messengers urging me to move my habitation nearer to his, that he might be better able to visit me when sick.

" A peculiar feature of this slow intermittent fever is sleep-lessness. I spent long sleepless nights, when the mind, wander-ing incessantly, was almost always at home. If I happened to fall into a dreamy sleep, I was at once there, perhaps in a sunny, snow-white bed, with a big fire blazing in the room, and my mother bringing in a tray full of most delightful jellies, etc. All my sickness would disappear, and I would delight in the miraculous return of health and strength. Opening my eyes I found nothing but a dark, dreary, confined hut around me, and the wind blowing through piteously, and moaning in the branches of the tree above. My days, however, were not spent unhappily, or my nights, for that matter. I had much quiet peace of mind and pleasure in the study of the Word, which indeed was my chief employment, as I was not able to do much out of doors

" My hope is, that the Lord will give me grace and patience to hold the ground until others come forward to help in the work, and that I may be enabled to remain by them for their help and encouragement. Time, indeed, seems to be nothing so long as He gives the grace and patience to wait. Last night, when in prayer, I was greatly refreshed by a realisation of the exceeding abundance and sufficiency of His grace in every possible emergency—in ' every time of need '—and I was enabled to ask for perfect and enduring contentment under all circumstances.

" I and my boys are entirely alone, all the Bihéans having gone off. The Garenganze are exceedingly slow in coming to me ; still a few do come. We are longing intensely for rain ; the sun is scorching, and the ground gets as hot as coals in a fire. To add to my troubles, Dick has been taken ill, and is quite laid aside.

" To-day I have had two men employed in covering my house with grass ; it is much better now, and I hope to have it finished within another month.

" *Oct. 3rd.*—This morning Dick came hobbling on a stick to greet me with a smile on his face. This is the first day he has been able to get out.

" *Oct. 21st* —Have just returned from a week's trip to the Lufira. I shot two zebras with which to pay the men who had carried me in my hammock. Not having sufficient strength to go out hunting, the men promised me that they would carry me in my hammock to where the game was to be found— a much more arduous task than carrying one along a beaten track. Seeing they persisted, I was willing to give them a chance of having some fresh meat. We started early in the

morning, the men pushing their way through the colossal
grasses. The jagged roots punished the feet of my men severely,
because of the heavy weight of my hammock pole in their
shoulders. After travelling some miles in this manner, those
who had gone on ahead returned to say that we must go softly,
as we were near some game. Soon we came in sight of a large
herd of zebra. The men thought that I had better get out and
do the rest of the hunting on foot   But this I gravely declined
doing, saying they must carry me alongside of the herd. The
zebras had not been accustomed to be stalked in such a daring
manner, and gazed upon us with astonishment, allowing my
hammock to be carried to within fifty yards of them. I then
quietly got out, took my gun, sat down on a little ant-hill, and
shot the biggest and fattest of the troop. Whilst some of the
men skinned and cut it up, the others carried me safely back
to my sleeping quarters. The heat was excessive, and in
returning we were compelled to travel by night, as the men
could not endure the sun. At the Lufira I could not go out of
doors during midday hours. On my delightful little hill, however, there is always a breeze, and the shade is always cool.
'Oh, for rain !' is the cry in everyone's mouth. All the trees
that but a short time ago looked green and fresh are beginning
to wither and droop.

"I was much struck during this trip, while traversing the
'Mukurru,' by the number of villages, especially in the eastern
part. In the course of two hours I counted 48, within sight
from the road, all of fair size, and all the land between was
under cultivation.

"*Nov. 4th*—Since recovering from my last fever, Dick has
shown signs of true conversion. One evening when we were
talking together he seemed to receive a peculiar measure of
joy. Our theme was the Cross ; and though naturally he had
a dull, heavy countenance, his face lightened up marvellously
and both mouth and heart were filled with the spirit of praise.
That night I learned that my dictatorial ways had been that
which had previously hindered my boy, and had produced only
a lifeless confession. That very night the thought occurred
to me that my boy would despise me, and serve me with less
respect, seeing I had humbled myself with him. But very
much the contrary has been the case, for never has he served
me more joyfully and thoroughly than since then.

" After this Dick became very anxious to learn to read and write, a study for which he was mentally unfitted. I did my best to instruct him, but he was so anxious about it that sometimes when he came before me to read he would so tremble with excitement that I had to send him away to some outside work. Latterly he began to complain very much of headaches ; fever symptoms set in, then great wandering of the mind, which increased so that for ten days he was quite insane, though active and vigorous. I had to do all but bind him, watching him night and day, and was the only one who had any power whatever with him. On the 2nd of November he had so far recovered as to be able to sleep quietly at night, but during the day he went about in a stupid way, not a smile crossing his face ; yet occasionally I could see a tear stealing down his cheek. There was nothing for it but to give him plenty of hard out-door work.

" Dick comes from the Zambesi, and has been with me for three years. As you will well understand, many fresh cares and anxieties rise in my mind for him, which I can only cast upon the Lord, who alone is able to make any to stand, to restore, and to uphold those who fell."

CHAPTER XIV

THE PEOPLE

"*NOV. 6th*, 1886.—We have had heavy rains lately, to the joy of everyone. It is in such a place, and at such a time, that one realises the blessings of rain. Six months of drought under a tropical sun had blackened and scorched the very stones; the earth, cracked and gaping all over, was at any hour of the day at a higher temperature than my bare foot could endure, and during the heat of the day I could not even hop on it without running the risk of raising blisters on my feet like half-crowns. Now all is cool, green and refreshing, my hill is covered with a magnificent show of flowers, and the grass is already from two to three inches high. How such baked earth could ever again yield grass, and that at the first sprinkling of rain, is marvellous

" The rains have, however, put a check on my daily routine; my patients have to be visited now during whatever part of the day is likely to be dry, instead of in the afternoon. Because of rheumatism I am quite nervous about being caught in the rain. To-day I was caught in a shower when out dressing the foot of a wounded man, page to one of Msidi's head wives; I had to go back to my house, so the queen offered me her blanket to put round me. I gladly accepted it, and marched home in my glory, robed in her coloured blanket. I have sent my hammock, however, to bring the suffering man to me; his friends come with him to-morrow to build a hut near me, and two will remain with him here. His foot is in a fearful condition, and will need much attention. This will be my first 'hospital hut.' The Lord works His own plans in His own way, and this seems to be the sort of auxiliary work that He is leading me into. I have had remarkable success with all sorts of diseases since coming here, fully nine-tenths being cured within a very short period. I have done little as yet in the way of school work.

" Kagoma, at the Lukuruwe River, sent word a few days ago

that he intended sending men to carry me in my hammock to pay him another visit, so you see I am busy, and, I can add, happy ; indeed, most happy.

" Since the hot weather has set in, my health has improved wonderfully My appetite knows no bounds, and is satisfied with the coarsest of foods. One could not imagine a more repulsive dish—'tis so to many, and was so to me until lately— than Kaffir corn porridge mixed with red palm oil, of which soap is made—yet I can enjoy it right heartily. My eyes give me little trouble now.

" *Nov. 15th* —Dick was out with me visiting a patient. On the way we were caught in a heavy shower. The next day he was complaining. A cough and a slight fever followed, lasting for two or three days. Since then he has been quite insane. I can't tell you how it cuts me to the very quick to put this word on paper, but so it is. I am sitting up now watching him, and am almost worn out. This is the third night of positive madness, trying to run off into the bush from the great serpents he sees hanging all round, and attempting to set fire to my huts. It is only when he is directly under my eye that he is at all quiet. Then indeed he crouches more like an animal, and is ready to cry if I say anything harsh to him, but no one else can control him. There is no other symptom of disease that I can discover. He eats well, and his head is quite cool, though in his quieter turns, during the day, he complains of a pain somewhere in the back of his head. At first I thought it would soon pass off, but now I go about like a man bereaved. Long twangs of loneliness come over me. I had just begun to find a joy in Dick's companionship, when it seems, for the time at least, to be snatched from me by his renewed illness and suffering in mind ; yet I can say from my heart, that God's perfect way, though hard to the flesh, is not hard to love ; for with Him alone is companionship, and all else is desolation and darkness.

" The chief sent for me early this morning, asking me to visit his brother, some distance off, who is ill, and whose wife had gone out of her mind. I trudged off with the king's page, sent to conduct me, returning late in the afternoon, throbbing all over with the excessive heat of the sun. This heat, however, I must confess, suits me ; I have grown stronger during these last six weeks.

" In going about from place to place, I better understand the

size of this Mukurru, or inhabited plain. It takes a good day's
journey to traverse it, being between eight to ten miles in
width   The ground is chiefly covered with fields, in the midst
of which the River Bunkeya runs, but the clusters of huts are
many, and scattered all over. Here and there are centres, in
which the king has his own houses, where, to the extent of half
a mile or so each way, the houses of the people are built
together.

   " In the midst of all these people the amount of quietness
and peace that reigns is remarkable. The fear of Msidi is
great. He is sharp and severe in his government, though I see
or hear of nothing in the way of torture or cruelty inflicted by
his orders as a means of punishment ; yet executions are
common, but death is inflicted at once, and in the most expedi-
tious manner.   All the cases of which I have heard particulars
have been those of actual crime, and not of witchcraft or any
other mere superstition.   The king has a long iron chain,
which he uses for punishing minor offenders. To this they are
bound by the neck, perhaps ten or twelve at a time, and are
sent out to his fields to work—a very sensible arrangement,
I think, and much better than the cruel flogging so common
in Africa.

   " October is the hoeing time, and it is a pleasure to see everyone turning out to the fields. The men indeed, so far as I can
judge, do a large share of the work ; and the husbands tell me
that after all their hard day's work, it is dangerous to return
home in the evening without a heavy log of wood to keep up the
night fire. The part which Msidi takes in this is very commend-
able. Not only does he go to the fields with his people to
labour, but he encourages his own sons to work, and so makes
labour honourable. I have seen him go out every day, with a
large band of hoers, for weeks together, and often stand in the
middle of the field when rain was falling heavily, watching the
workers. At other times his people would have left their work
for shelter, but when Msidi was there they had to be ' wet-
weather soldiers.'

   " One would suppose that there is abundance of food all the
year round, but it is not so. The prodigal waste of corn in the
dry season in brewing beer passes description. They make
beer of the strongest kind, filling large bark vessels, holding
as much as 20 or 30 gallons. It is free to all-comers, and

drinking is kept up night and day in the yard until the vessels
are emptied ; and then in two or three days the fruit of weeks
of toil in hoeing, and months of weeding and watching, has
vanished like smoke. A dull, sleepy state, rather than levity
and quarrelling, seems to be the effect of over-drinking this
heavy beer. I have only seen one man who had any appearance
of being a sotted drunkard, in spite of the amount of drink
consumed I suppose this is because it is always taken fresh.

" The cruel raiding on other tribes which is kept up, in which
many of the men are killed and the women captured, has
brought into the Garenganze an immense number of women,
so that the proportion of women to men is very unequal ;
consequently polygamy is carried on to a shameful extent.

" Marriages are made, not by purchase exactly, as in Zulu-
land ; neither do the wife and her children continue to be the
property of her brothers, as among the Ovimbundu tribes, but
a present is made to the father of the bride, who forthwith
disposes of his daughter ; she, however, may leave her husband
at any time, if she cares to do so. The case may then be
brought to the chief, and if the wife be at fault the present
must be returned ; if the husband has ill-treated his wife, then
he has driven her from him, so there is no one to blame but
himself. In disputes among themselves, the people undoubtedly
receive fair justice at the hands of Msidi ; and he is ready to
listen to all who come.

" *Dec. 18th*, 1886.—Dick is now so far recovered but goes
about in a mournful way. I notice the tears roll down his
cheek at times, but I ask him no questions, only seek to cheer
him up, and keep him employed in a light way. The desire to
learn, coming after the decided spiritual awakening, has I
think been more than he could stand. I will need to be very
careful now lest I again lead him beyond his mental depth.
The crouching affection he showed toward me during those
days was most touching, more like that of an animal He
would go to sleep a little at nights at the side of my cot bed,
with my hand upon him. You can well understand that this
has been and is a trial to me.

" *Dec. 25th.*—On Dec. 10th I started for the wood to look
for game as I am much in want of meat. In the evening I shot
a wart hog. I reached the Lukuruwe River on the 12th, where
I spent 10 days shooting and drying meat. I shot in all eight

antelopes, three zebras, and two hippopotami   I have returned with abundance of dried meat enough to last me for several months.

" While at the Lukuruwe I had a narrow escape.   I had been resting during the heat of the day, my bed being on the ground   When about to get up I reached out for my hat, intending to go outside, when whiz came a spear into my hut, cutting through the rim of my hat, which was in my hand, and sticking into the ground not three inches from my side.

" At another time a man and I were out alone in the woods, when the call of a honey-bird attracted us.   On going but a short way it halted on a tall tree.   We were looking into the tree trying to find the honey, when, from the grass which lay between us, out sprang a leopard and bounded off.   The wicked bird had led us to his lair.

" The people I met were nearly all of the Basanga tribe, the original occupants of the country, of whom there are now but few.   I scarce understand a word of their language as yet. Going north-west, nearly to the Kalasa mountains, I had a good view of the famous cavern mountain, which is inhabited. The great cave has two entrances, a distance of five miles or more apart, and within is a running stream.   There are also many smaller caves and dens in this mountainous country in which the natives hide themselves.   The entrances to these caves look like rabbit holes.   They form such perfect retreats that Msidi could extort no tribute from these people.   Near the mouths of the caves they have millet gardens.   They greatly feared my inspecting the caves, and I had to promise that I would not do so, or none would have come near me.   In going amongst their villages I seldom could get more than two or three together at one time.   When, however, I succeeded in killing the two hippopotami in the river close by my camp, and had sent round an invitation, I had no less than 100 of these poor people, who gathered together and were willing to remain with me as long as the feast lasted.   It was really a big Christmas dinner that we had in the heart of Africa, the two hippopotami forming the centre dish, with zebra and antelope as side dishes.

" On my return I found that the Arab traders with whom I had intended sending letters had gone.   This was a great disappointment.   I found also that my hut had been broken into.

A large blanket, a towel, an undershirt, a sack of corn, etc., are gone.

"*Dec. 30th.*—To-day I moved into my new house. I am very glad indeed that it is so far forward. With a portion of the dried meat I brought with me I was enabled to employ labour and finish the mudding of the inside.

"*Jan. 1st,* 1887.—A New Year has come round again ; the past one has been a blank to me, so far as home and the outer world are concerned, the last letters I have received being dated November, 1885.

" I find myself well housed, in good health, and seem to be in a measure settled after five years of hut and camp life. Yet my God alone knows.

"*Jan. 2nd.*—Before so many of the people gathered to my camp we had a rather stirring adventure. Two of our men, while out hunting, were benighted on the other side of the river. Night set in very dark indeed, and after waiting a long time for the absent ones the men in camp crossed, and made signals to guide them to our whereabouts ; and above the rushing of the river we heard their voices replying to us on the other side. I ran down to the river bank in order to guide them, but finding that my voice was not loud enough to make them hear me, I called to my men in camp to come down that we might all shout together, and so cause them to hear us All accordingly left the camp and joined me. We had only shouted once or twice when to my horror I heard a great noise in the direction of the camp, which seemed to be alive with howling demons. The truth was that the wild animals of the forest had taken advantage of our absence, rushed in, and were devouring the meat they found there. Some parts of a zebra were lying in the middle of the enclosure, and a family of hyenas, accompanied by two dog-leopards, were fighting and quarrelling over it. We had to act instantly, and having no fire or guns in our hands, it was impossible to remain out of our shelter. So taking the lead, and calling to my men to come on, I rushed at full speed back to the camp. Taking care to avoid the doorway, we sprang over the little brush barricade, so alarming the animals with our shouts and yells that they left the meat and fled

" *Feb. 5th,* 1887.—A company of Arab traders arrived here a few days ago. Yesterday being the reception day for them, the king sent for me to come and sit by him; and many of his people came together. Each of the three Arab master-traders brought a handsome shawl with him with which to deck Msidi. A military review was then held, after which speeches were made by the Arabs and by the king and his chiefs. Msidi then gave me an opportunity of speaking, which I would most gladly have taken had I been at all equal to it. I was glad, however, to find I was able to understand nearly all that was spoken in Seyek; but I fear my address would be no more popular here than at Liwanika's court among the Barotse. The sum and substance of their speeches on such an occasion is flattery; past events are rehearsed and discoursed upon, and all things greatly exaggerated and contorted to suit the occasion.

" Yesterday morning a woman was caught here by a leopard while in her field. She was a ' small wife ' of the king's, and through her cries assistance came, and the leopard was chased away but the woman died shortly after. Msidi at once sent to me for some poison to kill the leopard should it return, and I gave him some strychnine. Instead, however, of killing a goat or a dog to be used as bait, they preferred the dead woman's body. ' She is now dead,' said the chief. ' What can we do ? Let her redeem her fellows ! ' i.e. from the leopard's paw. A great deal of man-eating by wild animals goes on. The number of people massed together—more given to cultivating than to hunting—and the custom of throwing out the bodies of dead slaves, has given these animals a taste for human flesh.

" In my small compound, yet unfenced, it is not safe for any-one to be out of doors after dusk Little Johnny was very nearly caught by a hyena one evening. A little boy, left here sick by one of my Bihé carriers, was in the habit of coming over and eating with my boys of an evening, and sometimes sleeping with them. I missed him for a few days, and on inquiring, found that he had started for my house one evening, and had not returned. He doubtless was carried off by one of these beasts of prey.

" Old lions, which no longer have teeth strong enough to pull down large game, come round and prey upon the people, and they are very audacious. A woman close by us left her child sitting in front of her hut for a few minutes. On returning she found that the child had been carried off by one of these retired monarchs—his footprints, of course, telling the tale. Out in the bush, where game is abundant, it is quite different, and people sleep freely out in the open country. There they have simple mat doors to their huts; here they require doors of reed, strongly barred.

"I got a pleasant message from Kalolo, the village which I visited last year, and where many were so afraid of me as to sleep in the field all night. They wanted to know when I would return The description they gave was, ' Ah! that was the good white man that visited us, that gave us feastings of meat.' It is a rough, hilly country that lies between, but I must be off to them again, ' if by any means I may win some.'

"*Jan.* 15*th.*—After the mournful report as to Dick given before, I must needs refer to him again. He is decidedly better An unwonted nervousness is the only sign left of his former derangement. His happiness as a Christian is fully restored and he has set himself most bravely to learn to read. He was always much opposed to this. In knowledge of the Scripture, from what I have been teaching him, he is also progressing well I had repeatedly referred to baptism, explaining its full meaning to him as carefully as possible, but I avoided urging it upon him, preferring rather that it should be indeed with him ' an answer of a good conscience toward God.' Last night, however, he told me that he wished to be baptised. It seems he had been hindered by something that I had said about its not being done secretly, and he shrank at the thought of a large company of people being present. But for a sore which he has on his foot I would have him baptised at once. When he gets over this we shall not delay.

"*Feb.* 13*th*, 1887, *Lord's Day.*—This morning I baptised my lad Dick in a pool here. I fully realise the responsibility of my doing so alone, that is without the testimony of another as to Dick's conversion. It has not been done hurriedly, but after months of waiting, since his profession of conversion, during which time I have been daily more persuaded of its reality. Susi, my other lad, is applying for baptism.

"Before going down to the water we had a solemn time in my house with Dick, Susi, and another man who is deeply interested, though I cannot as yet say under any especial conviction.

" Well ! we had a solemn time by the pool out on the flat to which we went. To get down to the water we had to break our way through long rank grass, and close by I noticed the fresh footprints of a leopard that had drunk water there in the morning. After a short prayer in Umbundu, Dick was baptised in the name of the Father, and of the Son, and of the Holy Ghost It was a solemnly glad time, and all seemed to feel it. We then returned to my house and spent a long time in earnest conversation.

" When parting, six years ago, with dear Mr. Dyer, he remarked, in his usual solemn way, that ' it would be a day never to be forgotten by me when the first one was baptised under the dark Zambesi waters.' To-day a dark Zambesi sinner has been baptised in the Garenganze waters, and it is but the beginning of God's kindness to us and to these people ; there are more to follow.

" Until very recently the chief thought that presented itself to me in connection with baptism was that of death and burial ; but now it seems to me that the thought of resurrection and new life is by no means to be omitted, but rather to take the leading place. In 1 Peter iii, 21, it is directly connected with the resurrection of Jesus Christ , and baptism, being called ' the interrogation of a good conscience towards God,' implies *life*. As the new-born babe cries, so new-born souls call upon Him who is the source of their life.

" My relationship with the people, though very good from the first, is if anything improving. I find that both the king and his people make every effort to please me, and seem desirous to give me every encouragement to remain among them, giving their consent to everything I suggest, and shutting me up with flattery. Augustine, referring to Proverbs xviii, 21, remarked that ' our daily furnace was the tongue of men.' Paul and Barnabas found grace to resist the flattery of those who cried out that the gods had come down among them ; and afterwards grace, to resist their slanders and stones, was not withheld from them. Still we have much reason to rejoice and to give thanks for a quiet and peaceable life in what is generally considered to be the heart of savagedom, and the haunt of every cruelty.

" Though outwardly things are thus quiet and agreeable, yet there lacks not opposition from certain quarters. The Arab traders who come here have done what they could in spreading

Near Bihé

evil reports and lying stories about the ' designing English,' etc. The rains were exceedingly late this year, and when a regular drought was threatening, some of the ' doctors ' of the land would fain have laid the blame at my door ; but the story did not take. The spear, also, that was thrown at me in the bush close by the Lukuiuwe River shows that the enemy, though he lurks snake-like in the grass, is present, and will doubtless watch his opportunity for raising more opposition.

" Difficulties have arisen because I have not followed the custom of giving presents to bands of drummers in camp. I have refused to do so, and have often had trouble in clearing my camp of these boisterous musicians. In the first place, I cannot give lawfully the Lord's money to the support of such folly, and to do so might lead to the annoyance of all servants of the Lord who come after me, by encouraging and perpetuating the practice. The custom also of giving presents to headmen, minor chiefs, etc., who have no lawful claim to tribute, I have opposed, thus raising no little amount of dissatisfaction. At the Barotse I gave, with little discrimination, all I had ; my chief thought was to be acceptable to them, and to be liked. I succeeded in this. I fear, however, that it was not a godly success, or one to God's glory. I have but little with me, and with that little I am bound to see to the needs of the men who have patiently come this long way with me, and to speed them well on their return to their homes.

" I am in my house at last. Plastering the walls has been a slow and tedious process Indeed, the house stood so long with its heavy thatch covering, and with walls of poles, through which the wind could play at its pleasure, that the roof got somewhat twisted, and the thatch dishevelled. I have tried to make the mud plaster as perfect as possible, and with a good plank door I shall hope to be able to regulate the atmosphere inside, which I think will help greatly towards a more even condition of health.

" *Feb. 20th.*—Paid a visit to a camp of Arab traders, and was quite astonished at the number of slaves they have already bought, chiefly full-grown men and women, all secured by their necks with heavy forked sticks While there I saw the Arabs buy a man for ten yards of calico. They give, they told me, twelve to sixteen yards for women and young lads Full-grown men were not so valuable, as they are untameable, and liable to

o

make their escape. After the bargain had been completed three stout Zanzibaris came forward, seized the man they had bought, threw him on his face on the ground, drew his hands behind his back in the most cruel way, and bound them tightly ; then, with a blow on the side of the head, they ordered the poor fellow, who never uttered a word all this time, to get up and go before them. He would have to lie bound with this cord until a taming stick was manufactured to place on his neck. The weight of these sticks is very great, but to my mind the discomfort of their position during the day, when they are allowed to sit up with the end of the stick resting on the ground in front of them, is nothing compared to what they must suffer at night. Then they are made to lie down, the stick being kept fixed, and pinning their neck between its fork to the ground, its upper end fastened to the roof of a hut, shed, or branch of a tree.

" *March 17th*, 1887.—A young man, who lived a gunshot from my house, was carried off to-day by a lion while resting in the shade behind his hut.

" *March 18th*.—At eight o'clock this evening, just in the twilight, a leopard, which seemed to have followed my boys, seized and carried off my dog from the very centre of my yard.

" *March 25th*.—On going outside last night, about eleven o'clock, I encountered a large animal just in front of my door. He seemed to be waiting his opportunity to pounce upon some-one, but I tumbled back indoors and disappointed him. A few nights later, while sitting under the veranda of my house, I saw another of these creatures coming straight for my cottage, evidently attracted by the goats. Stepping indoors, and picking up my gun, which stood loaded in a corner, I fired at him, and the ball passed through his heart. I found it was a full-grown hyena, of the man-eating sort. My boys and the neighbours had a dance round it the next day. At this time of the year the grass is so long that these animals are emboldened to go round the villages and prey upon the people.

" *March 26th*.—Last night my boy Johnny died He had been ill for a long time with diarrhœa, brought on by eating maize corn. After a short prayer and a few words with the rest of the boys, we buried him in the garden. Poor little lad, he was of an exceedingly sweet and tender disposition. Among the rest he was pre-eminently my boy. Nothing, however, that I could possibly do or say could control his appetite for green corn. I whipped him and even tied his hands with cords, but as soon as he was released, or found the slightest opportunity, he was off to the field eating the corn green and unroasted. My first acquaintance with him was in the Lunda country. Kasoma bought him there, unknown to me During the long, tiring march before we reached the Lualaba River, this little lad completely broke down ; and as all the men were heavily burdened, only two courses were open to us—either to leave him by the roadside, or allow him to ride my ox. Accordingly he was carried on ox-back for several days, until he recovered somewhat. When Kasoma left for Bihé I was not willing to part with Johnny, so he left him with me. Johnny was always an example to the other children, and now all feel very much the death of their little playmate, and I hope the event will be blessed to them.

" To-day I had an opportunity of sending letters to the coast. As can well be understood, it is easier to send letters from a place like this than to receive them. All native traders go to the coast, but few from the coast come here ; and those who do are often uncertain as to their destination when leaving their homes. My mind naturally follows Cinyama and the little party, and sometimes I ponder the result of his journey with a measure of anxiety. When I left Natal alone five years ago, I never for a moment dreamed that it would be for so long a time as this, yet in looking back it does seem very short indeed ; and considering the wonderful goodness of the Lord to me, I have little reason to doubt as to the future. If Cinyama returns alone it will be well. If an English fellow-labourer should come with him I shall be very thankful. Meanwhile the Lord wonderfully makes up to me for all I lose in being without the immediate fellowship of brethren in Christ. My days are spent, I may say, in unbroken quietness of mind and peace within. Although I have joy, yet I do not say I am always rejoicing. There is much to depress me in such a field as this. Heathendom in all its nakedness, cruelty, and depravity is far from being exhilarating in its effect ; but yet, in comparison, the condition of these people is happy when placed alongside the state of the unsaved in home lands. How dark and hideous is the ignorance around one here ! but how guilty the ignorance of British sinners who close and harden their hearts against the light, and strengthen themselves with false hopes ! Here also they are never at rest, seeking after vain hopes and refuges of lies.

" On behalf of a caravan about to start for Bihé, Msidi and his fetish priests have been at work a whole month, preparing charms, etc. The process in such a case is first to divine as to the dangers that await them ; then to propitiate with the appointed sacrifices to forefathers (in this case two goats were killed) ; afterwards to prepare the charms necessary, either as antidotes against evil or to secure good. The *noma*, or fetish spear to be carried in front of the caravan, with charms secured to it, was thus prepared : the roots of a sweet herb were tied round the blade ; then a few bent splinters of wood were tied on, like the feathers of a shuttlecock. In the cage thus formed were placed a piece of human skin, little bits of the claws of a lion, leopard, etc., with food, beer and medical roots, thus securing, respectively, power over their enemies, safety from the paws of fierce animals, food and drink, and, finally, health. A cloth was sewn over all, and finally the king spat on it and blessed it. After all these performances they will set out with light hearts, each man marked with sacred chalk. Such is the ' fool ' in all lands ; he finds a refuge in his own imaginations.

"*April 1st*, 1887 —Three Bihé caravans arrived here this morning. They have brought no letters, but report American missionaries in Bihé. My first impulse was to bemoan the lack of pity on the part of my American brethren, in that they did not seek this opportunity of sending in letters. The matter, however, is surely in higher hands ; and when I looked at much work that, months ago, I had laid out to be done, scarce commenced, I felt ashamed of my impatience. The Lord, I know, does not forget me for one moment but chooses His own ways and means, not in order to disappoint our desires, but to exceed them.

" At present the languages are occupying most of my time. My chief interruptions are caused by having to go off occasionally to the bush to procure a supply of meat, which I dry and use, not so much as food, but to flavour my maize or millet corn porridge, which is my staple article of food ; but as this dried meat does not keep very long, I have to exchange large quantities of it with the natives for corn.

" Formerly my shooting greatly distressed me, as I wounded

many animals without killing them. Now, however, I believe in answer to prayer, I seldom fail to secure the animal I aim at. This searching for game takes up four or five days every three months. I might ere this have taught Dick, my lad, to shoot, and have given him this occupation, but I fear his being carried away with the excitement of hunting, and becoming a regular hunter—an occupation most unsettling and unprofitable.

" The field of corn and beans which my boys have cultivated has borne remarkably well, but I fear comparatively little of the crop will be secured, thieves and wild pigs having the larger share. There is no way of checking the thieves but by catching and cruelly beating them Of course, I will not hear of this being done, but, on the contrary, I have been moved to give a meal of food at my house to the poor hungry creatures caught stealing. So insensible, however, are they to mere rebuke, or even to kind treatment, that they will go off quietly, and again begin filling their baskets with half-ripe corn so soon as they think they are not observed.

" *May 5th*, 1887.—Returned to-day from a three weeks' outing which I thought would brace me up a bit after the past months of rain and consequent confinement. I took the precaution to have a native hunter with me this time to save myself from the extra toil of hunting for meat. The villages, by the way, do not grudge giving meal and other food, in fact it is a recognised institution here that strangers and travellers be entertained free of charge, so I purposely avoid, on all such trips, taking anything with me in the way of barterable goods.

" The first villages we reached were those of Mirambo, a little way beyond Kagoma's on the Lukuruwe River. We rested there one day, and then went down the river, making for a company of Ba-na-lunda villages. The long grass tired me out, so we went into camp about midday, sending a hunter on.

" At this spot we had quite a remarkable adventure with a lion, which but for the protecting care of God would have ended more seriously. All night we were kept awake more or less by three lions serenading us, and the lads had enough to do to keep their bivouac fires burning. I, however, got a good night's rest. Next morning when passing through a clump of long reedy grass I heard distinctly in front the low angry growl of a lion. The man who was before me stopped, saying it was a buffalo, and asked for my gun that he might shoot it. I urged him to push on, and tried to prevent the three boys from stopping, but it was too late to avoid the brute's charge. He made straight at the hindmost lad, who was carrying my mat and blanket. I ran back and succeeded in intercepting him, so that in his spring he fell short a few feet from his intended victim, and before my very face, too near indeed to allow me time to use my rifle. The man and the three lads dropped their loads, and were off like deer, leaving me and my royal friend alone in the reed thicket face to face. For a moment it was a question what the next scene would be. He was raging fiercely, and would fain have sprung on me, but seemed to lack the nerve. Holding him hard with my eyes, and slowly cocking my rifle, I lifted it to my shoulder for a steady aim, when he suddenly gave in, his huge tail dropped, and drawing his teeth under his lips he made off. I sprang after him, hoping to get a shot at safer range, but the grass was so dense that I could not sight him again ; so I started in search of my companions. I overtook Dick several hundred yards on by the river's brink, and then the others, but not one would return for his load, so complete was their scare, although I assured them that the lion had gone clean away. That, however, was no assurance to them that his wife or some of his relatives might not be hanging about the same lair. Shortly after we met some men returning from their fishing grounds, who were willing for a small consideration to return for the loads with my brave crew.

" The lad whose life I thus saved belongs to Bihé, and I overheard a young Bihéan say to his fellows, he would ' go anywhere with such a white man, who would throw his own body between a lion and a black lad of no account.' The young man who said this, is a nephew of the chief Kapoko, who told the carriers I had engaged at his village two years ago, not to go with this white man, as he was an Englishman, and would carry them all off to the other side of the continent and enslave them, the result of which advice was, that most of them left us.

" Two weary days' tramp across the flat brought me again to my comfortable house. On reaching the capital I met Msidi. He received me very warmly, and seeing I was very tired, sent one of his wives to cook a dish of rice and honey for me. It was dark ere I reached my house. I found that in my absence Susi's father had died. He was a mulatto from Loanda and came here seeking employment from Msidi as Secretary. He took part in the robbery of my goods at Nana Kandundu. Two months ago he took ill, and being in a wretched condition of poverty, etc., I sent and brought him to my village, when he recovered somewhat, but in my absence had a relapse and died. Before I left I pressed upon him for several evenings ' repentance toward God and faith toward our Lord Jesus Christ.'

" Msidi paid me a visit shortly after my return, and was most agreeable ; indeed, he is a thorough gentleman. The other day he told one of his courtiers that he had one true friend, and that was Monare, for in his heart he did not find one single suspicion of me ; and, strange to say, I feel very much the same towards him. I have no suspicion of his friendship ; he most carefully avoids asking anything of me, and all his family do the same.

" Matters have been settled between Bihé and this country, and the 'road ' is virtually open again. Msidi's two sons have not returned yet, but they were awaiting the arrival of goods from the coast, and will come shortly Two large caravans have arrived for trade, bringing no letters, nor any news for me, except that the American missionaries are re-established in Bihé. I suppose they did not know of the departure of these two caravans. I am expecting a large budget when it does come. My last home-letter dates are all in 1885."

CHAPTER XV

"*MAY 8th*, 1887.—Yesterday I had another child brought to me   The poor thing belonged to a blacksmith here, who some time ago sold its mother for corn to the king's executioner. The corn was not enough to cover the price of the child, so he kept it out of the bargain. The fact was, the ' hangman ' did not wish a slave with a baby on her back, so would not buy the child, though an extra basket of corn would have sufficed   The blacksmith, who has no wife, found he could do nothing with this baby, and instead of knocking it on the head, as the custom here is—for who would buy so young a thing ?—he sent to me, asking me to give a goat for him. I could not help myself in the matter, so sent a young goat in exchange. Poor little boy (we will call him Willie), he had been deceived, for they said they were taking him to his mother, and he cried long and bitterly, ' N twala ko mama ' (' Take me to mother '). In Luba the word for mother is exactly like our ' mama, the *a's* being very broad and emphatic. He is a plump, healthy little chap, with a fine-shaped head, awfully afraid of me as yet. I shan't give him up to his mother where she now is, but I will do so if I can redeem her.

" The question of these children harasses me a good deal, and often I don't know what to do. Little children here have really no market value, and a woman burdened with a child is a less desirable article of purchase than one with hands and shoulders free. The raiding parties kill off all small children found among their captives   The body of a fine little boy was picked up only a few days ago beside the Arab camp. The owner had doubtless taken him the round of all likely purchasers, probably including me among the number, and then thrust a spear through him as a useless burden on his hands. Another little boy, whom I refused to take

216

last year, was deliberately starved and thrown out to the wolves.

" A young man named Cilombo had charge of a field close by my cottage. Being interested in meetings held at my place, he moved his hut from the far to the near side of the field. His wife was a slave woman, and had a little child to whom I had taken quite a fancy, and in passing my hut on the way to the villages I used often to take the child in my arms and spend a few minutes in playing with it. During my absence on one occasion the mistress of Cilombo's wife carried out a threat she had made long before, and sold her with her child. The husband was powerless to intervene on behalf of either. One of a company of traders bought the woman, and started at once for Bihé. Another man, however, hearing that this woman had been sold, wished to exchange for her a younger slave, who was perhaps of more value, though less muscular, as he wanted an able-bodied woman to cultivate his fields. The Bihé trader was willing to make the exchange, but reminded the man that he had brought nothing for the child. The latter at once said that he did not want the child; but as it was so young, he thought it ought to be included with the mother in his bargain. The men were unable to come to terms, so, to prevent more ado, the child was taken from the mother's arms, its head was dashed against a tree, and it was thrown into the river. Thus the difficulty was got over, and the women were exchanged! The poor mother's grief at the loss of her child may be imagined. Had I known the peril that this little one was in I certainly should have secured it in some way or other.

" But to know where and when I ought to draw the line baffles me. I cannot allow myself to be involved in slave buying; that is clear. What are the points of difference between buying and redeeming? If it is lawful to buy, it must be equally lawful to sell. One can redeem a grown-up person and let him go, but this cannot be done with a child whose parents are enslaved; the owner of the mother might take him at once and sell him again. Of course, alone, I cannot look after more than a very few, and that settles the question so far. The little girl Chinze, whom I took last year from a Bihéan, when unable to travel because of boils on her feet, is again covered with a loathsome disease peculiar to this country, called *monona*, and has to be kept entirely separate. Among the natives this disease generally runs from two to five years. With a free use of sulphur internally and caustic externally, I hope to cure her soon.

" The following is the story of two little girls that were added to my family: One year, when Msidi's warriors were ransacking the district around Katapena, Lubaland, they surprised and carried off a number of children who were playing and bathing in a pool near their village. Among them were two girls, Mwepo and Delunga, who had been fast friends and constant playmates ; but the rough hands of Msidi's soldiers now separated them, and they were carried off in different directions. Three years after, I happened to be sitting in Msidi's yard talking with him, when a company of slaves were brought in. They were the belongings of someone who had recently died, and were brought to Msidi to be distributed among the relatives of the deceased man. The youngest of the slaves, a little girl of nine years of age, was suffering from painful ulcers on the soles of her feet. After giving away the healthy ones, Msidi turned and asked if I could do anything with this suffering child ; so I took her up to my cottage, dressed her sores, and after a little care and nursing she recovered.

" A few months later I happened again to be sitting beside Msidi, when a little girl entered the yard and threw herself down at some distance from the chief's feet, rubbing dust on her forehead and arms. Msidi told her to look up, and asked where she came from and what did she want. She said that she had run away from her mistress because she had been severely beaten the day before. It seems that she had travelled all night from the Lunsala, six or eight miles down the Bunkeya. Some of Msidi's breakfast was in a dish , this I handed in pity to the poor thing, and in a short time I rose up and left. Upon looking back, I saw the little girl following me, in charge of one of Msidi's young men who told me that Msidi had sent the child after me, saying that if she was afraid of being beaten she had better follow the white man. So on she came with me to my cottage. I handed her over to the care of the other little girl, Mwepo, when, to my astonishment, they flew into each other's arms, embracing one another and weeping. The two Luba free-born children had met again in my cottage after each had passed through her own three years of unmixed sorrow and hardship.

"So much for family matters and perplexities. Dick is in everything my good man ' Friday.' Susi, the other lad, is useful in taking messages, medicines, etc., but is very handless and of little use about the house. My other little one, Segunda, is getting on well ; it took about six months to get him out of the decline he had fallen into through neglect and bad food.

" My own health keeps excellent ; ever since moving into my ' house ' I have not had a single day's illness of any kind, and nearly a year has passed since I touched quinine or any other home medicines, although I have occasionally used the herbs and medicinal berries of this country. In fact, I am quite a naturalised African. The heat of the sun in no way affects my head as it used to do. I prefer wearing a light grass hat, of native manufacture, to my heavy pith-helmet, which is shaken out of its dust only on state occasions. My joints, however, have been stiffened a good deal with rheumatism this season, which has been an exceptionally wet one ; not that my house is at all damp, but after weeks of rain the very atmosphere becomes saturated.

" Dick and Susi are great helps to me. They thoroughly enter into sympathy with the work, and though neither ventures to talk much to others, they are not slow in going about and inviting the people to come to my house on the Lord's-day morning. I speak chiefly in Umbundu, consequently those who come are for the most part natives of Bihé ; many besides understand Umbundu, but do not come so freely to my house. The variety of excuses made, and obstacles that come in the way, are marvellous. If a man is sick, it is sure to be on the Sunday ; if a slave runs off, it is certain to be on a Saturday or Sunday ; and the most I have gathered at one time is about a dozen men To-day I went off to a village where Umbundu is the chief language spoken, the people being mixed. I planned to be there by midday, so as to find them resting during the heat of the day, but I was disappointed ; they had pressing business of their own on, so I returned. You see I have need of patience here, and of grace also, that ' I be not weary, though in weariness oft '

" I have been much cheered by a blacksmith who was at one of my Sunday morning meetings, and who responded in

a remarkable way to what was said. He declared before all
the rest that he had received new light that day. With an
honest expression, and in a sincere manner, he repeated afterwards, ' Is it so ? Is it so ? Is that what God is ? Is that the
nature of God's love ? ' This was the Sunday before I left for
the three weeks' tour. On returning, my feet were so sore and
blistered that on nearing the capital I sent on for my hammock,
hoping someone about would volunteer to carry me. The
blacksmith heard of the opportunity, and did not lose it. He
met me with four other volunteers, and taking hold of the pole
behind, the heaviest end, he would let no one change with him,
and left, when my door was reached, with a hearty ' Good
night.' It was for no present or pay that he thus gave his
cheerful aid. This act was like a fresh, cool breeze to one.

" *May 23rd.*—Yesterday was Sunday, when we had a most
profitable day. I had quite a houseful of grown men at the
morning service, which was continued until midday. Our
subject was, ' Repentance toward God, and faith toward our
Lord Jesus Christ.' I don't think I ever had a meeting at
which the people showed less difficulty in understanding, and
when in every way I had more liberty in using the Umbundu
language.

" This morning Dick got an unmistakable rebuke. Yesterday, someone in the village happened to remark that there was
little chance of Cinyama being here next month ; that he had
just come from Bihé, and knew how matters stood. Thoughtfully considering our empty corn bin, and that we had no more
beads or cloth to buy with, Dick remarked, ' If Cinyama does
not come next month we shall die of hunger.' I checked him
at once, and reminded him that they had not a day's hunger
during all the months gone by, when many people of the
country had actually perished from starvation. (The past
season was a very hard one for the natives.) That day a drinking cup had been stolen from my boy when on the way to draw
water, and the king had sent to kill the chief   I ran down to
prevent this, and obtained Msidi's consent to his being put in
chains for a few days instead. When I entered the king's
house and greeted him he drew out from behind him a roll of
eight yards of calico and gave it to me, saying, that perhaps I
was in need of it to buy corn, as the crops were ripe. Where
now were Dick's doubts ? I believe that this calico was given

especially for Dick's sake. He had mentioned the matter of food in prayer last night. I had not mentioned it , indeed, it is seldom in my thoughts, much less in my prayers. And here the answer comes the very next day, at early morning—calico to buy corn ! Msidi had never given me anything in that way before, except perhaps a basket of corn or rice.

" Not only to the boys, but to myself, this time of waiting upon God for our daily need has been greatly blessed ; indeed, it is only then that one can realise how truly this desert country might, in the experience of faith, become as a well-watered plain, and what seems only a way of discomfort and poverty prove a path dropping with fatness.

" *May 27th*.—I have heard to-day of the death of Mokobe at Kalolo. I visited his town last year, and was very well received. About two months ago or more he sent a message to me, asking me to repeat my visit. I had intended doing so very soon, and now hear of his death. Alas, for the stiffness of my neck, and my unwilling feet ! It was the rain that prevented me, or I might have gone when his message came. Surely I have not yet learned to endure hardness for the Gospel's sake. But there is scarcely a place I have been to that messages have not followed to repeat my visit. May the Lord of the harvest send help here soon, is my heart's prayer.

" About this time six years ago I was preparing to make farewell visits. It is not a long time, but it is long to be away from all those whom the affections hold as near and beloved in this life. It is a long time to be a stranger on the earth, without a companion ; yet, strange to say, it is only when I sit down and think of it that I feel it at all ; as a rule the days go by without a shadow of loneliness. The good Lord has wonderfully made up to me for the lack of Christian fellowship by giving me Dick and Susi ; and the other three little black faces keep alive somewhat the dear old home memories of nursery days and of love for love.

" *June 26th*, 1887.—Returned to-day from a trip to the Lukuruwe, and found a fresh caravan had arrived from Bihé. I hear that someone has come to Bihé *en route* for the Garenganze, intending to join me. May the good Lord speed him. It is no vain thing to wait upon God.

" *July 14th*, 1887.—To-day a son of the great Kazembe, of Lake Mweru, an old friend of Dr. Livingstone's, was executed.

This man, a tall, handsome fellow, came to Msidi's town as a refugee after the break up of his father's power. Conspiracies against him in his own country compelled him to seek a friend in his father's old enemy. He, however, acted very unwisely when staying with Msidi, who tested his fidelity by employing him in subordinate positions. Young Kazembe would not submit to such tests, seeing he himself was a king's son, and he preferred to remain idle at the capital. But his head was demanded by a daughter of Msidi as a marriage dowry on the occasion of her marriage to the brother of a former husband of hers who had been killed in a war against Kazembe. She had done all in her power to bring him into trouble, and at last he gave her an opportunity of speaking unguardedly, in a drunken fit, in the presence of Msidi, and implicating himself in the death of one of Msidi's favourite generals. He was withal so defiant to Msidi, that the king saw the wisdom of handing him over to his daughter. The condemned man was allowed to return to his hut and prepare himself, choosing his own time to hand himself over to the executioners. I sat with him outside his hut door while his wives and young men shaved his head and beard, trimmed his finger and toe nails, and washed his body and limbs, anointing him with scented palm oil. He sat through it all without moving a muscle, or showing the slightest concern. I spoke to him repeatedly, and my last words were, ' Whosoever shall call on the name of the Lord shall be saved.' The four executioners were sitting meanwhile in a row. When I rose and shook hands for the last time, Kazembe rose from his seat, and as I left him he quietly walked over to the executioners and gave himself up. They threw him roughly on the ground, bound him like a pig to an extra long pole—as Kazembe stood considerably over six feet in height—and with groans and animal grunts they carried him off to the bush where they struck his head off as he lay fastened to the pole. I had hardly reached my house ere the doleful procession of executioners passed by on their way to Kangofu, with Kazembe's head on a pike, carrying it to the offended queen.

"*August 9th*, 1887.—I had long been planning to revisit the town of Kalolo, where the people were so afraid of me as to go off and sleep in their fields all night. This time I carried nothing but my gun and blanket, intending to give the people the benefit of entertaining me to their hearts' content. I went a different road to the one previously taken, and called at the town of Likoko, a brother of Msidi. In doing so I had to pass the town of Kapapa, Msidi's chief wife. In going along a little path leading up to her town, I was astonished to see close by the gateway what I at first thought was a young man buried in the ground up to his neck, a mode of punishment common in these parts, as prisons and handcuffs are unknown, but to my horror I found it to be the head of a young man, freshly decapitated, placed thus on the path as a warning to all evildoers. The headless trunk was lying a few yards away, by the side of the road. At once I suspected that Msidi was at Kapapa's town. I found that he had arrived there very early in the morning, and had caught the young man skulking. It seems that Msidi had ordered him some days before to join a war party that had already gone out, and as it was his third or fourth offence Msidi ordered his immediate execution.

" After formally saluting the king, I went on to Likoko's town, where I slept for the night, and we were entertained with their best. We reached Kalolo in the afternoon of the next day. The people there were hearty indeed in their greeting, and, instead of bringing me food uncooked as before, they all took to cooking, so delighted were they to observe that, on my last visit, I ate their native food, and had no supernatural ways of existing. About five in the afternoon a woman came with a dish of thick porridge, and small pot of *ombelela*, or relish, which is often made of cooked beans or other things calculated to give the food a taste. In a short time another came laden in the same way, and then another, until for about half an hour there was a constant stream of women bringing to my hut dishes of cooked food. The whole village had brought me their own suppers, and all were assembled in the yard outside, evidently intending to partake of my feast. I at once fell into their little plan, called in my own boys, and told them to carry the food out and lay it before the people, so that I became their entertainer, and all were my guests for the evening. Remaining with them the next day, I had a pleasant and profitable time. There was a general holiday, and about a dozen young men offered to accompany me for the rest of the journey. Remembering the happy time I had at the Lukuruwe with the crowd who gathered to my camp when I killed the two hippopotami,

I thought I would adopt the same plan with these young men. We started into the bush, built a camp in the neighbourhood of the Lufira River, where there was plenty of game, and we spent six days together. Others joined our company from the neighbouring villages. Sufficient food was supplied to them, and the young men attended to their own cooking, and everything that was needful. I embraced every opportunity of explaining to them the truths of Scripture, and all appeared intensely interested in our morning and evening readings.

" One learns at such times that there are compensations in lonely service in Central Africa. The privilege of being enabled wholly to engross oneself from morning to night in the business of reaching the hearts of these people is very great indeed. In fact, I often feel that the present compensations quite outweigh any sacrifice made. All that draws us nearer to God is rich and fertile in reward ; yea, it is good at times even to be cast down, for the Lord comforteth them that are so.

" On returning to my house I found that a company of Bihé traders had arrived. They reported the death of Chipongi, the chief of that place, and also told me that there was a white man in Bihé, known as ' Monare's brother,' who was planning to reach the Garenganze. Their not having letters of any kind, however, made me rather suspicious of their statements, and their extravagant accounts of the immense following that this white man had, and the great amount of goods in his possession, and other cock-and-bull stories with which they filled my ears, made me still more doubt their truthfulness.

" When we go to any people, Jew or Gentile, as the Lord's ambassadors, they have surely a right to ask for our credentials. The early missionaries when preaching to the Jew appealed to Scripture. When preaching to the Gentile their preaching was accompanied with miraculous power. But are we to-day so left to ourselves and our own resources that we have nothing to say to the African challenge coming more or less directly, ' Where are your credentials ? ' It was always with a peculiar sense of triumph that I was able to quote John's words, and assure my hearers that it was so, He Who had sent me was with me. With me, making it impossible for any man to injure me in any way without His consent, with me to make them feel in their hearts that what I said was true, and with me to answer my prayers and give me all that I asked for.

Well, I was able, or rather enabled, on a few occasions to ask God for something publicly, and on each occasion was not ' put to shame.' Recently I employed six men to go with me on a Gospel tour, hoping to revisit several villages down the Lufira, but heavy floods of rain had driven man and beast away so that we splashed about for two days with a handful of rice for my first day's rations, soup made from old buffalo bones well gnawed by the hyenas for the second day's rations, and on the third day we hoped to arrive at villages that we knew were well above flood marks across the Chansamne Plains, but the men were hardly equal to it. However, we splashed along and I tried to cheer them up, but they had been thinking, and were still thinking, since last night's talk round the fire, how it was that the God they had come out to serve had served them so badly. So I replied that no doubt I had made a mistake in not seeking His guidance when we left home. But even although we had made a mistake God would give us food there and then in the midst of that great plain as easily as at the villages. So we stopped, and I prayed God, for the sake of those standing by, to give us food in this wilderness of water. All then shouldered their loads with a lighter heart and on we went. I then noticed that close by there stood a clump of dwarf palms grown on an old ant heap and just as we approached them an antelope sprang out, stood dazed for a moment in the bright light, then started to run towards us, but finding he was coming into the danger he had sniffed, he stopped again, giving me the opportunity of killing him with one shot. So that there on our path lay God's answer, and within ten minutes of our asking. I ought to add that this was the second antelope we had seen during the three days, and the other was quite out of reach with the rifle.

" *Sept.* 16*th*, 1897.—To-day has seen the end of a little episode in the history of my stay in Garenganze. Msidi tried to force upon me one of his own wives that she might be in my village to cultivate and grind for me. Seeing I would not consent to marry any of his daughters he seemed to think this the next best arrangement, and one he could carry through without my consent. My efforts at first seemed useless, but on sending a point blank refusal, when the matter seemed to be coming to a head, he threatened to beat my messenger. This made me think that he was possibly suspicious of me, and that

P

when other whites might come, we together would dispute the ground on which my village stood. But by placing his wife in my village he would thus have a foot inside. This morning I found the opportunity I had been waiting for of getting him alone when everything was talked over. I tried to explain why I had come here, the nature of my calling, his own need of the Gospel, etc., and the ' wifie ' question was completely talked out. As I left he gave me a little girl, about 10 years of age, who had been brought in as tribute, saying I might take her to my village.

" One of Msidi's hunters came to my house to say that there was a troop of antelopes out in the plain to the north of the capital, and urged me to go at once with him to the spot. As myself and boys were in need of food of some sort I started for the plain with this man as guide. We found, however, that the herd had gone further away Following on for some time, we made up to them about ten miles from Msidi's town I succeeded in stalking the herd, getting within 150 yards of them, and from behind a small tree I opened fire. Although I had only five cartridges in my belt, three of these antelopes were brought down. They were about the size of oxen, and are very good eating indeed. Two of them lay together, and the third about a hundred yards off.

" By this time the sun was just disappearing, and considering the state of my larder at home, I could not think of leaving all this meat in the plain. I therefore sent off my companion to the village for fire, and to bring more cartridges, and some men to cut up and carry the meat back. I remained by the carcases, armed only with a long hunting knife, having no ammunition for my rifle.

" Night had scarcely set in when I heard in the distance the whoop of a hyena, which was the signal for all night prowlers to gather round ; so I determined to march up and down, and if possible hold my own against them. Unfortunately there was no moon. It was a pitch-dark night, and I could only hear the animals as they came walking round in the dry grass. Having no fire with me, I was compelled to keep shouting at them, making as much noise as possible, to keep them from the carcases of the antelopes. They seemed to increase in number, and feeling unable to defend all my spoil, I gave up one animal to my hungry visitors, thinking that would satisfy them, and they would leave me in peaceful possession of the two.

" Feeling the cold intensely, I took out my hunting knife and skinned one of the antelopes, rolled myself in the borrowed hide, and lay down on the ground. But soon I heard the stealthy tread of some animal coming towards me. Springing instantly to my feet, I rushed to the place where I had left the one carcase, and found that in the course of an hour these hungry brutes had devoured it, and were now preparing to pounce upon either me or the other two. By dint of rushing up and down, and shouting for hours, I managed to keep them off. About three in the morning some men came, bringing fire with them, and I got a little sleep. The daylight revealed, by the footprints, that my companions had been five large hyenas and three cheta or dog-leopards ; and not only had they cleared off every atom of the flesh and bones of their antelope, but they had licked the very ground clean of the blood. We carried off the meat of the other two triumphantly to Msidi's town, giving him a quarter of one of the animals as we passed. He was quite astonished when he heard of the night's adventure. Indeed, he professed to be very angry at what appeared to him foolhardiness, and when I explained that necessity had compelled me, he wanted to know why I had not applied to him for food. I told him that I certainly would not do that, but he made me accept a large bin of corn, which contained more than a six months' supply for me and my boys.

" *Oct. 10th*, 1887.—Kasule, an old native trader from the Quando district, who has been living here with Msidi for many years, fell into a fire and burned his right hand He did not come to me to have it dressed at once, and mortification set in. When they brought him to-day I found the hand in such a state that I was compelled to amputate it. Taking him out to the bush close by, I set him down on the ground, and, with the assistance of my boy, Dick, held his arm across a huge stone, and with a razor and a little penknife I managed to sever the hand at the wrist joint. The poor old man stood the operation wonderfully well, and seemed very grateful for my help ; but he was quite overcome when Dick dug a hole in the ground and buried the hand. I kept the old man under my care for some days, and the wound healed completely. He seemed very unwilling to leave my village again, so I told him he had better bring his wife, build his hut close by, and I would take charge of his little boy and bring him up. I thought he might look after the village in my absence, and would be useful for going messages and other light work.

"*Oct. 13th.*—Msidi sent another little girl to my village. She had run off from her owners who had beaten her. Msidi sent her to me as I did not beat people.

"*Dec. 14th,* 1887.—Dick had just prepared my usual afternoon meal of corn porridge, and one roasted pigeon to flavour it, when two men came hastily up in front of my house, and without waiting to knock pushed their way in. Before I had time to remonstrate with them for their seeming rudeness, the foremost one thrust into my hand a packet of letters. I handed to him and his companion my porridge and pigeon, and, opening the packet, I found that, during these two long years of silence as to the movements of the outer world, I had not only been remembered by many friends at home, but that two brethren were actually close to me in the heart of Africa. Messrs. Swann and Faulknor, after many delays, difficulties and perplexities, had arrived safely at the Lualaba River, from which they had forwarded my letters, and in a few days they would be with me. What was I to do? Should I remain and make the house as comfortable as possible for their reception, or start at once to meet them? I decided to adopt the first course as being the most sensible.

"Home letters tell me of dear Nigel's death, the Nathaniel of our family, an Israelite indeed in whom there was no guile, for guilelessness was his special characteristic.

"Pedro, the bearer of these letters, had also brought for Msidi a piece of handkerchief and a message from the two brethren. To deliver these he at once started for the king's court. At that time Msidi's wife, Mataya, one of the queens of the country, and her eldest son, were being tried for having bewitched her younger son. This younger son was more liked by the chief than the elder, and had gone to Sombwe in a war party (under the command of the chief's nephew, Molenga), where he was shot. The diviners declared that he had been bewitched by someone, that his body had been stripped of its charms, and he had thus become exposed to the enemy's bullets. Suspicion fell on the lad's mother and elder brother,

who were consequently brought to trial. The evidence against
them was, that on the day of the departure of the war party,
the elder son hid the gun of his younger brother, and, when
the latter demanded his gun, he refused to give it up, saying,
' Neither of us is beloved of the chief, why then should we go
and fight his battles ? ' The mother interfered, and said,
' Give the lad his gun ; if he be killed, what matter ? Certainly
the chief won't weep for him.' The elder brother was condemned to be shot, but Mataya's sentence was deferred for
a final day of deliberation, when all in authority were to be
gathered. This court was sitting when the news reached
Msidi that Messrs. Swann and Faulknor were at the borders
of his country. Mataya was at once pardoned, and the sentence
of death passed upon her elder son was commuted to one of
banishment for life, the chief joyfully declaring that no human
blood should be shed upon the arrival of these his white guests,
and the piece of coloured handkerchief that the brethren
had sent was handed to Mataya by Msidi as a proof of her
pardon.

" Msidi sent one of his own sons to meet the caravan, bearing
with him Msidi's welcome, as well as letters of greeting and
hearty welcome from me , and I at once turned my attention
to making things as comfortable as possible for their arrival.
Some mats that had been made for me out of plaited strips
of palm leaves were sewn together to form a ceiling, and racks
and shelves were made to receive what goods these friends
might bring, in order to place them above the reach of the
white ants. To obtain the wood we had to make excursions to
the forest. The legs of a round table I had been making were
already in the rough, and these I had to dress down and fit
together.

" While busy with my preparations, tidings came of the near
approach of the white men, so leaving everything in the hands
of my boys I started off to meet them, going along the usual
caravan road. After proceeding for some distance without
hearing from the natives any report of their advance, I became
concerned, but thought that possibly they might have taken
the by-way over the hills, and I therefore returned to my
cottage to await their arrival. At such a time it was impossible
to do nothing, so I began to rig up a flagstaff. With a long
bamboo rod bound to my hammock pole, I made an awkward-

looking flagstaff, which I fastened to my pigeon house, and a tattered Union Jack was got ready for hoisting.

"*Dec.* 16*th*.—The first signal I had of the arrival of the strangers was the firing of three pistol shots in the distance. Running out of the door, I tried to hoist my Union Jack, but the line had got thick and twisted with the heavy rains, so I only succeeded in getting the flag half-way up. Starting down the hill as quickly as possible, I met Mr. Swann some little distance from my house. From letters forwarded from the Lualaba, I knew his name, and his object in coming, so we rejoiced to meet as brethren. His companion, Mr. Faulknor, remained with the caravan, expecting to follow in a couple of days, and Dick and Susi at once started with a hammock to help him on. On his arrival with the caravan, we were able to rejoice and thank God for His mercy to us. What a day we had of real Gospel triumph! There in the heart of the continent, standing holding each other by the hand, we sang, ' Jesus shall reign.' "

CHAPTER XVI

HOME AND FAME

HAVING introduced the new arrivals to Msidi, Arnot stayed a further two and a half months, until they were somewhat familiar with the work, and then, on February 27th, 1888, started for the coast and home. We confine ourselves to three extracts from his diary dealing with the journey to Benguella.

"*Nana Kandundu, April 12th,* 1888.—Have had a good journey thus far. I took a different route, coming more south, where food was plentiful. For several days we travelled along the Zambesi—quite a large stream, though near its source. Here I found that this female chief had gone off to fight with Kangombe, a Lovale chief, who has been raiding down the Zambesi with quite a large army. Her ladyship of this place objects, and goes to defend her subjects.

"*April 13th.*—The contending forces, we hear, have met twelve miles or so from here. All are much alarmed by many conflicting reports, and the sound of distant firing ; armed men are pouring in and going on to the fray from all directions. Her ladyship's litter has come to her town ; so she means to fight like the ancient heroes who burned their bridges behind them.

"*April 14th, midnight.*—A messenger from Nana Kandundu is calling me and my men to her aid. Five camps of Ovimbundu have gathered round me, mustering in all four or five hundred. I declare neutrality ; at the same time promise to protect her ladyship's person, should she be worsted and come to my camp. She has done well in going out to protect the down-trodden Lunda tribes along the Upper Zambesi that Kangombe has long been preying upon. She effectually demonstrates the superior humanity of female government, and I hope to welcome her victorious return."

Benguella was reached in August, and England on September 18th, 1888.

Quite a new kind of work now awaited the traveller. Missionary addresses were delivered in various parts of England and Scotland, a great correspondence was carried on, recruits for the field were obtained and provision made for the enlargement of the work.

Though, as his diary shows, Arnot was not thirsting for fame, it had come to him and he was quite one of the lions of the season.

Under the heading of " A New African Explorer," *The Times* gave a brief account of Arnot s travels soon after his return. Amongst other things, this article said : " His outfit was of the most slender character. He travelled practically unarmed. He was almost everywhere received with friendly welcome by chiefs and people, who clearly appreciated his confidence. If he had any grievances, he never took the law into his own hands , he invariably appealed to native tribunals, such as they are, and never without receiving practical justice. . . . Mr. Arnot struck north-west (of the Barotse) through that wonderful country of rivers, to Bihé. The hydrography of this strange region he has helped to unravel. One can stand almost on the very spot where rivers rise that flow north, south, east and west. . . . One thing he seems clearly to have proved, that Livingstone's Leeba, coming from the north-east. is the real Zambesi, and not the river which comes out of Lake Dilolo."

At the request of the Royal Geographical Society, Arnot read a paper before its members on January 7th, 1889. This summarises his journey from Natal in September, 1881, to Bihé and Benguella and thence across the Central Plateau of Africa to the sources of the Zambesi and the Congo and was printed in the *Proceedings* of the Society published in the following month, together with a map which the Society specially prepared to accompany it This map not only showed Arnot's routes but the discoveries of other well-known African travellers, such as Commander Cameron, Herr Reichard, and the Portuguese officers, Serpa Pinto, Capello, and Ivens. Livingstone's journey from the Zambesi to Loanda, which attracted Arnot's attention to this part of Africa, is also marked. From this map one can see that the journey from Peho to the Garenganze capital was over fresh ground ; the names of many new places and rivers appear for the first time, the true course of the first part of the Zambesi River is traced as running from east to west. To Arnot belongs the honour of being the first to locate the sources of this great water highway.

An interesting discussion took place after the reading of Arnot's paper, from the report of which we make the following extracts.

" Mr R. N. Cust said that Mr. Arnot was a stranger to the Society, but some of those present had watched his progress for the last seven years About five years ago he (Mr. Cust) sent the first notice of Mr. Arnot's existence to the *Proceedings* of the Society, in which he said there was a young fellow named Arnot walking across Africa on his own resources. Mr. Arnot had the two great characteristics of a thorough African traveller —pluck, and kindness to the natives. He must have had many a disagreeable quarter of an hour during those seven years, prostrated with fever, suffering in his eyes, wanting food, often within a few inches of losing his life, but his British pluck carried him through. In his kindness to the natives he was only equalled by the Society's gold medallist, Mr. Joseph Thomson. The natives found him to be their friend, and they still possessed that nobility of character which recognised a man who was good to them. In March next he was going back to Africa in the strength of an evangelist, and would take with him the best wishes of the Society.

" Sir Francis de Winton said that even from a merely travelling point of view Mr. Arnot had accomplished a most remarkable journey, considering the limited means at his disposal ; but he had also added to geographical science. With reference to the slave trade, which it was desired to stop," Sir Francis said, " blockading the coast and bombarding peaceful villages was only like scratching the surface. The true secret was to attack the trade in the centre of the country, and by making friends with the great chief Msidi, Mr. Arnot was doing something towards putting a stop to the inhuman traffic. It was an important fact that he had made the name of Englishman respected wherever he went."

The President, General Richard Strachey, said : " He trusted that the valuable ethnographical information Mr. Arnot had collected as to the distribution of the races, and the distribution of the power of the various chiefs, would be placed on record in a manner which would make it available for future travellers in the same country."

In the course of his reply, Mr. Arnot said : " With regard to the secret of his own success, he wished to use the words of one of England's worthies, George Herbert, who in his 'Thanksgiving ' said,' If they give me honour, I shall let them see that all the honour doth belong to Thee.' The one reason for his success in Africa was the reality of the presence and power of God with him night and day."

The above simple and courageous testimony is embodied in *The Proceedings of the Royal Geographical Society.*

The Society honoured their guest by making him a Fellow. It also presented him with a medal for his discoveries in connection with the Zambesi, and awarded him the Cuthbert Peak grant in recognition of his seven years' travel. The Murchison grant was also entrusted by the Society to him for the purpose of conveying a suitable present to Chitambo for the latter's care of Livingstone s body. In connection with this latter event, Mrs. Bruce of Edinburgh (daughter of Dr. Livingstone) had a medal prepared which was committed to the care of Arnot, together with other gifts from Scotland, for this great African chief.

Amongst other functions arranged for Arnot was a reception given by the late Lord Radstock at the Eccleston Hall, London. At this gathering the traveller was introduced to the Duchess of Teck. After the reception, the Duchess, together with her daughter, then Princess Mary—now Queen Mary—took him for a drive round Hyde Park, pointing out the places of interest and at the same time hearing his stories of travel On bidding farewell, Arnot left his map in the carriage, and the Princess, jumping down, ran after him and returned it to him.

In a very homely letter to his mother, Arnot thus refers to this experience : " I had no less than three meetings yesterday : Noon, Aldersgate St. (R. C. Morgan in the chair) ; afternoon, Eccleston Hall (Lord Radstock). What an ado ! Swell carriages kept driving up in quick succession ; the ante-hall was being prepared for a reception ; grand ladies were arriving, and poor me, with my trussy head, etc., did not exactly know what calamity was about to befall me, when Lord Radstock called me off and told me that H.R H the Princess Mary was coming, and that I must be prepared to be presented to her, and sure enough in came the cortège. Sudden swells ! a long alley was formed of curtseying ladies, when Lord Radstock came forward with, ' Allow me to present to you '. . . . Angles ensued. The Princess asked most interesting questions, and sat through the lecture. Then we all had tea in ante-hall (Princess, nobility and poor me only). Then the Princess would have me drive off in her carriage with herself and another Princess, and asked about you and Dad and was so glad to see me, and would never forget me, and was so helped. She dropped me at Lady Beauchamp's, where I had tea."

A good deal of Arnot's time in England was taken up in preparing *Garenganze*, his first book, for the press. This was published early in 1889, and had a good reception. Three editions were soon called for. The book certainly did much towards stirring up missionary enthusiasm.

We quote from two of the reviews which appeared. *The Times* said : " In a modest volume of 270 pages Mr. Arnot tells the story of his seven years' work in Africa. He makes no pretensions to literary grace. . . . One feature of the work accomplished by Mr. Arnot is the small expenditure of money which it has involved. The total outlay for his seven years' work has not exceeded £500, a marked contrast to the thousands which have been expended on other expeditions, covering much less ground and extending only over a few months. Mr. Arnot, of course, had to pay his way ; but his following was at all times small. . . . It is needless to say Mr. Arnot travelled practically unarmed ; he certainly had no hesitation in shooting game when necessary, but among the natives he, like Gordon, never showed any weapon more formidable than a cane. . . . In his journey eastwards Mr. Arnot passed through a region of great geographical interest, the greatest river region, indeed, of Africa, what Livingstone very appropriately designated the ' Great Sponge.' In the Lovale and Lunda country, the region around Lake Dilolo, one finds within an hour's march of each other streams flowing in nearly all directions of the compass— north-eastward and northward to the Congo and its tributaries, south-eastward to the Zambesi, westward and north-westward to the Atlantic. . . .

" Mr. Arnot has been able to lay down with greater precision than has hitherto been the case the courses of many of these streams, and has pretty clearly shown that the Leeba is the real Zambesi, which comes from the plateau on the west of the Garenganze country."

The Glasgow Herald said : " Mr. Arnot s book appears to-day. It is a modest volume of 270 pages, issued at the moderate figure of 2s. 6d., Mr. Arnot being determined to obtain as wide a circulation as possible for his narrative. The first edition of 5000 copies is, I believe, all taken up already, and it may be three weeks before a second is ready. Mr. Arnot confines himself to what came under his own observation. He is now, and has been for some time, taking lessons with the scientific instructor of the Royal Geographical Society, so that when he returns to Africa in a few days he will be in a better position than before for collecting important geographical data. He will also take with him a photographic apparatus. . . . As a book one misses here the stirring encounters and restless movement of Stanley's narratives, or the tactical manœuvring of Joseph Thomson's, or the eloquent description of fuana, flora, and scenery of H. H. Johnston's. Mr. Arnot has neither scientific training, nor military instincts, nor great literary gifts. His book is compiled from letters and diaries, and it is bald, insufficient, fragmentary, and by no means a fitting memorial of a memorable achievement. Nevertheless, every page of it is filled with living interest, for in every page of it we see the heart of the writer. Simple and unassuming in outfit as in character, strong in faith as in physique, this young man quietly sets down the memoranda of his travels as if he were doing nothing out of the ordinary."

Arnot's six months' stay in England were marked by his engagement in October, 1888, to Miss Harriet Jane Fisher, of Greenwich Neither had known the other till they met shortly after the missionary's return from the Dark Continent. It was an ideal match, and the marriage. which took place in March, 1889, added much to Arnot's comfort, efficiency and usefulness.

Many friends were interested in hearing of the open door given for missionary work along the comparatively healthy watershed lying between the Zambesi and the Congo River systems. From amongst the many, twelve were willing, in answer to what they believed to be the Lord's call, to rise up and leave all.

A large meeting was held in the Exeter Hall, London, on

March 19th, 1889, to bid these (fourteen in all with Mr. and Mrs. Arnot) farewell. Each of these missionaries went forth on his own responsibility to his Master, though not independently of fellow-Christians with whom he had been associated at home, and who gave their fellowship and counsel. The party were all closely associated with " The Brethren." They went out in two sections, the first of which consisted of Mr. and Mrs. Arnot, Mr. Dan Crawford, Mr. Geo. Fisher, Mr. F. Lane and Mr. A. Munnock.

A report of this meeting was published in one of the current newspapers as follows .

" On Tuesday two meetings were held in Exeter Hall, to take farewell of Mr. F. S. Arnot, and his companions, who are now *en route* for Africa, as well as various friends destined for other spheres of missionary work. The interest in the proceedings was wide and deep, as shown in a remarkable attendance. In the afternoon the body of the large hall was filled, though it had been intended to meet in the lower and smaller hall. . . Mr. Arnot . . . spoke of the narrow paths which have to be trodden, through thick jungles, and along mountain ridges. No beasts of burden, and no ordinary vehicles can be employed. Some novel trucks, designed by Mr Edward K. Groves, of Bristol, will, however, be taken out, and it is hoped the native porters will use them. The big Exeter Hall was not big enough comfortably to contain the eager crowd that desired to have a share in this memorable farewell. Galleries and gangways were packed with people glad to get even standing room, and an overflow meeting had to be held in the hall below. Leading members of the community of Brethren were prominent all along the platform, but there was a goodly sprinkling of other Christians. The great audience ' could scarce forbear to cheer ' when Mr F S Arnot rose to speak, but the platform effectually imposed a wet blanket, and hushed the people to silence. Why the speakers should have unfettered freedom to liberate their souls in glowing speech, and the thousands in front of them should have rigidly to repress their emotions we fail to understand. Can there be anything dishonouring to God in a hearty cheer ? "

CHAPTER XVII

THE SECOND JOURNEY

WE now come to a new era in Arnot's life. Hitherto his African experiences have been unique. His first period of travel, covering seven years, was one of pioneering, and during the greater part of this time he was alone amongst the natives. Probably no other African traveller came nearer to the experiences of Livingstone than did Arnot when spying out the land. But now his story is merged with that of others. In fact, it belongs to the establishment of one of the greatest of the missionary bodies operating in Central Africa. It is somewhat difficult to disentangle the thread of Arnot's life from the skein with which it is associated. And this difficulty is enhanced by one of the outstanding features of Arnot's character, viz. his great humility. His letters and records from this time onward have more to say about the labours of fellow-workers than about his own. But as the purpose of this book is to tell the story of his life, rather than the story of the missions he did so much to found, we shall now only seek to trace his footsteps, and in doing this we shall be satisfied with much less detail than when following him alone, and in paths that were then altogether new.

Arriving at Benguella on May 9th, 1889, the six missionaries were faced with great difficulties in the matter of transport, and it was necessary that those following should be acquainted with the situation. Fortunately, the Eastern Telegraph Company had just finished laying a cable along the West Coast of Africa, and the first paid message from Benguella was one from Mr. Arnot informing the second party of the state of matters As things seemed to grow worse instead of better two other telegraphic messages were sent in order to make sure that the new-comers should not set forth blindly on a path beset with so many difficulties.

At last, with the help of six men, a horse, a donkey, and a

mule, Mr. and Mrs. Arnot, Messrs. Lane and Munnoch, and Dick, Arnot's old boy, who had come to meet him, a start was made for the interior, Messrs. Crawford and Fisher being left at the coast to await the arrival of the second party.

On the second day out Mr. Lane was down with an attack of fever and dysentery, and after a delay of another day he and Mr. Munnock returned to Benguella, Mr. and Mrs. Arnot pushing on to Bailundu to procure carriers Travelling through the passes leading to Chisanje these latter had to walk most of the way. In clambering over huge boulders the horse fell once or twice and got badly cut, and the donkey was very obstinate. At last late one afternoon they struggled into camp, Mrs. Arnot having fainted twice from the heat and the exertion.

The few men they had were engaged to go only as far as the Chivulu country, which was safely reached on July 6th, after eleven days' journey from the coast. Here they remained for a few days whilst Dick went on to King Ekwikwi's war camp to ask him for carriers to take them to Bailundu. He sent nineteen, so Mrs. Arnot was able to enjoy the luxury of riding in a hammock, carried on the shoulders of two men. Three days' travelling brought them to Ekwikwi's camp. "This great man," Arnot says, " was able, it seemed, to block the caravan road for a year or two at a time, and only by paying a heavy blackmail was it possible for the Portuguese to take their ivory and rubber to the coast. After travelling for fourteen days we arrived at the war camp, where all was drunkenness and great swelling words of brag and boast as to the prowess of Ekwikwi, and of how the white man was tributary to him. At my first interview I did not make much progress, but he gave us a hut and we settled down to the difficult task of trying to soften his hard heart. It so happened that a friend in Demerara had sent me a very fine hammock, made entirely by Indians. When the chief saw me hang it up he coveted it greedily. So next day I repeated my request and gave him the hammock. Nothing could have been more effective. He granted all I wanted. '

Mrs. Arnot had fever for a few days in this camp and it was thought the wiser plan to take her on to the American Mission Station in Bailundu, after which Arnot returned to the Chivanda country, where, during August, 1889, he was alone, as of old " For several weeks," he says, " I toiled about from village to village on my poor horse, sometimes covering sixty miles a day collecting or trying to collect carriers. One night would find me lying curled up by a fire in a corner of a native hut, with seven or eight long black fellows stretched out all around me, and the next night perhaps making the most of some deserted camp in the bush. At last, little by little, hope began to rise , but even when promises were given, second and third visits had to be made. Then came the final assurance, ' Yes ! let me see, to-day my wife has gone to the field barn for corn ; to-morrow she will soak and hull it ; on the third day she will pound it into meal ; on the fourth day she will dry it and put it into a skin bag—why on the fifth day I will be ready.' ' And what about your two brothers you promised to bring with you ?' ' Oh ! they have gone to a spirit dance at our mother's village ' This one definite promise, however, gives me something to work upon. I start off several paid agents to scour the country and call at all the villages visited by me with the final announce-ment · ' After four days Monare will form a camp at the meeting of the three paths by the two rivers in the Ohumbe district of Chivanda.' I post off for a good-bye visit to my wife in Bailundu, and am ready waiting at the appointed place on the fifth day. The delay of a few more days was still required with a little humouring of the first batch or two of men who had joined me. One day I bought them a goat, another day we went off and fired a stretch of reeds by the river, and shot some water-buck as they escaped , and so I kept the men happy until all who were coming with us had joined the camp. Then came a talk over the recognised rules and by-laws of the road. A crier was appointed to call out each evening instructions as to the next day's march, and a start was made in regular order for the coast."

Arnot reached Benguella on September 1st, with one hundred and eighty men. At first sight this seems to be a large supply of carriers, but when one considers that there were thirteen Europeans for whom everything needful for a stay in the interior had to be taken, it will be seen that the caravan was far too limited, especially as hammock bearers had to be deducted. On the men's shoulders all supplies had to be borne, including bulky cloth currency, tents and bedding for cold nights on the hills, cooking utensils. supplies of food to take them over long stretches of

barren country where no provisions could be bought, changes
of clothing, tools for building houses or rather huts, medicine,
etc., etc. In addition supplies had to be taken for Messrs
Swann and Faulknor, who were alone in the Garenganze.

The second party had arrived at Benguella on August 7th.
Amongst the members of this was Dr. Fisher, brother of Mrs.
Arnot. The landing had been a sad one, for Mr. Johnston,
one of its members, had caught a chill at Loanda and had died
shortly after the ship had cast anchor at Benguella.

The journey inland was full of sorrow. On reaching the
Utalama camp two of the lady missionaries had slight attacks
of fever, and the carriers, finding that they could not continue
the journey on the day appointed, became demoralised. Many
of them refused to go to Bihé, and fresh men had to be obtained
to take their places. At last, after three weeks' waiting, they
were just on the point of completing arrangements for a start
when Mr. Morris, who had come with his wife, leaving four
children behind in London, was suddenly taken ill. He had
been along the banks of the Keve River the day before with
another member, hoping to get a goose or wild duck for supper,
and, after wading through several lagoons, returned much
exhausted from the heat of the sun, which had been intense.
Upon the first symptoms of fever Dr. Fisher gave him the
usual medicinal treatment, which seemed to check the disease,
and he got up from his bed, and was preparing for the journey
to Bihé. Just then the shed used as his kitchen took fire, and
in a short time his tent was riddled with holes by the shower
of sparks from the flames, and but for the efforts of all present
the whole camp would have been destroyed. The excitement
and exertion proved too much for Mr. Morris in his weak state,
and he had a relapse, and gradually grew weaker. On the day
after the fire, Mr. Gall, another member of the second party,
who had strained himself to the utmost to save the camp,
complained of headache, and Dr. Fisher had him carried into
his own tent. For several days he was delirious, and then sank
rapidly. After barely a fortnight's illness, Mr. Morris passed
away, and Mr Gall, after a still shorter illness, died a few hours
later.

Mrs Morris, the broken-hearted widow, decided to return to
her four fatherless children in England, taking one of the ladies
with her, and Mr G. Fisher also decided to accompany them

Q

home. So the original party of fourteen was reduced to eight within two hundred miles of the coast, a fifth of the way to the interior.

With staggering, bewildered steps the diminished missionaries turned to the duties of the day and resumed the journey.

The necessity for the establishment of a depot for the various articles required by those already labouring in the centre of Africa, and by others who might follow, led to a decision to establish a Mission Station at Kuanjulula, in the Bihé country A few days' journey from Bailundu brought the missionaries to the new site in safety. Supplies were sent forward to the Garenganze for Messrs. Swann and Faulknor, and hut building was proceeded with at Kuanjulula. After a couple of months Arnot writes, in December, 1889 : " A dark cloud now arose on the political horizon of Bihé. The king, Chindunduma, declared himself suspicious of so many white people coming to his country, and blamed Senhor Porto (who had put in a special plea for us) for inviting the ' Englese ' to Bihé. He also sent a letter to Kuanjulula commanding us to withdraw forthwith. This it was imposible for us to do without throwing away all we had with us, and, what was more serious still, leaving Swann and Faulknor unprovided for in Garenganze, for the king would not allow us to go toward the interior in our flight. We spread the letter before the Lord, and committed ourselves to His protection and disposal. Next morning Senhor Porto arrived at our camp in a very excited state, saying that an army was coming to plunder us and drive us out of Bihé, and with undoubted kindness he had come over to do what he could to prevent bloodshed. In a short time the army came, consisting of a company of the king's young men in charge of three captains, two of whom I knew well, Chikuya and Ukuesala. The former, when in charge of a trading caravan from the interior, was attacked and plundered by a section of the Lovale tribe, and I found him, on my first journey, detained as a prisoner in the village of the chief, who had robbed him of everything. I was able at that time to help him with a small gift of cloth, so that he obtained his release and returned to Bihé, professing himself under lifelong obligation to me. I told Senhor Porto that we had nothing to fear, and going forward I greeted Chikuya, who replied with a downcast look, and, after consulting his companions, said, with all the authority he was able to command, 'We have been sent by the king to enforce his letter ordering you all to leave Bihé at once ' I replied, 'The king has sent the wrong men Had he intended doing us any harm he would have sent strangers, and not friends. The king has only sent you to talk over the matter with us. Chikuya,' I added, 'you are responsible for the conduct of the warriors you have brought with you. You had better order them to sit down together there (pointing to a corner in our yard), and I will have some food brought for them while we talk matters over.' Chikuya did what he was told, and three goats were handed over to the young men, while I prepared some food hastily for the three captains in a hut close by, and, with the Gospel of John in my hand, replied to the king's letter. Those African braves—like a wild beast missing the prey in his first spring—had no longer any heart for plundering our camp, as their first intention clearly had been. Chikuya pleaded with his fellows against doing so, saying that he was sure the king had had his ears filled with lies against us. A compromise was at last come to. I gave them a handsome present of trade calico for the king, and presented each of the warrior bands with four yards of check shirting. Then, with tents and such-like improvised accommodation, we made them all comfortable for the night, and next morning they departed in good order without having robbed us of even the value of a pin.

" As soon as the king's young men had taken their leave a number of smaller chiefs in our immediate neighbourhood took the opportunity of making a demonstration in our favour. No less than five appeared with their followers, armed to the teeth, dancing and shouting, and declaring that the king of Bihé had openly insulted them all by sending his warriors into their province, etc. Finally a big palaver was held, and two chiefs were appointed by the others to go to the capital to contradict the lies spoken against their white men.

" The day after Chikuya had returned to the king a messenger came to our camp calling me to the capital. I, with my wife and Dr. Fisher, called on Senhor Porto, who kindly accompanied us to the king's town, where we were received with ' white chalk,' meaning acquittal, and not with ' red chalk,' which would have meant guilt. After quite a formal palaver the king presented us with an ox for food as a token of good feeling, giving Messrs. Thompson, Lane, Crawford, and myself an open road to the Garenganze, and permission to collect carriers for the journey. This trouble seemed to be thus well got over, and we went on with our preparations for the journey to the interior when rumours of fresh political disturbance reached us.

" About this time a Portuguese expedition, under Captain Couceiro, arrived in Bihé, bound for the Okavangu River. The king of Bihé refused to give Captain Couceiro, and the 150 soldiers who accompanied him, permission to pass through his country, declaring that an understanding existed between him and the Portuguese Government to the effect that no black soldiers were ever to be quartered in Bihé, and that he only welcomed white strangers to his country. Senhor Porto did his best to allay his fears, but without avail ; and seeing nothing but trouble before himself and his countrymen he settled up his affairs, spread thirteen kegs of gunpowder on the floor of his house, and, opening one keg and lying at full length on the other twelve, he struck a match and deliberately ignited the powder. The explosion threw him a great height into the air, through the roof of his house. Dr. Fisher was at once sent for, but the poor old man died after twenty-four hours. By this time Chindunduma was collecting his forces and threatening the Portuguese encampment. Captain Couceiro withdrew, his camp was ransacked by Chindunduma, and the Portuguese settlements of Belmonte and Boavista were plundered and destroyed.

" It can be easily understood that the Portuguese became suspicious of us, seeing we were ' English missionaries,' and had been allowed to remain safely in Bihé while their own subjects had been driven from the country. When we remember that at this particular time they were in open conflict with the British South Africa Company touching their East African territory, we must be thankful for the thoroughness with which they ultimately enquired into the matter, and for the justice shown to us   I received an official letter from the Captain-General of Bihé and Bailundu, advising us to withdraw from Bihé, and after a little while a second letter came, more strongly worded, saying that if we remained in Bihé we did so at our own peril. Later still a third official letter was sent, in which this Captain-General clearly stated that the Portuguese officials at the coast were in possession of evidence sufficient to convict me of being in league with Chindunduma, the rebel chief of Bihé.

"By this time Messrs. Thompson, Lane and Crawford had gone into camp at Kalusia, and several headmen were out collecting carriers to accompany them to Garenganze We felt the parting with our three brethren much, yet longed to see them finally off to the relief of Messrs. Swann and Faulknor, and were thankful that they had learned sufficient of the Umbundu language to enable them to collect and manage the carriers *en route*.

"Dr. Fisher remained in charge of our mud and wattle compound at Kuanjululu, while I returned in company with Mr. Munnock to Benguella. At Bailundu I was told by the American missionaries that a warrant was out for my arrest. It was so ordered that the very day I reached Benguella the Governor-General of Angola arrived there from Loanda to talk over Bihé matters with the Governor of Benguella, and both gladly listened to my story, and acquitted me af all the charges brought against me. I was asked to protect the children of Senhor Porto and other Portuguese subjects still in Bihé, and was informed that a well-armed force had left Mossamedes to chastise the king of Bihé, and that the officer in charge, Captain Paiva, was commissioned to make full enquiries into the cause of the revolt.

"I got back to Bihé as quickly as possible, leaving Mr. Munnock in Bailundu, and found all well, though anxious for my return, as they had been disturbed during my absence with rumours of war, and of the coming of the force under Captain Paiva.

"Captain Paiva with his army, composed chiefly of Transvaal Boers, from the colony established near Mossamedes, arrived at Bihé on November 4th. He attacked the town of Chindunduma, who made a very feeble resistance, and soon took to flight. Many of the natives were shot down by the mounted Boers, and so long as the chief was at large Captain Paiva scattered fire and sword throughout the country.

"On November 6th, Mr. Sanders, of Kamondongo, succeeded in procuring a few days' truce by forwarding to the Portuguese camp a promise from several chiefs that Chindunduma would be delivered up to the Portuguese. They failed, however, in persuading the fugitive king to deliver himself up. The days of truce expired, and the burning of villages and shooting of the flying people began again. I made an imploring appeal to the chiefs over the northern district of Bihé to combine in some way to save their country, for every moment was of value. In twelve hours' time over twenty chiefs had collected in our yard at Kuanjulula to discuss the matter. I wrote to Captain Paiva their request for an eight days' truce, accompanied with their promise to do their utmost to capture and deliver up Chindunduma. The Captain in his reply thanked me for anything we were able to do to prevent further bloodshed, and promised the assembled chiefs nine days' truce. In six days the native force, twelve hundred strong, returned with the runaway king. Peace was at once declared, and arrangements made for the permanent occupation of Bihé by a Portuguese military force.

" When the king's town was taken Captain Paiva seized his papers. These Ovimbundu chiefs, being unable to write, employ as a rule some Portuguese mulatto as secretary. In his official report to the Portuguese Government, a copy of which I saw at Loanda, Captain Paiva had copied verbatim several letters that he found written by me to Chindunduma, in order to show how harmless they were. One referred to a present of cloth that he had asked of me, and another was a refusal to send him a present of gunpowder. At the same time, sufficient evidence was found to incriminate a Portuguese trader and rum distiller, who, it seems, had been sending presents of rum to the king of Bihé ; and it was thus evident that it was not me but he who had sought to stop the Portuguese advance toward the interior, evidently fearing lest his own business at the coast should suffer if fresh centres and channels of trade were opened up."

Whilst Messrs. Thompson, Lane and Crawford were pressing on to the relief of Messrs. Swann and Faulknor in the Garenganze, the party of five Europeans (including Mr. and Mrs. Arnot) at Kuanjulula were solving the problems connected with the transport of goods from the coast to the far interior. They also felt the need of making known the Gospel to those natives in their part of the large district of Bihé who were out of the reach of the American missionaries. Buildings and enclosures for the Station were erected, and an effort made to provide food for the workers by farming. The study of Umbundu was prosecuted and sick ones were cared for.

In November, 1890, news came from Mr. Dan Crawford of the safe arrival of Messrs. H. Thompson, Lane and himself in Garenganze, and their joyful welcome by Messrs. Swann and Faulknor, with whom they were housed in the little Mission Station at Bunkeya under the sway of the great chief of that country. The trials of the long journey were now over, but they were confronted with fresh difficulties, which might be summed up in one word—Msidi.

"African despots," says Arnot, "such as Msidi of the Garenganze, Lobengula of the Matabele, Liwanika of the Barotse, have no ancient hereditary claims to their extensive empires ; but their power has to be retained by the same brute force by which they or their immediate predecessors obtained it. And, so far as I can find out, these empires had their beginnings about the time of the introduction of guns and powder into Africa. Any chiefs, who were able in those days to get a monopoly of the trade in arms could carve out for themselves enormous kingdoms. Lobengula is perhaps an exception to this rule, his father, Mosilikatse, having conquered the Makalaka and Mashona tribes with the spear. But in Central Africa, so long as the spear and the bow were the only weapons, the balance of power seems to have been fairly well maintained between the small tribal chiefs. Now that the power of these African despots is being curtailed by European rule, it is well to remember that they have indirectly played an important part in the opening up of the interior of Africa.

" Dr. Livingstone was led to undertake his journey to the Zambesi through hearing that Sebituane, with his Makololo followers, had marched northwards from the Baltaping country and had established himself in the Barotse valley. Sebituane soon brought the tribes all around under his sway, and by the aid of this great chief Dr. Livingstone was able to obtain boats to ascend the Zambesi. He also provided carriers, and ivory for the purpose of goods ; and Livingstone was encouraged to make his first great journey from the Zambesi River to St. Paul de Loanda in 1854.

" The great African chiefs have generally invited and welcomed missionaries into their countries, perhaps with the idea of making friends with the white man, from whom powder and guns might be obtained, but they have jealously watched against any possibility of their own influence being weakened by that of the missionary. For forty years missionaries laboured in the Matabele country without apparent fruit, simply because Lobengula quickly called to his capital Gubulowayo (i.e. ' the killing place '), and disposed of any of his people who seemed to come under the influence of the missionaries' teaching.

" In the Garenganze, Msidi from the beginning protected and befriended us, so that while we laboured at the language of the people, and then went about from village to village telling our story for the first time, our lives were ' quiet and peaceable.' Mr. Swann and I were, however, repeatedly apprised of this, that though Msidi allowed us a measure of liberty, he had no intention of giving his people one inch of it. And he seemed to take pleasure in proving to us that our presence in his country put him under no restraint. In order to rule over so many tribes he had to make his name a terror, and perhaps only by comparing him with other African despots are we able to discover his virtues. I would give my testimony as to his having an uncommonly kind side to his cruel heart, and that with all his rapacity and greed he was at times lavishly generous."

In 1891 seven new workers from Great Britain, Canada and Demerara were added to the force often stationed at Kuanjulula and the Garenganze. It was therefore decided that an attempt should be made to establish a third centre, and in August of that year Arnot accompanied some of the new workers to Nana Kandundu. He thus describes the events :

" Making a start from Bihé is always tedious work. The villages, where the men whom we hire as porters reside, are widely scattered, and their friends expect them to give a visit all round, and to drink beer with them before leaving home. No shipmaster in the olden days could have had greater trouble or required more patience in getting his own crew together on the eve of a voyage than we have in collecting our men for a final start. We crossed the Kwanza in canoes, August 31st, 1891. Since the military occupation of Bihé by the Portuguese the natives everywhere were found more easy to deal with, and although we exchanged presents with the chiefs, they no longer plagued us with peremptory demands for tribute at every camp.

" On the way we sought to bring the Gospel before the many carriers from different parts of the Bihé district, who composed our caravan.

" We reached Nana's on October 15th—only six months after Mr. and Mrs Bird (two of the new missionaries) had left London. The absence of delays at the coast and at Bihé allowed of this exceptionally quick journey ; but it had its disadvantages, for they found themselves in the centre of Africa, comparative strangers to the language, the people, and their customs.

" Nana seemed very doubtful as to our real intentions, and was fearful of losing her position as chieftain. After several visits to our camp, however, she became more assured, and came down one evening with an ox and a number of her most important people. She said that if I would kill this ox there and then, with her hand resting on one of my shoulders, and her husband's hand on the other, all her fears would be dispelled and she and the whites would be friends for ever. We gladly agreed to her proposal, and I took my gun and went out to the bush with Mr. Bird, and the ceremony of shooting the ox was gone through, greatly to the satisfaction of Nana and her people. Next day we sent her a handsome present of calico (96 yards) and arrangements were at once made by Mr. Bird for getting a house built, for which we went in search of rafter poles Three more happy days of fellowship closed my stay at Nana's. The altitude of Nana Kandundu above the sea we found, by boiling point thermometer, to be 3690 feet.

" The story of the rescue, on this journey, of a little boy named Ngoi is full of interest, giving, as it does, a glimpse into the horrors of Central African slavery. Socitota, a well-known Bihé trader, had gone to the Luba country to obtain slaves, and while engaged in his nefarious traffic was killed by a company of Congo Free State soldiers. The remnant of Socitota's large caravan arrived at Nana Kandundu in charge of his brother, having managed to escape with a number of slaves. One man had carried a little boy on his shoulder for over a week—not from kindness to the boy, but hoping to exchange him at Nana Kandundu for a goat or a pig. He had cut the throat of the rest of his slaves, he said, but this child escaped a similar fate because he was light and easily carried. This man had hawked the child round the Lovale villages for some time before I heard of him, but no purchaser was found, and I gladly gave the man the price of a goat for him. Little more than skin and bone, Ngoi was unable to stand upright from sheer weakness, and because of a twist in his back from being carried so long over the man's shoulder, but I did not despair of pulling him through. He rode behind me on the mule all the way to Bihé, clinging with his sinewy little arms to my back, much as he had done to his mother's only a few months before.

" As the child gained strength and confidence he told his touching story with great pathos. He was given by his friends as security until a certain debt they had incurred was paid. Meanwhile the native traders from Bihé came along with their guns and many-coloured calico, and the temptation was too great to the man who held Ngoi as security, so he sold him to these ' Ishmaelites ' of West Central Africa. After long months of waiting in camp, where Ngoi was tied with a lot of other slave children, a start was made for Bihé, but they had not gone far when they met the Free State soldiers. Ngoi's master at once fastened a wooden shackle on his feet to keep him from running away, and he was put into a grass hut with other slaves, of whom, he said, there were hundreds. Then the fighting began. The bullets whizzed through the camp, and Ngoi was very much afraid. Struggling to free himself of his shackle, he succeeded in knocking out the pin that held his feet in, and off he rushed to the bush. In a hollow tree near by he found refuge, but several bullets struck the tree. At last Socitota's camp took fire, and little Ngoi, from his hollow tree saw the flames and heard the shrieks of the poor slaves, all fastened together, as they were burned to death. Then night came, and all was still , the hyenas came round, and poor Ngoi thought he would never escape their jaws. Towards morning one of Socitota's men stole back to the burned camp in search of his master's body, which he found and buried, and also released Ngoi from the tree and carried him off after the retreating caravan. All this must have been a terrible experience for the poor little boy. They had to travel very quickly, and from morning till night. All the other children in Ngoi's company were killed one after the other. His master lifted his axe time after time to give him the fatal blow, and followed him with it over his little head, saying, ' Now, if you stop I will kill you.' He was, however, brought on to Nana Kandundu, and we trust that he will also be freed from the bondage of sin and Satan.

" Leaving Nana Kandundu with Ngoi, my journey to Kuanjulula was quickly and safely accomplished by November 27th, and I was very thankful to find all well and the work progressing.

" It was a pleasure to find the new workers applying themselves successfully to the study of the Umbundu language. I have often observed that, unless new-comers apply themselves closely to learn an African language during their first few months in the country, they rarely so master it as to accurately understand what the natives say, or to express themselves with ease or fluency, even though they may have years of residence and of desultory and interrupted study.

" ' I have set before thee an open door ' was brought forcibly to my mind as I saw, on returning to Kuanjulula, the access that Dr. Fisher had to the surrounding villages and people. It became my joyful privilege to unite with him in this work, which came as a restful and refreshing change after the bustle and arduousness of travel. When on the march with carriers there are, it is true, opportunities afforded us of preaching to the men night after night, which we always embrace ; but gospel work among the villages is in every way pleasanter and more satisfactory, inasmuch as we are free from the distractions peculiar to ' the road '—paying off and engaging men, disputings as to pay, rations, etc. At Kuanjulula we arranged to hold special meetings during the moonlight nights, at which we could get together from 20 to 150 hearers every evening. During these village preachings we had our full share of exercise of heart, both of joy and grief, among those who heard, and some of whom we are thankful to add have believed in Christ. One young woman, D——, has been a typical case of the ' good ground,' for not only has she received salvation herself, but by her prayers and zeal she has gained her cousin for Christ. Another, C——, has proved the power of the Word of God in the heart to stimulate the mind to study the art of reading and writing, and thus he has been able to read the Scriptures for himself. Another, S——, for whom much intercession had been made, after the preaching of the Gospel in his uncle's village, confessed himself a sinner in the sight of God. Since then the poor man has lost nearly all his children, five of them dying within a few months. Of course his friends ascribe these deaths in his family to the displeasure of the spirits of his forefathers, who, they say, are enraged at him for associating himself with the white man and his religion. To some extent poor S—— has been brought to a standstill by this overwhelming trial, yet he not only continues to come to the meetings, but also his friends with him. We had our own suspicions regarding the death of all these children.

"On the other hand there are those who did run well, but who now walk no longer with us. One who was baptised publicly as a Christian, has not only been put away from the Lord's Table, but also prohibited the premises of Kuanjulula because of his wicked and depraved example.

"Some have sought instruction, and professed themselves enquirers after God, merely with a view to improve their temporal condition. The tendency of the African to be inflated and uplifted presents a great difficulty to the Christian teacher. How to instruct the mind, and yet humble the heart; how to clothe the body, and yet strip the soul, are problems that continually confront us. The effort to awaken any conscience toward God ever reminds us of our dependence upon His Holy Spirit. Suppose, for instance, that you visit a sick man; he may possibly tell you that he has a bad conscience; his heart smites him; he has done wrong; and that is why he is sick. At first sight it would seem that the man was, from a Christian's standpoint, in a hopeful condition, but upon further enquiry you will probably discover that his omission of some act of gross wickedness is really what is troubling his mind. He thinks, perhaps, that he has offended the spirit of his grandfather, because he has not avenged his death at the hands of some witch long since dead, but whose children are still alive, and to this neglect of revenge against them he attributes his present sickness."

After Arnot's return from escorting the small party to Nana Kandundu, the state of his health caused much concern. The first visit home in 1888 had failed to remove the effects of fever contracted in the Barotse Valley. Acting on the advice of his brother-in-law, Dr. Walter Fisher, Arnot accordingly left Bihé with his wife and little girl, reaching England in June, 1892. In the following March, 1893, he was able to write .

" In looking back to the time when I took my solitary journey to the centre of the continent in 1886, I can only thank God that He has stirred up the hearts of not a few to care for *this* part of Africa. The steps of 27 persons have been directed thither, and though three of these were only permitted to lay down their lives in the Dark Continent, the rest are yet alive, and nineteen are now at work. My wife and I hope to return as soon as possible, and more labourers, we trust, will follow."

CHAPTER XVIII

THE THIRD JOURNEY

IT was two years before Arnot was able to return to Africa He quite hoped to return to Bihé and merely visited his doctor to get his approval. The doctor, however, was very firm in refusing permission, so although it cost him much he at once made up his mind to make his home in England until more definite consent could be given. With his wife and child he settled at Waterloo, near Liverpool, that being the port for the line of steamers which was used at that time to take the missionaries of the " Brethren " to Benguella. All goods for these workers in Central Africa were also despatched from this port, and Arnot was able to supervise the shipping arrangements. Whilst engaged in this work he was able to initiate, in conjunction with the late Mr. Brooke Broadbent, what afterwards proved to be a series of missionary conferences which were held yearly at different centres in the North of England. Many were stirred by means of these gatherings to go to the foreign field, and others were stimulated to give the necessary help.

In the early part of this interval at home Arnot paid a short visit to the United States. He met Mr. Moody in Chicago, and this enterprising leader wanted to secure him for the Northfield Convention. A severe attack of influenza, however, prevented this arrangement from being carried out, and Arnot returned to England sooner than was originally intended.

During 1893 and the early months of 1894, letters from the field told of new trials and difficulties besetting the workers. The hope had been long entertained that the workers in the Garenganze would be able to receive all their supplies from the West Coast, and that the opening of the station at Nana Kandundu, and probably another in the Chokwe country, would greatly facilitate their doing so. A porterage, however, of twelve hundred miles through native territory, with the constant risk of tribal warfare blocking the route, was from the beginning a precarious undertaking. But now in addition to this the station in the Garenganze was in danger of complete isolation, owing to the occupation of that country by Captain Stairs on behalf of the Congo Free State. A letter from Captain Stairs to Arnot told of a new order of things there, and of the possibility of the West Coast trade route being stopped Msidi had been killed during the proceedings connected with the occupation The Zanzibaris, attached to Captain Stairs' expedition, would not rest until the head of the once great enemy of the Arab trader had been cut off. Mwenda, the son of Msidi, was recognised as chief in his father's stead, and a Belgian officer was installed as magistrate. The Congo Free State Government at first forced the natives to scatter. In addition to this dispersion a suspicion was aroused in the minds of many of the Va-Garenganze against the missionaries. A section of the people looked upon the conquest of their country as a very clever piece of deception and generalship from the time of the arrival of the first missionary in the country to the cutting off of Msidi's head. Messrs. Thompson and Crawford decided therefore to remove to Lake Mweru, taking with them a host of adherents, men, women and children. The isolated missionaries hoped that from the new site it might be possible to open up communications with the East Coast. In the meantime they were greatly in need of supplies and were feeling the pinch keenly. Arnot decided that these circumstances constituted a new call to proceed to Africa, first to take supplies to the stranded workers, and secondly to ascertain the possibilities of the East Coast route and its possible advantages over the West Coast.

Leaving his wife and two children (a second child, Nigel, having been born in England) in Liverpool, Arnot left England in August, 1894, with Mr. Benjamin Cobbe, a man whom Arnot described as possessed " of much quiet, constant zeal, and habitually prayerful and studious."

Proceeding to Durban, Arnot called at Capetown and Port Elizabeth, and was welcomed by the assemblies of the " Brethren " in these centres and established a fellowship with South African gatherings that bore rich fruit in mutual spiritual help and in practical support of the work in the mission field. Writing to his wife from the home of Mr. Trill, Arnot said :

" The first night ashore was very enjoyable. I lay awake nearly all night listening to the ring-doves, the tree crickets, the frogs and other night insects. Then just before daybreak the night-jay set up his shrill call, that used to wake one up so often to the scramble and hurry-scurry of an early morning march. Then the clear, still air ! There is nothing or no place equal to it. You must come along, love. . . . Mrs. Trill is asking me to promise that you will stay here on your way to join me next spring . . . All are delighted with the babies' pictures, indeed I have only to produce them, and they act like the proverbial ' touch of nature.' "

Whilst waiting at Capetown for a steamer for Durban, the late Cecil Rhodes sent Arnot an invitation to meet him. Concerning this meeting, Arnot wrote : " Mr. Rhodes had many questions to ask about the Garenganze country, and hoped that the brethren there would be willing to train young men as telegraph clerks, etc., so that they might earn good wages and be useful to the large commercial companies and European governments It was not very easy for me to explain to him that we were rather hoping to find ways and means of teaching the native boys trades that would keep them at home. The African native cannot be employed on trading stations and Government posts without developing a strong inclination to pick up the white man's vices ; and even when congregated in mining compounds, or on plantations under the best control, they are still exposed to what might be called ' barrack life ' temptations. The natives can weave and work in metals, as well as farm, all of course in a rough way. Our ambitions, therefore, I explained to Mr. Rhodes, lay rather in the line of stimulating these industries, and in preserving African village life."

Writing from " off East London," Arnot said : " We went ashore at Port Elizabeth for two days and met with several very nice people. We had two prolonged conferences. An ' Exclusive ' evangelist has come along teaching household baptism, with the result that the leading brother in the open meeting had all his family baptised. The ' Exclusive ' evangelist was present and tried to defend his theories. I do not know what the result will be, but I think our arrival there was opportune. . . . I am getting on nicely with Swahili. There is a native of Zanzibar on board who speaks English. It was very soon evident that my way of learning languages is by conversation, and through contact with the people, for in a short time I was talking with the man. The bookwork is very slow work to me."

In September, 1894, Arnot and Cobbe embarked at Durban in a flat-bottomed coasting steamer able to cross the bar of the Chinde mouth of the Zanzibar. At Chinde they went on board the African Lakes Corporation's steamer *George Stevenson*. They went as passengers of the African Lakes Corporation from Chinde to Tanganyika, " entirely at our own risk," Arnot said, " as the Arabs were giving the British Administration a good deal of trouble, or *vice versa*. This Company (A.L.C.) was promoted with a view to assisting missionaries with their transports, and of promoting industry and legitimate commerce among the natives. The A.L.C. bears the brunt of the conflict with the Arabs of Lake Nyassa over their slave dealing propensities. . . . River travelling in Africa is always restful and interesting. We often ran aground on sandbanks and remained fast for an hour or two. At such times the crew would have to jump into the water and help to push off, the Captain leaving the bridge and urging the men to ' pusha ' with a long stick."

From Katungas, on October 9th, 1894, Arnot writes to his wife concerning the possible changing of all that they had planned for the future on account of a return of his old troubles : " We have got to the end of the river journey, 14 days. I am greatly pleased with it. It is a much better channel than I expected to find, and it is surprising what an amount of traffic goes on. From this port to Blantyre goods are carried by porters, and about 500 men come down on an average per day for work. . . . My own stupid spleen has been getting bigger, which suggests very gently that I may not be able to remain in the country for over a year or so at a time. I have not had a single touch of fever. So it is probable that I will arrange with the A.L C. Manager for any coming out next year for the Garenganze, probably better be brethren only, then go on with Cobbe to Mweru, see Dan Crawford and then work my way by tepora to Nana Kandundu and Bihé, where I may be helpful to all. In this case you will stay on at Waterloo with our sweet pets until Pe-pe comes back. There would be no use my coming back this way unless it were to meet you, and I could not hope to make you comfortable and help others in a semi-disabled

R

condition, as this spleen trouble seems to amount to. . . . This will be a great disappointment to you, but were you to come out and I not able to remain more than a year or two in the country it would be very sad indeed."

The following extracts from letters to Mrs Arnot tell of the progress of the journey, and of incidents *en route* :

" *Upper Shire River*, 16*th Oct*, 1894.—I was asked to preach in the church at Blantyre on Sunday evening, when nearly all the white people turned out. The church is a wonderful building, and the service decidedly ritualistic. I took substitution for my subject. . . . My only objection to this route is that there are so many missionaries along it that one is not so much needed. . . . The only advantage of this route is the transport. The changing from river to land journeying, the bustle and traffic at the stations, the tin fare and the protracted exposure to the heat of these river-ways is a long way inferior to our pleasant journey with our own Ovimbundu up to Bihé, and were carriers only sufficiently plentiful nothing could equal the West Coast route in comfort.

" *Karonga*, 31*st Oct.*, 1894 —Your own hub is wonderfully well again. Since getting out of the Lower Zambesi I have felt very well in spite of the heat. I am very glad, however, I wrote you not to come this way. Honestly I don't think you would stand it. The heat has been in excess even of Benguella heat, and day and night ; then fever seems to be as common and deadly as on the Congo. Certainly none of our bairnies could stand it. Then there are so many missionary societies contending for every inch of ground, I was going to say, right on to Lake Mweru. The East Coast route is not to be compared to our West Coast route provided carriers were only more plentiful at Bihé, so that I think I am right in planning meanwhile to go out to Bihé and test the matter afresh by spending a month or two there and getting a caravan together. This might lead in all probability to our taking up our quarters again in Bihé.

" Tell Ray that coming up in the steamer we had six Sikh soldiers on board and they were all seasick, so that there were six seasick Sikhs.

" The little river steamer we travelled in was not able to take us very far up the Shire River, so we were compelled to complete the journey to Lake Nyassa by boat. As we neared the lake we had to run the gauntlet of one or two hostile villages. At one point we had to land, as the channel was completely blocked by hippos. I shot one, hoping that the others would move off. But the old bull of the herd landed in a rage, and came running along the sandy shore of the river to destroy our boat. I ran to meet him with my rifle, Cobbe following me with cartridges. My first few shots seemed of no avail; they glanced off his great skull, so, as a last effort, I knelt on one knee, and was able thus to sight his chest and to plant a bullet in it that must have pierced the heart, for he rolled over sideways, to our great relief, and fell into the river. When our men began to cut up the hippo, throwing the offal into the river, with parts of the meat they did not want, we witnessed a most extraordinary sight. About twenty large crocodiles came racing through the water from all directions and fought over the meat.

"*Fife Station*, 13*th Nov.*, 1894.—I am not going to say anything more about our future plans, whether our home should continue in England, Garenganze or Bihé or anywhere else. I am just going to leave it. At any rate I feel sure it will be my duty to come home for you. . . . My spleen is still in evidence and I had one sick spell after riding Cobbe's donkey for a forenoon. . . . I have been travelling mostly in a tepoia, although on this side one needs to employ ten men, and then keep very wide awake. They rush you along and bring you against all the tree stumps in the country and bob you up and down like a pea on a pan. They hardly know how to carry an ordinary load, and boxes weighing about 60 lb. require two men."

Writing at a later date concerning conversations during this period, Arnot said :

"The missionaries are not united in their work. Some quite laugh at the idea of doing anything by means of preaching and think education and industrial work to be the most helpful. I point out to them that our fellow-countrymen, with education and religious training, and some even with Christian profession, living immoral lives, having no more strength to resist sin than the Portuguese or Arab, prove beyond all question that all are in the same natural condition and that all must be born again, recreated, and that this spiritual change can be as truly accomplished in the most ignorant as well as the learned.

" When we reached Lake Nyassa we went on board the s.s. *Domira*. Mr. Chalmers, the Captain, an ' 1859 revival ' convert, was a delightful man , he gave us a hearty welcome. In his younger days he had owned a fishing smack that sailed from Rothesay, but a storm swept all his nets away one day, and he had to compromise with his creditors, to his great regret. With the one desire to pay them back in full, he faced all the trials and privations of Central Africa. The happy day at last came when he paid them their 20s. to the £, with interest. And he showed me the watch his creditors had subscribed to him, with a suitable inscription upon it. No matter who came on board Capt. Chalmers' steamer, all had to join in the evening worship.

" Lake Nyassa was still in the hands of the slave dealers, and Arab dhows were to be seen cutting across the lake. One morning we saw from the deck of the steamer a large impi of Bangoni—a far-wandered, Zulu-speaking tribe—with their long shields and short, stabbing spears, raiding a village of Atonga. We landed at Bandawe and spent a few hours with Dr. and Mrs. Laws, but, a storm coming up, we had to return to the steamer and run before it to a sheltering bay.

" Disembarking at Karonga, we were greeted by swarms of Kakonde women, wading into the water, offering to carry our bag and baggage over the long shallow stretch of water, lying between the steamer and the shore. Karonga is the beginning of the Stevenson road, made in order to unite Lake Nyassa and Lake Tanganyika, another example of disinterested interest in the opening up of Central Africa, the late Mr. Stevenson deriving no benefit from the outlay this engineering project involved.

" An Arab trader, Malose, had built his fortified village at the very back door of Karonga   Mr. Cobbe and I had not much difficulty in slipping past Malose's stronghold, and we were soon passing by the head waters of the Chambesi River on our way across the plateau.

" Lake Tanganyika was a grand sight. The south end of it appeared to be a vast, deep sheet of water, surrounded by mountain ranges, furrowed with deep ravines down which fierce storms rush, whipping the lake into white squalls. After some delay we were able to employ sufficient carriers to take us over the hundred miles that lie between Lakes Tanganyika and

Mweru. Being entire strangers, the Ba-mwanga did not trust us But by turning my attention to the women, and giving them fair prices for the meal they brought, and small presents to their children, I proved again that ' the hand that rocks the cradle rules the world.' The women returned to their kraals singing our praises, and their men-folk soon turned out.

" Crossing Lake Tanganyika in a boat belonging to the L.M.S. we landed at the head of Cameron Bay on the west shore. . . .

" The political condition of the country to the west of Tanganyika is peculiar. We have to go back perhaps thirty or forty years ago, before the Arab began to cross the Lake. Then it would seem to have been a well-peopled country. The Arab does not attack a country, as a rule, in such a way as to compel the people to band together in self-defence, but appears first as a trader, then chooses some fertile spot near to the village of some chief with whom he has ' made friendship ' and whose daughter he marries, and asks permission to build a camp there, while his people go to the coast to bring more cloth. The temporary camp is gradually made stronger, a good store of gunpowder is secured, and the Arab gradually becomes more insolent and exacting to his friend. One case in point was brought before Mr. Knight, who is in charge of the Administration Station at Sumba, the other day when an old man besought him to release his daughter who was in the clutches of an Arab of the name of Meso. Meso years ago had been his sworn friend. One day he had asked the old man to pay him a visit and bring all his wives and children with him, as he wished to give them all presents of beads and calico. ' Get meal ground and let us carry a present to Meso,' said the old man to his wives, and so off they set. Meso made all the women and children prisoners, gave the old man a severe thrashing and sent him away. All had been sold, too, at the coast with the exception of their one daughter, whom Mr. Knight was able to restore to her father. Thus little by little the country has been depopulated. Mr. Cobbe and I visited one of these Arab camps the other day. A large square was found with huts of slaves, roofed with earth so as to be proof against fire. The huts in the centre of the enclosure were all built in the same way, also the chief's house in the centre. Mats and rugs were spread for us on his verandah. Since the British occupation these Arabs have lost their power, as well as many of their slaves, and in

the Belgian territory their camps have been broken up and
many of the Arabs killed. The man we visited deplored in a
lamentable way the cruelty of the white man, and the barbarous,
unjust warfare he was waging against the innocent, unoffend-
ing Arab, who always treated him kindly, gave him rice, helped
him on his expeditions, etc.

" From Cameron Bay we had to bore our way through a
perfect tangle of rubber vine, the men creeping on their hands
and knees and pulling their loads after them. Grassy plains
then opened up before us as we travelled westward   The bones
of thousands of buffalo and other animals lay in patches here
and there, victims of the terrible rinderpest plague that swept
the country of cattle and game, from Uganda southward.
Further on we came to a pool of water in a dried-up river bed,
with about 50 hippos in it, all trying to keep themselves wet
until the rains should fall again. An Arab invited us to spend
the night in his boma rather than expose ourselves to the lions,
which, owing to the death of the game, had turned to man-
eating   Indeed, lions, zebras and elephants seemed to have the
veldt to themselves. One day our men came on a troop of lions
that had pulled down a young cow elephant. They drove them
off, and brought the meat and tusks of the elephant along with
them.

" The Vinanwanga, who inhabit this country, seem to be
pure Bantu ; they extract the lower front teeth like the Baluba,
and the women cut and draw out the lobe of the ear to such an
extent that they are able to insert a circular ornament as large
as a billiard ball in circumference, and about half an inch in
thickness. Curiously enough this tribe is not used to the hoe for
cultivating their fields ; although they are, or used to be, large
manufacturers of iron, judging from the number of upright
smelting furnaces found throughout the country. They live
chiefly on a small red millet. The fields in which this millet
is grown are prepared by heaping together a great mass of
timber and branches of trees, till the ground is covered to the
depth of two or three feet ; when thoroughly dried, the wood
is burned. At the beginning of the rainy season the seed is
scattered over the wood ash. The same field, I am told, is
seldom sown a second year ; so it is easy to understand how
a very small community can destroy immense forests. The
fact is that there is very little of the better class of woods

found in this country, showing that this destructive process has gone on for long. The better roots of wood, which are always slow growing, have not a chance to renew themselves, while the softer trees, piactically useless for building purposes, have sprung up.

" *Nov. 18th*, 1894.—Arrived at French R.C. Mission Station, and had lunch and dinner with the seven ' White Friars ' we found there. They all seemed to be living together in a peaceful sort of a way, reminding us very much of those I met on the Upper Zambesi about twelve years ago. One hears continually, from Colonial traders and others, of quarrels among the Protestant missionaries, that have become public scandals ; but one hears nothing of quarrels among the Roman Catholic missionaries, the perfect order and discipline undoubtedly the reason ; each ' Father ' or ' Brother ' has his allotted place and work ; there is no room left for striving as to who should be the greatest, for all their relative positions of importance are already allotted to them ; but might not our Lord have done the same and for ever settled the question as to who should be the greatest and chief disciple. His only answer was, however, and in what startling contrast to all human wisdom, ' He that is least, shall be greatest.' What scope we have for continually exercising ourselves in becoming less. The Divine path and plan after all are only possible to crucified and slain men.

" *Nov. 19th* —Great trouble in getting our men along. They are so hungry that every fruit tree we come to makes them halt in spite of all my urgings. I managed to shoot three antelopes, however, just as we arrived in camp, so the men got a good supper.

" *Nov. 20th*.—Arrived at the large village of Kera. It was refreshing to see so many people together, even though I was not able to speak to them. They belong to the Mambwe tribe, formerly wholly subject to the Va-wemba, but since the British occupation they are free. We passed the ruins of a large village that had been burned to the ground. It had become infested with the jigger, or penetrating flea, and as this insect, so well known on the West Coast, has just recently found its way across to these parts, the people do not know how to deal with it, and in this case, I suppose, in despair, they set fire to their houses and built their village on a fresh site.

" *Nov. 26th*.—What Kipling sang of the Imperialists is true of the army of pioneers who are now bleaching in Africa on account of the callousness and forgetfulness of home friends :

"'In the faith of little children they went on their way,
Then the wood failed, then the food failed, then the last water dried
In the faith of little children they lay down and died
On the sandbelt, on the veld side, in the fern scrub they lay
That their sons might follow after by the bones upon the way.'

" As we approached Lake Mweru the forest became more dense. One morning, to our great delight, we met Mr. Thompson a few hours from the lake shore. He had kindly come to meet us, leaving Mr. Crawford in his camp at Chipungu.

" Mweru has nothing of the grandeur of the two great lakes we had just left behind us. But it is a beautiful sheet of water, and the hills around are covered with forests. We walked round the sandy beach to the north end of the lake, crossed the Lualaba, and climbed up to Chipungu. To our surprise we found that, during Mr. Thompson's short absence, Mr. Crawford had been joined by Mr. D. Campbell from the West Coast, so we had much to talk about. An excursion was made to the south to look out for a better site than Chipungu, as Mr. Crawford was anxious for more room for his people to build and cultivate. Finally, Luanza was decided upon, and there, sitting on the stump of a tree, the local chiefs gave their consent to the laying out of the station

" I recognised quite a number of old faces among the natives that had built at Mweru. One young man, who had been a faithful friend to Crawford, was one of Msidi's junior executioners. He had often heard the Gospel, and had grown very hard and indifferent to it, but the gentle words of a woman dying under his cruel hands, as she pleaded with him to 'deal kindly with her child,' impressed him in this way, ' What the missionaries say about me is true, I am indeed a very wicked man.' At one of the meetings, he stood up and publicly confessed that ' now he knew the blood of Jesus was sufficient for the washing away of a black man's sins as well as those of a white man.' He told us that for months he had been wrestling with the devil, who kept telling him that ' a black sinner like him, a shedder of innocent blood, could not hope to be forgiven as easily as a good white man.' Poor people, I am afraid their early notions about ' the good white men ' have been sadly upset in those remote parts since those days ;

so that the devil has been robbed of at least one argument. Far from making it our business—as some of our enemies say we do —to persuade the black man that he is as good as the white man, we often have enough to do to prove that he is as bad as the white man, and in need of the same Saviour.

" The after life of Mishe-mishe proved that this confession by the lake was real. The story, too, of how he got over the difficulty of having five wives, as told by Mr. Crawford, is most interesting. Finding that Mr. Crawford was not prepared to advise him as to what he should do, and only persisted in assuring him that God knew, and by His Holy Spirit would enlighten him, he went home and did not come again for advice. Calling his wives together, he said that if *one* were willing to remain with him he would divide all his property between the four. One chose to abide as a poor man's wife, and the others gladly carried off their portions to their paternal villages. Mrs. Crawford taught Mishe-mishe the elements of ambulance work, and of cleansing and doctoring ulcers, so with a linen bag over his shoulder, he visited the many villages around, reminding the people of what he was at one time, but now that he was a Christian he was willing to wash out and bind up their sores.

" *Chipungu, Lake Mweru, 7th Jan.*, 1895.—(To Mrs Arnot.) If you only saw the long, long screeds of letters that I had written to you, and now I am tearing them all up Well! the story is soon told. I was completely carried away with things here : site, prospect of work, etc., that I decided to remain, wrote out a telegram for you to meet me at Natal, and spent two days writing you instructions, orders, commands, entreaties, advices, etc. Well! we waited. That night I was laid aside with severe pain in spleen; next day prolonged agony. Crawford and the others began praying me home. Now I am over it. But my spleen is as large nearly as ever it was, so that I have lost in a few months what took eighteen months to repair. I may start back in a month or otherwise. . . All seem happy about it. In fact Crawford and the others seem to think that my place is at home, health or no health. So we will be more settled now. I am exceedingly thankful that I have come and got fairly in touch with this route. . . . It has been a hard decision to come to, that my African days were gone by, but now that it is so let us live for the work at home.

" Spending those happy weeks at Mweru, and hearing the story of the cross told out so fully, in the very heart of Africa, as the only point of meeting between sinful man and a sinless God, was to me an abundant reward for all the toils of pioneer and transport work that had fallen to my share.

" Mr. Campbell accompanied me as far as Lake Tanganyika ; I was thankful for his company, as a serious illness overtook me. At Cameron Bay I rested and recovered sufficiently to allow of our crossing the lake, in the middle of which we were caught in a twirling storm of wind and rain, and sent flying back towards the west shore. How we kept afloat that night is a mystery to me, as the waves were literally covering our little ship. By one o'clock in the morning we found we were nearing a rocky island ; we managed to control the boat sufficiently to bring her up under the shelter of this island and drop anchor. When morning broke we completed our voyage.

" *Lake Nyassa, on board ' Ilala,' 2nd March,* 1895.—I have crossed the plateau safely and quickly in spite of the continuous rain. . . . I came on board the *Ilala* on the 28th February. We had to row in a boat for hour and a half to Kambe Bay, where she was lying. . . . We had supper and a big crocodile came up close by and I shot it. Night fell. We were preparing to turn in ; the native crew getting steam up and ready to start about three or four in the morning when ' boate,' ' boate ' comes from the shore. It was now pitch dark, but the boat which the *Ilala* tows behind her went off in the direc-tion. Shortly it returned. A black hand thrust in to me through the window a letter rolled up in calico. I opened it and there was your telegram. Well ! Imagine my delight. The O.C. Co. agent at Kituta, Lake Tanganyika, had sent it back after me. What a relief ! What a mercy ! Next morning I was awake at four and lying thinking of the Lord's goodness and mercy that had indeed followed me. I asked in prayer for some promise for this dear little boy that I had not seen. . . . I began to wonder how the answer would come, I thought and thought, and at last getting up I turned up the lamp, opened my Bible ; my eyes fell on Isaiah xliv, and there in the third verse read : ' I will pour water upon him that is thirsty, and floods upon the dry ground. I will pour my spirit upon thy seed and my blessing upon thine offspring.' In the little steam cabin, by that flickering lamp, in the dark early morning. I heard God, as it were, speak this word of promise to me. It came a direct answer to my request.

"*Inhambane, 23rd March.*—I met a young man at Chinde who had just come up from Natal. I heard him whisper to another, ' That's Fred Arnot.' Then he came round and asked me if I was Mr. A. Whereupon he began consoling me upon the death of my father. I could hardly believe it at first. However, I have since seen a Natal paper dated March 8th, with notice of father's death. How I did wish to be able to wire home to mother. I wonder how the dear old mother has stood it. It was quite a shock to me."

On the voyage home from Capetown to England Arnot met the late Rev Dr. Andrew Murray for the first time. Mr Murray was then for the fourth period Moderator of the Dutch Reformed Church of South Africa. The Rev. George Robson, Wesleyan minister of Capetown, is fond of telling of the enjoyable and helpful fellowship he had on that occasion with these two men of God. The first Sunday out the service in the saloon was taken by a dignitary of the Anglican Church and was followed by a Communion Service. Mr. Arnot, Mr. Murray and Mr. Robson discussed together whether they should join in the latter. As Mr. Murray had presented himself for communion on a previous occasion on board ship and been refused participation, it was decided not to run the risk of a similar experience now but to break bread together in Mr. Murray's cabin. But the regular service itself they all attended. At this they listened to a sermon that for dreariness and childishness would be hard to beat. Mr. Arnot and Mr. Robson were anxious to get an expression of opinion from Mr. Murray about the discourse, so they asked him what he thought of it. After a pause, stroking his chin, and with a twinkle in his eye, the great saint said · " Well ! It is a poor hen that can't get a few grains out of a muck heap."

CHAPTER XIX

YIELDING to medical advice, Arnot remained in England for several years. For five years, from 1895 to 1900, he lived with his family in Liverpool. The time was spent in pastoral work, in giving missionary lectures up and down the country, and in helping missionaries by training them in dispensary work amongst the poor, and guiding them in their studies and in the selection of their outfits.

With the help of his friend, Mr. Nightingale of Shrewsbury, village work was started in the north of England. Many young men gave up the whole of their summer holidays to this enterprise, and many were the testimonies received of the good done in this way.

In 1897, Arnot visited British Guiana in South America, where there were a number of assemblies of Brethren, and where considerable interest in the work in Africa had been stirred up among the descendants of Africans, and from amongst whom not a few volunteered to carry the Gospel back to their own people.

To his fellow-workers in Central Africa, Arnot wrote from Liverpool, under date December 20th, 1897. "Notes on a visit to British Guiana," from which we extract the following·

" Knowing that there is much in common between the work in Africa among the Africans, and in British Guiana among descendants of the same race I thought the following remarks would interest you.

" Although the work in British Guiana is now in its third generation it is full of life and vigour. The foundations were carefully laid, not so much by men who were pre-eminently wise but pre-eminently godly and devoted. The work began, not among half-civilised blacks, or blacks who had the advantage of learning the English language, for the slaves as they were

brought over were put entirely under Dutch or English over-
seers who delighted in teaching them the little they learned
wrongly. What between the two languages, Dutch and English,
a strange dialect came to be used by them that must have
brought them much lower down in the scale of intelligence than
when they used their African dialects. When the older Christians stood up in the meetings, Mr. Bergin and I were quite
unable to understand them—they might have been speaking
Italian or Chinese. Then, what little morality that existed
in African custom was nearly entirely driven out of the slaves ;
there was no marriage of slaves ; mothers were not allowed to
bring up their children, but at once had to give them up to the
plantation nurses and turn to their work again. Fetish worship
survived, for the Africans brought it as a common inheritance
from all parts of the continent ; and the ' obea men,' or
witch doctors, are found to-day along the rivers of the colony.
The only thing that helped the Gospel in any way was their
wretchedness and misery.

" I was interested in coming across the record of a contract
made by the Dutch Co. with a Portuguese Co. at the Cape Verde
Islands, which lie nearly on the same latitude as British Guiana,
for the supply of so many ' Angola slaves,' so that this verified
my own impressions on landing in the colony that the black
people came chiefly from the Bantu tribes.

" Besides the descendants of the early African slaves, there
are many Africans and their children now in British Guiana
who were taken from Spanish and Portuguese vessels and
liberated on the high seas by British men-of-war. Probably
the bulk of these were brought from countries south of the
Congo. Four I met with in two assemblies were able to understand me when I spoke to them in Umbundu ; and in answer
to my questions I learned that one came originally from the
Barotse country, that she was brought out to Bihé by Sen.
Jao, Silva Porto's slave, and then when she was a young woman
was taken to the coast and sold and put on board a Spanish
vessel which was captured by a British man-of-war. Another
was a native of the Valumbe tribe. Two came from the Lunda
country and the fourth from Ambacca. Two of the women
spoke Umbundu perfectly, and are now giving lessons to those
who are exercised about going to Africa."

(Then follow descriptions of how the bitter cassava or manioc and the paupau are used as articles of food, which method Arnot urges for Africa, also remarks upon the different persons proposing to come out.)

" The interest in Africa stirred up by the going forth of Murrain and O'Jon has, they say, been a great blessing to all the assemblies. The colony is suffering just now from the low price of sugar, and still, with the greatest courage, they pray the Lord to raise up and send labourers to Africa. They collect what they can, and in some of the poorest of houses I saw boxes made up for Africa. On the other hand those who are coming forward to go are giving up something in doing so, and are not going merely for the sake of a livelihood."

Returning from South America to Liverpool, Arnot suffered, as he had also done in his previous residence at that centre, from repeated malarial attacks. Advised by a malarial expert to try a drier climate the home was removed to Clifton, near Bristol. Messrs. Wright and Bergin of the Muller Orphan Homes were especially warm in the welcome extended to Arnot in this new centre. Four very happy years of fellowship with the friends there passed all too quickly Help was given to the large assemblies meeting at Alma, Bethesda, and Stokescroft, and also to the smaller gatherings in the outlying districts.

The change south so improved Arnot s health that when in 1904 a party of workers from the United States and from British Guiana set out to pay their debt to the heathen he decided to join them at Lisbon, and to lead them to the vacant field in the Chokwe country, stretching far to the east of Bihé. Prior, however, to joining these workers, Arnot with his wife, made a trip to the continent of Europe, and contributed again an increase of interest in the cause of missions. His experiences are described in his diary as follows :

" *March* 14*th*, 1904.—The last kiss and hug all round with our bairns was the *real* farewell. A number of the many friends were at the station to see us off from Bristol at 2.7 p.m.

" Miss Jordan's farewell meeting was well attended, also the farewell meetings in the Devonshire House next day, afternoon and evening. Wednesday was spent in town shopping and making a few farewell visits. At 4 p.m. I visited, by invitation, Sir H. M. Stanley. Lady Stanley was very chatty, but poor Sir Henry, paralysed on the one side, was only able to speak feebly, but he seemed anxious to talk about Africa and was loud in praise of King Leopold, and of the purity of his motive in beginning the Congo Free State, but he could not be held responsible for all his officers. Lady Stanley was strong, however, in her denunciation of the rubber trading companies who had brought the Congo Free State, and her own husband's work and good name, into bad repute. Sir Henry asked for the members of Dr Livingstone's family, and was surprised to hear that Mrs. F. Wilson had gone to Sierra Leone.

"*March 17th.*—Last night's crossing was very pleasant. Antwerp lies on the banks of the Scheldt. A tower is pointed out where the Spanish Inquisition executed its victims. The city itself is strongly fortified. We went to a good hotel and visited all the sights. Rubens' original masterpieces are to be seen in the Museum and in the Cathedral, and although I am not an art critic, there was something unique about these great masterpieces that must make them stand out in one's memory from all the pictures that one has seen or is ever likely to see. Going on to Brussels we passed near to where Tyndale was strangled by the orders of Henry VIII, who promised at the same time to see that a better translation of the Scriptures was translated. According to Green's *History*, Tyndale was known as belonging to the sect of the ' Brethren.' Belgium has been the scene of two great battles. The heroes of both were British—Tyndale and Wellington. Liberty to read the Bible in our own tongue was the fruit of the one, political liberty, to some extent, the fruit of the other. The one was fought in the shade, in closet, and by the printing presses of Antwerp. Tyndale appeared to lose the day. His light went out in the dark. He was strangled miserably, yet how great and lasting his victory compared with Wellington's.

" The Congo Free State officials received me very well, and could not have promised me more, and say they will send a *personalité civile* to me to Lisbon. Trottie's (Mrs. Arnot) French helped me in getting about. We had meetings nearly every night, either in the town or the country districts around Waterloo, there being a bright assembly at Braine l'Alleud, Wellington's right, and another at Bransbeek, his extreme left. Now we have come on to Charleroi, and are going out with Mr. Gaudebert to see a glass tumbler factory.

"*March 27th, Sunday.*—The meeting is at Dampremy, one mile from Charleroi. There are over 100 in fellowship, and attendance about 250, and that in a grossly Roman Catholic neighbourhood. Only a. few hundred yards distant from the hall, built in the garden of a Christian, there is the shrine of a saint that works miracles, and we looked in and saw a great many garments, underclothing, hanging up on the wall, not to be disinfected, but to be infected with virtue and stored with health— salted, as the Africans would say, with good. The Christians seemed to be all fairly well off, and some were intelligent men. They collect about £6 per week.

" *March* 28*th*.—We took farewell with M and Madame Gaudebert and left for Homburg, Frankfort, at two in the morning, via Cologne. We were turned out at five o'clock to have our luggage overhauled at the German frontier. Later on we arrived at Cologne, and had two hours to spare. The Cathedral and the Rhine are the two great sights. It was Holy week, and many were bowing down to the images of saints and crosses all round. In Belgium we saw processions of ' sons of Voltaire ' escorting bands of children to the temples of science to be initiated as infidels, and it is difficult to say which was the sadder sight.

" The train journey up the Rhine was very beautiful, ruined castles on every hill-top, and modern fortresses abounded, and the river was grand, just like the Lualaba as it passes through the Garenganze. Vineyards covered the slopes.

" At Frankfort we changed for Homburg. . . . I had two meetings here, a very good attendance and signs of awakening exist, they say, over all that part of Germany.

" *March* 29*th* —We came on to Krishona, an institution for the training of missionaries that has been carried on for forty years on faith lines. Herr Rapard is quite a G. Muller, very warm and helpful. We met with some interesting people. Mr. Wartz, the Secretary of the famous Basle Mission, met us at the railway station and took us to dinner. When at Krishona we had our first view of the Alps, and slept with our window open to the snow-capped peaks. Our next night was spent at Bienne. The train passed through lovely mountain scenery, and over dizzy chasms, and one grand waterfall. The meetings at Bienne were very hearty. On Saturday we visited Grindel-wald, close to the Vaterhorn. It was the first warm spring day after a good deal of snow and long winter, so we were favoured above many in seeing a grand display of avalanches, a rare sight, over forty torrents of snow and ice rolled down the mountains and over precipices, sounding like thunder in the chasms below.

"*Sunday, April 3rd.*—Large meetings at Bienne. On Monday we came on to Vevey, and Tuesday to Montreux, where we met with a regular colony of English people, Dr. and Mrs. Neatby among others. The rest of our time will be taken up with visits around the Lake of Geneva. Sunday I spend at Geneva, and Monday Trottie will start for home. On Tuesday night I go on to Barcelona, Madrid, Oporto and Lisbon."

s

CHAPTER XX

ON arriving at Bihé, in August, 1904, Arnot, and the party with him, had a great welcome from the natives. Many still remembered him.

Writing to Mrs. Arnot from Chindunda, July 23rd, he said : " We are now six days across the Kwanza. This is a wonderful country we are passing through for variety in flowers and butterflies. As yet it is quite unexplored. I have crossed large rivers that have no mention in the latest Portuguese maps. The ground orchids are much in evidence and all different from those on the Benguella road. Some of the butterflies too are so pretty that I will keep them by me, I think, safely packed in tins, and bring them home to the boys. As the district is new some may be valuable. . . . I am not the hardened African I had hoped to be after my long stay at home. I have had two turns of fever and ague since crossing the Kwanza, the last with rather a sharp temperature, rose to 104 5, but it responded so quickly and well to treatment that I am not a bit cast down over it. I must have been inoculated at Lucalla; there are no mosquitoes this side of the Kwanza, and regular dosing with quinine will work the microbes out. Still I was a little disappointed when I found the temperature persistently going up, and I will not likely push on to the Chibokwe as I had half hoped to do.

" We have had meetings with the men around the fire, and afterwards Kashinda has come into my tent for a reading lesson. So I am trying to be both you and me this time. Before, you did the teaching and I the talking. Now all seems so different. I have no care with the men. The road is perfectly safe and peaceful, and I can give my whole time and thought to the work, sending the two Christians to visit the villages and to repeat what they have been taught. It is very delightful. The other day a number of the natives of the district attended

the meeting in camp, and came in the morning and thanked me
for ' preaching forgiveness. We slept soundly,' they added,
' after hearing your words.' This whole district has never been
touched or visited by anyone. There are three tribes between
the Vandulu and the Kwanza, and no missionary has so much
as visited their villages at any time. Surely the ' judgment
that must begin at the house of God ' will have something to do
with these unvisited—unevangelised ?

" *Sikado (within two days of Ochilonda), July 31st, 1904.*—
Sanders persistently visits around all these villages every
three months or so. We came on yesterday passing six or
eight villages, and it is remarkable to see how the people have
advanced in cleanliness and clothing. You would hardly
believe it. To-day we have had quite a large meeting with
our men and villagers. Sanders says, in one word, the great
encouragement lies in the fact that Africans are now being used
to the conversion of Africans.

" The whole district within a radius of twelve miles is linked
up by well-made roads and bridges, allowing of bicycle and
donkey travelling by night or day. These roads lead to 25
schoolrooms and preaching stations, all built and supported
by the native church. And now the Christians are building
two-roomed rest houses for the use of the European missionaries
as they come along. The central meeting room holds over 800
people, and on special occasions it is generally full 'inside and out.'

" Well, August 3rd, we arrived in Owhalondo and Ochilonda,
and what a welcome ! Strings of boys and men and women ;
then the volleys ; then a hymn in the bush ; then a long
procession formed up, and on we marched : I on Mr. Lane's
donkey. The Murrains do look well. . . . The family sang
us some hymns of welcome, quite touching. The hymns had
been specially learned for the occasion and the schoolroom
done up with mottoes and welcomes. The villagers at Owhalondo gathered round the spot where we, that is you and I,
pitched our tent when on our way to the Ondulu country, and
one said, ' I was standing just here ' ; another, ' And I was
standing across the river,' and so on and so on. Then several
of the leading boys are our old Kuanjulula and kitchen boys,
Sai Wimbo among them. Best of all the work goes on. Three
have been converted the last few days. . . . I am in Hill's
old house. He has a large garden enclosure.

" You speak of my being in the midst of great African problems, etc. But all seems very easy and simple now. Men come forward freely for carrying, both to the coast and inland. Lane is quite capable and quite at home in all transport matters. Then the Portuguese could not be pleasanter, and taking it all round, the old difficult times seem to be passed. Or perhaps I have learned to take things easier. At any rate, I quite enjoy the insects and beetles and butterflies, and wish I could pack all home to the children. To-night the air is alive with flying ants coming up in myraids out of the ground. Won't the hens have a feed to-morrow !

" *Ochilonda, Bihé,* 14th *Aug.,* 1904.—Well ! one matter had to be decided before going to the fort, and that was, Who was to go on to the Chibokwe with our brethren. Of course, I was willing to go, and was planning to go ; but Lane had been hinting that he thought he ought to go. At last he came out with it definitely that he would like to go and escort the party, and then go and visit Kavungu and Kazombo and return again, so I gave way to him, and now I am settled here for the rainy season. I know this will be a great relief to you, and I am so glad to think that I am able to relieve Lane, and allow him to go on with the party, and it will be a cause of thanksgiving if a beginning is made among the Chibokwe.

" *Sept* 4th, 1904.—We have had a busy day again, and the problem is to know what to do with the people. Our buildings are all too small. I am improving daily in my speaking.

" *Sept.* 6th.—The kindergarten for the little blacks is great fun. They do enjoy it and laugh at one another's mistakes. The rule is that all must wash hands and face, and a basin was provided, if you please, but after washing their dirty hands, all in the same water, Miss Gammon found the little wretches drinking the water.

" Some of the young men who were converted when we were at Kuan are now useful Christians. Then you had only three or four girls under a tree to teach—now there are hundreds of women and children coming to the schools and meetings.

" *Oct.* 15th, 1904.—Last Sunday we were cheered with three new converts, one man and two women. It was a very happy day. The morning meetings are most spiritual and helpful. The Christian natives take part freely and never make mistakes. . . . My days are very regular when I am at home. In the forenoon I look after the garden. Then school in the afternoon, and if I am not taking the evening meeting I spend my evenings alone, reading, and often finish up with a quiet game of chess, copying some of the games given in *The Times* . . . All I long for, all I claim for our children is God's blessing. It maketh rich and addeth no sorrow. And if I can only leave to them an example of subjection to God's will, what a fortune ! I don't mean subjection in the stoical sense, but after Christ's example, ' I do delight to do Thy will, O God. Yes ! Thy law is within my heart.' . . . I am getting on with my afternoon class, and have started an evening class in one of my rooms, two large tables, two lamps and chairs all round. Some writing with pen and ink, others at sums, and I am getting them to ask questions on portions of Scripture that are difficult to them, and so the evenings pass on until 9 30   I thoroughly enjoy settling down to this regular station work, and must conclude now that my place is quietly to stay on here and not go inland. . . .

Sunday evening, Oct. 30th.—A happy day. The morning meeting most spiritual and helpful. Then my old men's class. About twenty of the chiefs and headmen around gathered in my room. The forenoon gospel service, packed out before I got there with grown up men and women in equal numbers, all looking so clean and well clothed compared with the old days. Mr Lane and I spoke   A number were standing outside, and they had come as usual from groups of villages all around. It is most impressive to see them break up and leave for home in little groups in all directions. Then we divided up and took meetings in the afternoon in four different villages all round. . . . We had such a helpful meeting this morning. These young men do take hold of the Scriptures. More intelligent words one seldom hears at home.

" How to teach the native Christian honest trades is a great problem   One effort in this direction greatly interested me, because of its far-reaching consequences. The art of sawing planks out of trees is of course the foundation of all carpentry in a new country, and many of the young men have been taught the use of the pit saw. And several have set up as rough door, window and furniture makers. But making coffins gradually grew to be the most profitable branch of these little businesses. The Ovimbundu are accustomed to make much of funerals. The body is usually kept for weeks enclosed in a faggot of

sticks until quantities of beer have been brewed and friends
have had time to assemble from a distance. Then with feasting
and drinking and firing of guns the body is carried down to the
plain or valley, carried on the shoulders of two men   The chief
fetish doctor then asks questions of the corpse, ' How did he
come by his death ? '   And if by witchcraft, ' On which side of
the family was the witch to be found,' ' man,' ' woman,' or
' young,' etc., until by jerks and violent swingings from side
to side, when the two men who carry the body pore with perspi-
ration from fatigue and excitement, the dead man answers the
questions, so that usually the witch or wizard is smelt out
before the drunken feast is over. Now all this means expense,
and often ruin to the relatives, and the happy idea had taken
hold of the heathen mind that it would be more economical, and
certainly not less respectable, to be buried in a white man's
coffin. The Christian young men who found employment in
this way were also expected to bring the box along and
finish the matter by holding a religious service at the grave.
In this way the Gospel has been carried into strongholds of
heathenism.''

Having left a family of six children, with the mother, in ⌐
England, Arnot's correspondence now included letters to these ·
Rachel, Nigel, Winnie, Cyril. Aleck and Arthur. As these
present us with another side, both of his character and experiences, we give the following extracts, spread over the period
covered by the above record :

" *June 1st,* 1904.—Wake at 5, rub my eyes, think for a
little before I get up and say, ' Yes ! This is the day we sail
away to Africa.' I wish everybody was going with me, everybody at home I mean. How happy Noah must have been when
God told him that his wife and all his children were to be with
him in the ark. But I had to get up, for the man was coming
for my boxes, and such a nice man too. He was afraid that
some of my boxes were not tight enough so he brought some
strange string that he said the King uses to tie his boxes with.
You see Portugal is a little country and everyone knows what
the King does, where he gets his boots made, and the shop he
goes to for pencils and indiarubber

" There is a Society in Lisbon for the prevention of cruelty
to animals ; and I read in the papers of a Portuguese who
jumped out of the car to save the life of a cat that was run over,

and how the cat did not know that he was coming to save his life, and the cat bit him, and the kind Portuguese died."

After leaving Loanda on June 25th, 1904. " It is great fun watching the natives from the interior when they see the train. They look very frightened and come nearer so long as the engine does not move, but whenever the engine whistles and begins to move they rush off pell-mell, tumbling one over another in their flight. Others, I am sorry to say, dance round it as if it were a god, but that is only when it is standing still. If it gives just a little screech, off they dash for their lives.

" *July 8th* —This morning I thought I would take some ointment out of my medicine box to rub on my rusty throat. The ointment was in a tube covered with blue paper. ' Oh! Yes ! here it is,' but I had not put on my specs and I took up instead a tube of ' stickatine ' and was just about to rub my throat all over with the dreadful sticky stuff ; then I would have been in a fine state, and my shirt and collar would have stuck on so beautifully, just like Winnie's bought dolls, and I laughed so much at my mistake that I coughed up all the hoarseness.

" At Pungo Andongo we were shown the footprint of the ancient Linga tribe. By the side of the Queen's footprint we were shown the footprint of her dog, and another of her child, but of course all this is superstition. There are many human footprints in the hard path that could not have been carved and were evidently made when the rock was soft like mud, although it is hard rock now. I took a piece of paper and rubbed over it with a pencil, and here you can see an exact copy of the mysterious footprint.

" We stayed at an American Mission Station. This Station was opened by Bishop Taylor when he was an old man of 80. One day a chief came to visit from the interior and the only bed that Bishop Taylor had to offer him was one in his own room, which was a large room, and the Bishop's bed was next the door. The chief was very nervous and could not sleep, but lay and watched the old Bishop. When he knelt down to pray, his long white beard nearly touched the ground. The chief trembled and thought, ' Now has come the day of my death. This is not a man but a spirit.' When Bishop Taylor had finished praying he got up and took his false teeth out and put them in a glass. At this the chief trembled still more. But when the Bishop took off his wig and put it on a chair, the chief was nearly beside himself with terror, and as soon as the way to the door was clear he rushed out saying he was going home to return again with a present. But he never came back, and told everyone he met that he had seen a spirit. He had seen him ' take his bones out of his mouth, and then take off his head and put it on a chair.'

" Although I have a hammock, and men to carry me, I walk a good deal. I carry a butterfly net and catch butterflies. . . . The man who carries in front of my hammock is like the lookout man on board ship. He warns the man who carries behind. If there is a stump in front about as high as his knee he sings out, ' k'ongolo,' meaning ' knee high.' If the stump is higher then he shouts out ' k'ovimo yongombe,' which means ' to the chest of an ox.' If the stump should be quite small he will say ' ombeo,' meaning ' a tortoise,' and the man behind answers back to the man in front in his own way, as for instance, ' Tortoise is nice. It makes good sauce.' The carriers seldom get cross with one another.

" We had some nice meetings at Bihé with the natives. One native preacher said that if a man built a fine house he did not allow a pig to live in it. And so heaven was God's fine house, and God would not allow pigs to live in it. Then I thought of the hymn :

> ' There is a city bright,
> Closed are its gates to sin '

" *Oct. 6th*, 1904.—I am sending home a box of butterflies, about 100. Many are alike, but these you could sell or exchange. Do not open them yourself. You will break their legs and things and that takes all their value away. Some are worth pounds. . . . There are some very large butterflies here with four tails. They are as big as plates and fly so high that I can't reach them.

" I am writing in the early morning, big frogs are croaking in the brook at the foot of the garden, canaries are singing in the peach trees, humming birds are dancing round the banana flowers close to the door. I think I can hear you saying, ' Oh ! how nice. Wouldn't I like to go to Africa.' But wait a bit. I have killed four snakes in my garden since I came here. That is the other side, isn't it ? Still they always run away from people, and we never hear of the natives being bitten, although they always run about with bare feet. The people are very nice and quiet too, and always so pleased to see me when I call on them, and they ask for all my children, and who followed at the back of Ray's neck, and who followed again at the back of Nigel's neck, and so on down to baby Arthur. He, poor boy, won't know me when I come again He will run away, thinking I am a monster. Never mind, I will soon talk him over. Oh ! two such lovely young parrots were brought here for sale, and so tame. Then I had an owl, and old owl died, and there was no person with a shovel to dig old owl's grave "

Writing to Winnie on her tenth birthday Arnot referred to the letter received during his third journey, when on the *Ilala*, on Lake Nyassa, and said : " The letter contained the telegram that told me you were born, but I thought you were a boy ! And it was some months after that I found out my mistake, and learned that you were a girl after all.

" *Dec. 1st.*—I have just heard that my old boy Dick is on his way to Bihé. He followed me of his own accord from the Barotse country and was my faithful servant when wandering about all alone. When I left the Garenganze country in 1888 I left him there with Mr. Swann, but the first person mother and I saw when sailing up to the pier at Benguella, in the little boat that took us from the steamer, was Dick. He had travelled out 1200 miles to meet us. We left him in Bihé when we came home, to his great distress. But when he heard that I had gone out to Lake Mweru he travelled all the way from Bihé with his wife and two children, hoping to find me, but I had returned home. So he remained there with Mr. Crawford until now. And here he is on his way to Bihé to meet me with his wife and two children. How glad I will be to see him. His life would make a story of how faithful an African can be. When Rachel was born Dick got so excited that he started to dance a war dance At another time when mother was ill Dick ran seventy miles in a day and a night to tell Uncle Walter

' *Bihé, March 7th*, 1905 —When out walking about looking for the mail men one evening I came across a bundle of grass, and when I kicked it, it looked like a bird's nest. Then I took it up and examined it, and could find no hole opening inside, only a little hollow on the top for a bird to sit on. So I pulled the bundle of grass to pieces, and there was the nest inside and a young bird gaping away. A little closer study showed how

cleverly the passage was covered by a little trap-door arrangement that sprang to with the force of some stiff bits of grass
which acted like springs, so that neither mouse nor snake could
get in. I was sorry then that we had spoiled it. But this nest
had really two stories, one for the hen bird to sit on her nest
and one for the cock bird to sit and sing songs and talk bits of
chat to while away the time when the eggs were hatching.

" A black boy, a great friend of mine, said quite earnestly
that he wanted to trust Jesus now, and I said, ' Why ? ' He
said, because Jesus was standing at the door of his heart
knocking. I asked him how he knew that, and he said because
he had a pain there—pointing to his inside—and he knew that
it was Jesus wanting to save him.

" I must tell you of an adventure I had with a flying serpent.
Hearing a great noise among the hens I knew that a serpent
was trying to catch one of them for the hens make a different
noise when a hawk appears, or a dog, or a serpent. I suppose
it's their own language that they speak. So I left my writing,
took my gun and ran out to shoot the snake, but by this time
a crowd of little birds had come to help the hens, and they all
together were giving Mr. Serpent such a scolding that I am sure
he must have felt very wicked indeed. I thought these hens
and birds had more sense than Eve had, even although she was
our first mother. The birds grew more excited when they saw
me, and flew around the bush where the serpent was hiding,
pointing him out. At last I saw his wicked eye glancing through
the leaves. Then his body, which was of a fiery, copper colour.
' Don't go near him,' shouted my one-eyed boy. ' He is very
angry and very poisonous.' Indeed, from his copper, fiery
colour I felt sure that this serpent belonged to the same family
of serpents that bit the children of Israel in the wilderness, and
the brazen or copper serpent that Moses made and placed on
a pole was intended to be like them. But my one-eyed boy
was getting quite excited by this time. ' Shoot it ! Shoot it ! '
he cried, ' or it will fly at you.' ' What nonsense ! ' I said.
' Don't be frightened. It has no wings.' ' Oh, yes it has ! ' he
said. ' It has wings. Kill it, and you will see.' So I pulled
the trigger. Bang went the gun. A small bullet had gone
right through his head, and it was soon quite dead. Then with
long sticks we poked him out of the tree, and sure enough the
serpent had wings, for all along the sides of his body the skin

projected like a long fin. This long skin wing is only used when
the flying snake is up a tree, but he could not make any use
of it when lying on the ground. There is a flying squirrel that
has skin-wings stretched between his hind and fore legs on
either side. But both the snake and the squirrel have to climb
the tree first, like other snakes and squirrels, and then fly down.

" This month I have a story about a little boy, Kasinda, and
his sisters. They had no father, and their mother was sold by
the people of the village because they said she was a witch.
Well, Kasinda was only a little boy and didn't know anything,
but he grew to be a man, and when he heard of God and of
Jesus Christ he was converted His hard, heathen heart was
broken, and a new heart began to grow little by little into the
places where the broken pieces were, and he began to think of
his mother and that she was a slave. So he said to his sister
that it would be nice to redeem their mother, and she said that
it would be nice, and they began to work hard and save their
money. When Kasinda had forty yards of calico saved up,
which would be as much as ten bed sheets, and a pig that
Kasinda's sister had been feeding, he started away to redeem
his mother from the man that had bought her. But Kasinda
found that he had hardened his heart, like Pharaoh, and would
not let her go, and looked with scorn on the forty yards and
the pig. Kasinda then came back to his village, and his neighbours said that he should go to the judge, who would put the
cruel slave owner into prison. But Kasinda said, ' No ! I will
not go to the judge. I will pray to God to soften his heart.'
When one said to Kasinda that that would be very difficult
for God to do, Kasinda said, ' Has God not softened my
heart, making me to love my mother more than forty yards
of calico and a pig ? God can soften this man's heart too.'
So Kasinda gave himself several days' rest, when he prayed
every day. Then he started on the long three days' journey,
without adding any more to what he had taken before. This
time to his great joy the man said,' The price is enough. Take
your mother and go.' And so Kasinda returned to his village
with his mother, in triumph, and now he is building a home for
her.

" *Dec. 5th.*—I have your letter telling of your having been
to Ovei, and having left your *overcoat* and of your having to
cycle *over* to *Over* to get your *overcoat*.

" *4th Feb.*, 1905.—Do you do any fret - work, or perhaps you are content with fretting mother, and Rachel, and Winnie, and all the rest of the people ? The last thing I killed was a puff-adder, a very deadly snake, but very lazy and sleepy. But this has been such a month for extraordinary animals. First, a flying serpent ; second, an ant-eater ; third, a tree-climbing otter with hands like men ; fourth, a skin brought to me of an animal with a head and tail like a fox, forepaws like a small ant bear, and hind feet like an antelope ; fifth, a skin of a boa constrictor, twelve feet long ; sixth, the puff-adder, which I have skinned. So you will have to start a museum, for I mean to send all these things home. . . . All the village dogs are barking furiously. Of course I know an old hyena is walking around. I wish the trap was here. I would soon snap his paw. But I have caught such a number of rats with a small spring **trap**; I find that if I wash the trap after each rat, the others walk in."

Arnot returned from the above journey via Broken Hill and the Cape, reaching England in August, 1905.

During the year and four months he was away from home, Mr. Wright, of the Bristol Orphan Homes, had passed away, and Arnot was asked, on his return, to assist Mr. Bergin with the directorate. This he did for a period of eight months. Then Dr. Bergin, who had been seriously ill for a long period after his return from China, sufficiently recovered so as to be able to help his father in the conduct of the homes. This set Arnot free to do what he had often planned to do, viz. to visit all the stations in Central Africa which had been started since 1889.

CHAPTER XXI

THE FIFTH JOURNEY

ARNOT started again for Africa in November, 1906, leaving his wife and family at Bristol. Arriving at Loanda, in December, he had several interviews with the Governor-General of Portuguese West Africa, and with the help of the British Consul was able to do some useful work with regard to the registering of the Mission Stations, and Government recognition of the position of the natives. Letters awaited him at Loanda, telling of an unusual amount of sickness amongst the missionaries in Bihé, and of the more serious illness of Dr. Sparks who had preceded him on this visit by several months.

Proceeding from Loanda by the Portuguese railway to Lucalla, his sole companion in the train for a time was an old leprous woman. Arnot wrote : " The Portuguese are not tied down with too many regulations ; natives suffering from all sorts of diseases travel freely, and a trader is allowed to fill up a compartment with slaves roped together. Looking at this poor woman, and feeling the discomfort of her presence, made me thankful for all, who, for Christ's sake, take up the work of ministering to lepers ; thankful, I say, not for the leper's sake only, but for one's own sake. To sit down and think of the unselfish and the humble, in this world of selfishness and pride, is both comforting and stimulating.

" Lucalla is the name of a large river that flows into the Kwanza. Dr. Livingstone crossed it on his first great journey from the Cape to St. Paul de Loanda, and the town of Lucalla lies east and west of the ferry used by the famous traveller ; indeed, I had been able to identify from my comfortable seat in the train several of the rivers and stopping places he wrote of in his first Journals. Here, at Ngulungo-Olto, he was delighted with the mountain scenery, and reminded of his home in Scotland ; there, along that oozy, muddy river Bengo, he had

285

fever on fever; there, his men, finding that they were within a few days of Loanda—the great slave port of those days—were all minded to leave him and return without pay to their homes in Barotseland.

Writing from Lucalla, December 28th, 1906, Arnot said: "Tell Mrs.—— how when we were all sitting at dinner a big poisonous spider came into the room, and a Portuguese rushed from the table in terror, saying, ' If it bites me I will be dead in six months.' I wondered why he didn't say in six days or in six minutes, he looked so frightened, but the hotel keeper came boldly to the rescue and put his foot on the hairy monster, and then burned it. . . . I am having my Christmas holidays waiting in a Portuguese trader's house. Oh! dear me! He has only a little room for us both, and he does like to be so hot and dirty, and no window open. But I get a corner open. The house hasn't been cleaned for a year, I think, and he doesn't think it worth while cleaning it for he is going to leave it in another year. . . . How my host hocks and coughs, and what sores he has to dress, and what groans and moans and violent tempers! But he tries to make one comfortable in his own way with fish and oil."

At Malolo, a sort of half-way camp between Lucalla and Bihé, Arnot was met, on January 12th, 1907, with the sad news that Dr. Sparks' state was very critical. Letters urged him to press on if possible. In five days Arnot covered, with his carriers, one hundred and fifty miles, arriving at Okapango, Bihé, the same day as Dr. Wellman from the West. " There was," says Arnot, "no hope. I went in at once to the sick room; Dr. Sparks, of course, looked greatly changed, but brighter and happier than perhaps I had ever seen him. While I held his hand, he asked what had delayed me, and added that my coming was to him a special answer to prayer. The end came in a few days without much pain or suffering The missionaries gathered from Ochilonda and Ohwalondo, as did also many native Christians, to attend the funeral. During Dr. Sparks' short service in Africa, he had succoured many, and saved the lives of not a few."

On January 29th he writes . " Mrs. Lane nursed me through my little fever, more the result of the hard walking and distress too at finding Sparks so low. Still I am quite myself again, and thankful to be here."

The opportunity afforded by the gathering of missionaries to the funeral of **Dr.** Sparks was seized to hold a Conference to discuss some important—and a few burning—questions of Church order and discipline among the African converts. " It was good," writes Arnot, " to be reminded that time was too short for mourning ; better brush the tear aside and press on. We had no ' Peter ' or ' James ' at our ' Jerusalem Council,' but the Lord was with us, and peace and harmony the outcome.

" Polygamy, with its many concomitant evils, lies at the root of most of our African church troubles. We were all of one mind in concluding from Scripture that no professing Christian *living* with more than one wife should be received at the Lord's table. At the same time such were not to be treated as under discipline, but helped on and cheered with the hope that God would soon open a right way of deliverance. My prayer is that all advisers and friends of the work at home will join with and support us in this earnest desire to preserve within the circle of the Church visible the authority and purity of our Lord's words in Matt. xix, verses 4 and 5, ' Have ye not read, that He that made them at the beginning, made them male and female, and said, For this cause shall a man leave father and mother and shall cleave to his wife ; and they twain shall be one flesh.'

" The Old Testament saints and their many wives, of course, perplexed the African, and he has many questions to ask, but the words '*at the beginning*' in verse 4, and '*from the beginning*' in verse 8, justify our passing over the heads of all these men as *examples in this particular*. Indeed, I have had no hesitation in telling the African that Abraham, Jacob, David, Solomon, etc., were clearly living in a ' time of ignorance ' as to the true meaning of the marriage bond ; the mystical and typical teaching of Adam and Eve remained hidden from the Old Testament saints, being bound up with the mystery of the Church, the Bride of Christ, revealed to us in the gospels and epistles.

" Then, the great question of the African convert's conduct towards his wives was considered under several heads. And here, as all can well understand, we felt ourselves face to face with our utter ignorance and helplessness, and *apart* from the Holy Spirit's personal help and interference in each *individual case* we had no hope. But surely His presence *is* hope and comfort.

" The importance of preserving ' a good report of them that are without ' was mentioned as a guiding principle, so that no wife could be sent away : (a) Without the wife's consent ; (b) Without the approval of her relatives and the elders of her tribe."

Under date February 5th, 1907, Arnot wrote to one of his sons · " A snake was in the boat I got into to cross a river, and it came for me, and I had my camera in my hand and snap- shotted it. The man who owned the boat yelled for flight for he thought my camera was a gun, and that I was going to shoot a hole in the bottom of the boat "

Writing at this time to the *Echoes of Service,* Arnot said : " When Portugal, over 400 years ago, threw off the yoke of the Moors, and pursued them into Africa, she began a line of conquest and exploration that led to her occupation of the West Coast of Africa, south of the mouth of the great Congo River. From their enemies, the Moors, the Portuguese also learned to value negro slaves, whom they found more docile and industrious than slaves captured on other coasts. There- fore Loanda, Benguella and other ports known to many of my readers were orginally slave markets, where the natives brought captives taken in war, to be sold to the white man in exchange for cotton goods, silks, rums, guns, salt, etc. One day a slave was brought to Loanda for sale, who afterwards persuaded his white master that he was the son of a great chief, captured and sold by a rival. This boy was taken to the Portu- guese Governor, who gave him a military training, and when old enough, Kangombe—for that was the name he was after- wards known by—was sent with a force of soldiers to reconquer his father's kraal and country, which country has since been known by the name of Bihé. Kangombe's descendants reigned over an intelligent and active people until about fifteen years ago, when the Portuguese took the country over, with other large tracks of West Central Africa. Now the name Bihé covers a large part of the great West Central plateau.

" The brethren and sisters known to readers of *Echoes of Service* occupy three stations in this region. The Portuguese have never encouraged their own missionaries ; indeed, two centuries ago they drove the Jesuits out of all their African possessions, so it was not to be expected that they would welcome Protestants. Little by little, however, without either

A STRIKING HEADDRESS

A Mashukalumpe man. Near the Kafukwe
River, upper N.W. Rhodesia.

A FETISH MAN

In a dress intended to represent a departed
spirit.

the invitation or the good-will of Portuguese or native, the Gospel has been preached and schools have been established, so that to-day Bihé might almost be a Protestant country, for certainly the preaching and the teaching of the Word of God has made it difficult for missionaries to find an entrance with any other text-book than the Bible."

From Okapango Arnot went to Ohwalondo and on to Ochilonda. His description of the work in the latter centre gives some idea of the progress of the work which he had done so much to found. We quote this simply as a specimen of what he found in all the centres : " Messrs. Sanders and Figg gave up much of their regular work to join me in visiting outlying villages where there are groups of professing Christians. Regular day-schools are carried on in six of these, as well as at Ochilonda, and in and around the other two Bihé stations. It is encouraging to see the amount of free labour given by Christian young men to this semi-secular, but most important branch of the work. Three fairly qualified men are each paid £5 a year by our brethren to teach in the more important schools. The village schoolrooms are also the meeting rooms for prayer and Bible reading during the week, and Gospel preaching on the Sundays. The native Christians in those districts seem to draw together into one village built close to the other villages of the group ; they have snug little houses with gardens and fruit trees. One morning I surprised one of these village homes, and thought I had never beheld a more beautiful sight. The father was reading a chapter from the New Testament, with his wife and five children sitting around, clean and decently clothed. These village Christians, especially the girls and women, have at times to endure a good deal of rough handling from their relatives when first professing Christ.

" Although the population around Ochilonda has decreased during the last few years, the Christians have increased, and the meetings are better attended than ever ; some came over ten miles to that held on Sunday morning. One young man, Buta, who was converted at the American mission station, some thirty miles off, has built a school and meeting room in his own district, where he teaches and toils at his own charges. He is indeed an example to all of happy Christian activity and contentment. The question now before our brethren in charge of the work here is how to encourage the older native Christians

T

to scatter themselves over a still wider area. For we have only to go three or four hours' journey from Ochilonda to five large villages and districts wholly without the Gospel. And Bihé, after all, is but one province on the great Umbunda-speaking plateau of West Central Africa, a district as large as Spain and Portugal, so that when the Ovimbundu tribe is spoken of it must be as a people almost wholly without the Gospel.

" To come down to the details of things is, after all, one great comfort when occupied with so large a field of service. The ordinary traveller would see nothing to encourage him in the great heaps of earth thrown up all around Kimberley, but a sight of the diamonds safely guarded by the manager—the result, perhaps, of one day's washing—would dispel all doubt as to the success of the mine. A tall native living at Buta's village had served as a soldier. When he professed conversion a few weeks ago, he said, ' When a soldier I obeyed my captain ; shall I not now obey my Master Jesus ? ' Since then he has destroyed a great store of fetishes and magic-working charms, and desired to be baptised. Recently a Conference was held at Ochilonda, when over 200 Christians assembled, and one present said it did his heart good to see such a number gathered to the Lord's name, and that they all seemed so happily to realise our unity in Christ. It may well do *our* hearts good to hear of it."

Journeying towards the Chokwe Arnot says : " I passed many Portuguese rum distilleries, and shops where also a little cloth and gunpowder are sold ; for although a European can with difficulty get 100 cartridges into the country, hundreds of guns and tons of gunpowder are sold to the natives. . . .

" My carriers know, of course, that they have set out on a long journey ; they may be a year from their homes. Some of them are Christians ; we have profitable meetings with the villagers living near our camp, and in their own simple way my men add a few words. One, indeed, is quite an orator, and drew lessons from the thunder that warned the women in the field and the woodman in the forest to gather their things together and start for home.

" The day before I crossed the Kwanza River, a Portuguese asked me to eleven o'clock breakfast with him. After sitting rather wearily through the many courses composed of the same African goat, boiled, roasted, fried, fricassee, etc., I was about to leave for camp, when he invited me to wait and listen to his gramophone. The first disc he took from the drawer was not the one he wished me to listen to ; so he put it back, with the remark that it was ' a discourse in a strange language,' but I urged him to let me hear it, and said the one disc would be as good as the other to me. Imagine, then, my surprise and delight when the machine began to give off Psalm xxiii in a fine English voice. So the Lord has His own ways of comforting and cheering one on.

" *April 17th*, 1907.—We are now among the Chokwe villages ; and to-day I was visited by Sama Kalenge, the chief who attempted to rob me at Peho 22 years ago. These Chokwe people seem to be by themselves in their pride and sense of superiority, even above the whites. That they are a superior sort of people there can be no question, and this also accounts for the fact that of all the West Central African tribes they have proved to be the most troublesome. The ' we are the people ' doctrine is not confined to white and ' Christian ' races. In the eyes of many Africans the ' white man ' is like the ' green plum ' blown too soon from the tree, while they held fast until they were ripe and vigorous.

" I left Boma on the 15th, and four days' good travelling, through a fairly populous country, brought me to the edge of the Chifumashi plains. Heavy rains were now falling—unusually so for this time of the year—and I and my men faced the flats with many misgivings ; however, we got through in five days with *much* damage from water, but it was an experience. Ant heaps were our only sleeping places at night and we had water knee-deep, and sometimes even thigh- and waist-deep, all the days with cold rain storms sweeping over us. At one river I had gone on in a cogly canoe to try to find another and larger dug-out, leaving my carriers standing in water up to their thighs, with no way of escape except by canoe. One of the men suggested that I was making off and would not return again, and when some marshwood trees hid me from them they gave way to panic. I sent the canoe back on reaching the other side of the swollen river, and my loads were literally thrown into it, until it sank with three boxes. Some called on their mothers and fathers ; the younger boys wept and wailed ; and but for one elder man's presence of mind and wise words all my loads would have been thrown into the water.

" On nearing Nana Kandundu, I met the old Queen Nakatolo, or Nana Kandundu, and when I complimented her on her youthful appearance, she returned the compliment by saying that she looked well because she saw me, her old friend, that day.

" Humanly speaking, there is much to suggest that the Balovale and Baluena would prove a fruitful field They are not a beer-brewing, drink-sodden people, nor aggressive and warlike, and some of their legendary stories have a touch of goodness about them. As, for instance, in a story they tell of two men who came to their god to beg for seed to sow as the drought had left them without food or seed. The god asked the first man his name, and he said his name was ' Mr. Help-Myself,' so he gave him boiled seed. The second man said that his name was ' Mr. Help-my-Neighbour,' so the god gave him good seed to sow.

" Then another tale, translated by Mr. Schindler (of Nana Kandundu), tells of two blind men coming to a river and hailing the ferryman to come and paddle them over. When in mid-stream the ferryman asked the first blind man why he was blind, and he confessed and said it was just what he deserved, so the ferryman gave him back his sight. Returning for the second blind man he brought him to mid-stream and asked him the same question, and the blind man declared that his jealous relations had bewitched him, and that God had dealt hardly with him, etc. He was allowed to cross over, but to go on for the rest of his life blind and groping.

" This is unusual, and suggests that away back in the history of the tribe some African Confucius must have lived and taught.

" I shall never forget one morning's walk Mr. Schindler took me through the forest. At last we came to a clearing and a few huts appeared Then some sweet potato patches and more huts. Then a shed-like erection, and a tall, sober-looking young man of about 30 years, the leader of a little group of five believers, who had built this room of the best wood they could find as their prayer room. In different directions similar groups are forming and becoming more visible, and begin to spread like the grafts of living skins on the bare raw flesh of Africa's, and the world's, open sore."

Writing from Kavungu, May 13th, 1907, Arnot said : "I have just returned from Kazombo, and I have enjoyed the beautiful Zambesi again and the scenery around.

" On Monday we went for a picnic to a hill three miles or so away. We passed a dead hyena. Miss Lindley said it was a dead ox. It was hidden in the grass, and her hammock men said, ' Oh, yes ! it is a dead ox.' The other men shouted out to them, ' You fool ! It is not an ox, it is a dead hyena.' ' Hush ! Hush ! ' was the reply, ' hasn't the lady said it was a dead ox ? Then if she said so it must be so. It's an ox, an ox.' So you see what good manners the Africans have; they don't like to contradict ladies.

" *Kavungu, July 23rd,* 1907.—I am keeping up my duties here, carpentering with converts in forenoon, and sitting with Schindler each afternoon helping him with translation of Luke. I help him with the English idioms. We look up the Greek too with helps, and compare Umbundu and Luba. I am able to help him out from these two translations very often. Then we have an excellent native sitting with us, so we look quite imposing. To me it is a great honour to have even this little share in the translation of the New Testament.

" Mr. Louttit is also making progress with the Chokwe language, in the hope of soon being able to begin to translate the Scriptures, while Dr. Stover (A.B.C F.M.) has practically finished the New Testament in Umbundu, and Dr. Laws and his friends in Chisanje, out east, so Lunda will be the last of the great languages to be enriched with the words of truth and life along this belt of Africa from West to East. Shall we not therefore continue more earnestly in prayer that this work may be completed. Already we can say that at least *parts* of Holy Scripture have been translated into every African dialect found between the West Coast at Benguella and the East Coast.

" Dr. and Mrs. Fisher are very hopeful of the work around Kalene among the Va-Lunda, as well as of the Sanatorium This, of course, as an institution, must be content with small beginnings, and probably it will be of no great service to missionaries over a hundred miles away until a railway is made. But it is, and will be, a very great boon. By eighteen years' constant service, Dr. Fisher has done much to improve the health conditions in Central Africa, and will make it possible for those needing change to obtain it, and also for any to have teeth attended to and renewed, or to have small operations performed, without being obliged to take the long journey to England.

" The more one sees of the Va-Lovale and the Va-Lunda tribes, the more one's interest in them increases. When at Kalene I visited some of the Lunda villages with Dr. Fisher. At one we found all busy worshipping the spirit of some ancestral hunter, who, it was said, had enabled one of the villagers to kill two large antelopes. By the time we arrived an offering had been prepared, consisting of native bread and cooked antelope meat. The lump of soft bread was held on the end of a stick, and looked like wool on a distaff. The chief of the village held the bread and all danced in front of a fetish horn stuck in the ground, behind which a hatstand-like tree stood, hung all over with horns, skulls and jaw-bones of animals killed in the chase. The chief then allowed each dancer to pick off a piece of bread, and with a little bit of antelope meat make an offering to the ancestral spirit ; after which all knelt down and, with clappings and bowings, gave to the spirit the honours due to a great chief The hunter then took his stand on the head of one of the slain antelopes, and all danced before him. The stick of bread was handed to him ; he ate a little and handed the loaf back to the chief, so the dance continued. Now a little boy was allowed to join in, and all went merrily on for a few minutes ; then the boy— playing his part well—seized the bread and rushed off with it, while the men followed in a mock chase until they reached the village bounds. The ' thief ' was soon joined by his companions, and all sat around in a ring, and ' partook ' of the sacred loaf. In this way these rude but clever savages got over their difficult question of disposing of what in their eyes was something ' consecrated.'

" The dance being now over, chief and people sat down to listen to and converse with us. ' How many ancestral spirits do you Va-Lunda worship in this way ? ' ' We don't know ; we have so many.' ' How many gods have the Va-Lunda ? ' ' There is only one God.' ' Which is the greatest—God or the ancestral spirits ? ' ' Of course, God is the greatest,' the chief replied. ' Then, if God is the greatest, why do you not worship Him ? Why worship only these ancestral spirits who were made by Him ? ' At this the chief turned to the group of men, saying, ' Listen to this,' as much as to say, Dr. Fisher and his friend have got me into a nice fix ; what answer can I give ? Then, turning round he said,, ' We would worship God if we

only knew how.' Of course we told him that the reason for
our coming to live among them was to tell them how to worship
God.

" On my six days' journey back to Kavungu I witnessed a
very touching sight.   On reaching a Lunda village we found
that a woman had died the night before, and they had set her
body up on a mat outside her hut.   A spirit-doctor was present
in full professional costume, and her husband was holding her
hands, and imploring her to treat him kindly, to remember
how he had clothed her in life, and was now heaping all his
wealth upon her body.   Then he wound long strings of beads
about her arms and neck."

Arnot wrote to his children from Kalene, August 11th,
1907 :

" I have had a very pleasant trip along the Zambesi Valley.
My Lovale carriers do not keep together so well as the Ovimbundu   We had a good time, however, and I hurried my men
up by giving a present of a bit of meat to each man who arrived
in the camping place during the first half hour or so.   I have
four men carrying my hammock, so I walk two hours, two men
carry me two hours, the other two carry me for other two
hours, so we reach camp.

" Although these Lovale men seem to live in the midst of
noises, drumming and dancing all night long until one's head
is sore and weary, I was surprised to find how they dislike
some noises.   For instance, the cover of my hammock was a
little loose and went knock, knock against the pole.   Because
of the thick trees I decided to remove the cover.   After a
while I was putting it on again when one of the men gave a
shudder, ' Ugh,' he said, ' Put on that wretched cover ? '
' Why not ? ' I asked, ' it is not heavy.'   ' Oh, no ! ' he
replied, ' but oh, that dreadful knock, knock.'   So I tied on
my jacket to the pole to pad it where the top knocked.   To
carry a box too with something rattling inside is most annoying,
and the poor man will bring the box and put it down with
such an imploring look.   I suppose they feel like the hippo
who had to get into the water to get out of the wet, or the
elephant with a hide so tough that he can push through the
thickest thorn bushes, and yet seems to be so annoyed when
a fly lights on him, for he pulls a branch of a tree to dust the
fly away,

" Kalunda and Kalene are the first stations to be opened among the great Balunda tribe. The Balunda are very shy, and so ready to move off at the slightest alarm that the work proved to be very slow at first   Their villages, however, are full of children. Although often hidden away in some dark thick forest we had to be most careful when visiting the villages not to take them by surprise, for with wonderful presence of mind every man, woman and child would suddenly disappear like a brood of young partridges.   Then as one's eyes became accustomed to the shade of the trees I could see a child at my feet hiding in a turf of grass, a feeble old woman under a cassava bush, a man or woman standing stiff and still behind each tree that had been left standing for such a useful purpose, and behind a hut or corn bin a mother, with three or four bairns, would all be huddled together, the anxious mother putting her finger into the baby's mouth to keep him quiet.

" Entering one of these Lunda villages to the east of Kalene I found we had made too much noise, and all fled, like a breeze of wind, into the forest. Only one old woman and her family were unable to escape, and sat huddled in the dark recess of their hut. When I knelt down at the door to beckon them, the poor woman shrieked with terror. I quietly kept my ground, however, and held out to the little boy of five or six a bright piece of calico. The child looked at the calico, then at his mother, then at the calico again, until at last the temptation became too strong, and with a rush and a grab he seized the prize. Then I tempted the rest of the children with salt, more delightful to them than sugar. At last all came out to the sunlight and scampered off to show their treasure to their friends in the forest, and soon I had, not only all the children, but all the fathers and mothers too. From among these wild, naked people some wonderful trophies have already been won. The difficulty, both at Kalunda and Kalene, was how to build meeting rooms large enough to take all in."

Crossing the Lualaba Arnot travelled to Koni Hill along a road cut as straight as a die. "All so strange," he says, " from the old days of thick forest and bog and marsh. To the west of the Lualaba the very path that I had cut through a bamboo forest, at the rate of four miles a day, with torn boots and bleeding feet, owing to the sharp bamboo stumps, was now a veritable highway."

Arnot arrived at Koni Hill in August, 1907, after twenty years' absence. " There," he wrote, " close by, stood the villages where the inhabitants had fled at my first appearance, saying that my feet were like zebra's hoofs, and where I had publicly eaten a potato to show that I was human. Now the Gospel is preached to them every week. Mrs Anton's school was a model one ; the houses of the missionaries and schoolrooms were of burnt brick and solid woodwork, and everything around spoke of skilled labour.

" The name of Va-Garenganze, given by Msidi to his people, has now fallen quite out of use ; the Congo Free State and mining companies use only the name Katanga for Msidi's old kingdom.

" How interesting every hill and river and village was to me 22 years ago, and how dreary this time. My spleen threatens to fill up all my abdomen, and I am reduced to a slop diet."

After a good rest here Arnot recovered and wrote : " I have been able to see a little of the native Christians, and also some who were on a visit from the Lufoi Hills, where quite a ' revival ' has been in progress, and about thirty professed Christians are struggling along in their own simple way, and amidst some little opposition, the local chief declaring it to be extreme forwardness on their part to profess conversion to the white man's faith while their big chief Mwenda still remains outside the Christian fold.

" Kapapa, the dowager queen of the country, was the first to visit me. She has since been baptised, and her good example has strengthened the cause of Christ among the women. I think we can safely say that unless the work of conversion begins among the women no beginning has been made. The men alone seem unable to shake themselves clear of the entanglements of polygamy and other evils."

From Koni Hill Arnot started " in company with Mr. Anton and Mr. Last for Mwenda's town The hammock ride along the east bank of the Lufira was very interesting, being all new country to me. We passed a series of beautiful waterfalls, and further on a hot spring heavily charged with salt, which is a source of wealth to the little chief in charge. My companions cycled, as the road is well made, and in the dry season forms an ideal bicycle track. By this means the thirty miles between Koni Hill and Mwenda's occupy only three hours, or even less.   But 'the lame duck gives the pace,' so on account of my slower rate of travelling we camped midway.

"*Oct. 6th*, 1907 (*Sunday*).—A great day !   Such a splendid turn-out and welcome at Mwenda's !   Every seat was occupied in the schoolroom, and there was a good hearing from chief, queens, and people.   This was not because of the presence of three white missionaries, for Kapekele, the converted raider and murderer, was the preacher the Sunday before, and had quite as many present to hear him.   The Katanga Co. estimate the population of Mwenda's town at **5000**, and taking a radius of about five miles, there must be ten times that number.

" On every hand I met with old Bunkeya friends, for here we have Msidi's old town divided pretty much as it was twenty years ago, and composed of the same people or their children. Many were the enquiries made for Messrs Swann and Faulknor, and one man was proud of a whole limb that the latter had ' mended ' when badly smashed by a bullet."

From Msidi's old town Arnot proceeded to Luanza on Lake Mweru, where the now famous Dan Crawford was stationed. " The whole school," Arnot says, " came down to meet us, and this was but the beginning of the boisterous welcome awaiting us all the way up the hill from hundreds of young and old. The Crawfords have a delightful wattle and daub house, thoroughly African, and yet most comfortable and home-like.   To describe Luanza and to give any idea of the changes that have been brought about since my last visit, thirteen years ago, would be a long task.   *Then* Arab slave raiders were scattering the people, compelling Mr. Crawford to turn from being a wandering cave, forest and swamp missionary, to reside more or less in one place and to gather around him the hunted and homeless tribes of Lake Mweru.   *Now*, first, we have here the inner circle of baptised believers, numbering 45, including several chiefs , second, a large company of pro-fessing Christians and ' listeners,' varying from 500 to 1000, meeting in the circular schoolroom ; third, the day-school of over 200 scholars, as well as several village schools—all too many at present for the teachers available ; and, finally, streets of comfortable, two-roomed cottage homes, spreading over the plateau.

" Messrs Crawford and Sims are anxious to push on with

the school work. Having now the New Testament and other reading books in Chi-Luba, the time seems to have come for extending the system of village schools broadcast, for only in this way will the work of the evangelist be supported by the written Word in the hands of the people. Old fetish superstitions are crumbling away ; Arab invasion and Mahommedanism have been checked ; and the European powers are not opposed ; why is it, then, that we seem so backward, so unwilling as a Church to advance and occupy these wholly unoccupied fields ? After all, Bihé, Chokwe, Kavungu, Kazombo, Kalunda, Kalene, Koni, Luanza, Johnston Falls, are only thresholds to vast regions, where the success of the few ought to encourage the many to follow on, and surpass.

" During my stay at Luanza I paid a visit to the graveyard where the precious remains of Benjamin Cobbe, William Gammon, John Wilson, Mrs. Higgins, Mrs. Campbell, Miss Jordan, Mr. and Mrs. Crawford's first-born baby, Lindsay, and the first native convert, Mishi-mishi, tell the tale of the cost of pioneer work in Central Africa."

Before proceeding home there was one more centre to visit, viz. the one at Johnston Falls on the Luapula River " Here," Arnot says, " the meeting in the evening surprised me ; I did not expect to find so many professing Christians. . . . The Sunday before I left was a very happy one. In the morning eleven converts were baptised in the stream close by, and in the evening we all dined together in true African fashion, sitting in groups round piles of native bread, or mush, and pots of cooked venison. I spoke of how, after our Lord's first coming and death and resurrection, the Gospel was preached all over the ancient world, and then came long years of silence as far as Africa was concerned ; but now East West, North and South, missionaries were coming, people were hearing what their fathers and grandfathers had never heard, and converts were to be found in nearly every country —what did it all mean ? Surely it must mean nothing more nor less than that the time for our Lord to come back again was very near. Then one of the young native converts took up the subject by reading the scripture, ' Blessed are the eyes that see the things that ye see, and the ears that hear the things that ye hear,' and in a very able, enlightened way, followed in the same strain, lifting all present into a fine spirit

of thanksgiving, in that through God's mercy the Gospel had
been brought to them, poor Va-Vemba sinners.

" Here also, as at all the stations, our brethren have great
plans and projects for the extension of the work ; and so it
ought to be, and ever will be, if we are serving in communion
with the Master Servant. As the ship can never overtake the
ocean horizon, so the missionary's hands and feet can never
reach as far as his eyes and heart.

" My journey now lay south for 200 miles to Broken Hill,
North-Western Rhodesia, and from there by rail and steamer
home. On the way I saw how that the ' Cape to Cairo ' railway was penetrating the almost wholly unevangelised North-
Western Rhodesia, and I felt strongly impressed with the
thought that the time had come to come back to my old South
African base of operations. Writing these thoughts and plans
home to my wife I was surprised to find awaiting me at Capetown a letter from her that must have passed my letter in
mid-ocean, expressing the same idea. So all other things being
equal we gathered that we had both been guided by the ' one
Spirit ' in the matter. And the few months I spent in England
were occupied chiefly in breaking up the home at Bristol and
in arranging for the removal of my wife and seven children
to South Africa where I could visit them as often as it was
possible to do."

CHAPTER XXII

THE SIXTH AND SEVENTH JOURNEYS

IN the latter part of 1908 Arnot took up his residence, with his family, in Johannesburg. Meeting with and speaking in the assemblies of the " Brethren " in that centre he was a means of spiritual help to many   The reverence and affection with which he is spoken of to-day are a tribute both to his character and work from that time onward unto his death. Other churches felt the stimulus of his missionary zeal and were helped to stretch out a hand to the " regions beyond."

As soon as the family was settled the call of Central Africa again took Arnot to the old scenes. The train took him as far as Broken Hill, at that time the terminus of the Cape to Cairo railway   Writing to Mrs. Arnot, in March, 1909, when on his way north, he said :

" I changed into the B.H. train and we were soon off. But some rough customers on board. In my compartment two hunters began drinking hard, then threatening to shoot each other. Then the big one held the little one down by the throat. But the little one watched his chance and jumped from the into the next compartment but the big Texas man kept hand-train, leaving his gun and kit and ticket behind him. I shifted ling his guns and trying the locks and preparing to fire on the enemy all night. I went in to try and calm him and unloaded two cartridges, but he soon put them back again. However, he was better in the morning. I hid his whisky away and he is no longer dangerous.

" *April* 18*th*, 1908.—This morning I awoke after a good night's rest to lie and listen to the doves and green parrots. My camp is in a lovely glade, with a village close by where an old rascal lives who tried to sell me three eggs as fresh, with feathered fowls inside. They had no hens either to sell, so just about supper time two doves came on the tree close by.

They looked very lovingly at each other and I looked lovingly at them, and soon had them nicely stewed on my plate. . . . My bike behaves fairly well, only thrown me twice, but I am breaking him in. . . . I had a four hours' wade in a marsh up to the waist and none the worse.

"*May 1st, Kalaso.*—I am very well, wearing nothing but my trousers and my singlet. You can imagine how sun-burnt I am. Still I am enjoying it, enjoying meeting these Bakaonde, all Lulu speaking, so I am quite at home. Oh ! the plans my poor brain works up. What a field for an entirely new start ! The Bakaonde are right up to the Congo frontier, where at Kansanshi the watershed rises to 5400 ft. We could have the benefit of Crawford's translation. Would be in touch with the railway at Kansanshi, if not actually on it, etc. A work might be begun that our own children could carry on. However, my work clearly is to help Walter (Dr. Fisher) this year, and Cunningham is evidently waiting for me. The sight of these utterly unevangelised cannot but affect one deeply. And the Coillards' heroic effort when older than we are is always a stimulant." Arnot was then nearing his fiftieth birthday.

Joining Dr. Fisher at Kalene Hill Arnot travelled on with him to a Conference arranged at Kalunda, Mr. Cunningham's station. Missionaries from Kavungu and Kazombo were also present. Difficulties were faced and overcome and much profitable work done.

The unevangelised condition of the country appealed to him all the time. To his daughter Rachel he wrote from Kalunda : " Uncle Walter came here with me. It took us five days, travelling all day, to reach this, the nearest Mission Station to Kalene, so that there are great fields to be filled in. We passed large districts full of people who never really hear the Gospel."

From Kalene Hill, he writes a month later to Mrs. Arnot : " We are not treading on other people's toes in all these great wastes of country. I should like to take a holiday with you on a Mission Station in Natal, and study Zulu, for right up to the Zambesi I can see Zulu is ousting Sechuana, and is to be the dialect of the natives of S. Africa."

His sense of humour crops out in the midst of all the pressing need he faces, and he passes on to his children the stories picked up around the camp fires. Here is one : " Tell the boys that I heard of an asylum that had a ward in it for motor car madmen. A visitor was being shown round the asylum, and when he was brought to the ward for motor men he saw no one in it and was much surprised. But the attendant said, ' Oh ! they are all here. There ! Under each bed ! Don't you see them ? Each one is mending his motor car ' ''

In his general report of this trip Arnot wrote · '' Leaving Kalene I travelled with a few men along the Anglo-Belgian frontier to Kansanshi. The only trace of European occupation, however, during the 250 miles' tramp was not the boma of an Arab slave dealer, but the den of a trader of German birth. (On the way I met with Balunda, Basamba and Bakaonde, and plenty of game. Indeed, in one district they seemed more interested in me than I in them. Craning their necks and snuffing the air, these big animals approached me to within fifty yards.) Tall and muscular. His frontier store was well supplied with gunpowder from Portuguese territory, with young women slaves from the Congo Free State (composing his harem) and with cases of whisky from British territory. Miss Wilson Carmichael caused a sensation by writing things as they are in India. I could write an equally sensational report if I were to write things as I found them in the den of this loathsome man. He is since dead. How can one account for the fact that in framing laws for governments and chartered companies, supposed to exist first of all for the protection of the native, not a single clause has been introduced empowering His Majesty's Commissioners in the field to protect the native from the scum of Europe ?

'' Night after night as we journeyed eastward I was enabled to spend hours in prayer for deserted and forsaken N.W. Rhodesia. But for the few missionaries in the Barotse territory and at Kalene and a small beginning near Ndola, N.W. Rhodesia is without the Gospel. Hitherto one had looked to young evangelists from the assemblies of the ' Brethren ' in Britain to come forward to fill these open doors. But surely we are unequal to this gigantic task. Men from ' other ships ' must be called upon to come to the help of the Lord.'' Since then Mr. Bailey, on behalf of the S.A. General Mission, has opened two stations here about ; and on behalf of the Baptists of South Africa, Mr. Doke of Johannesburg, with his son, determined to go north and see for himself whether these things were true, and although the journey to the valley of the Kafue cost Mr. Doke his life, the work he had it on his heart to do will be taken up by others.

Returning to Johannesburg, Arnot started on his seventh journey to the interior in 1910. A portion of this trip was occupied with assisting Mr. Bailey of the S A General Mission in settling at Kansanshi in North-Western Rhodesia.

On March 8th, he writes "Mr. Bailey and I have been talking over Kansanshi. He is keen, I can see, on my staying with him. At present he is finding it difficult to make a start at the language, and alone on a site without even trusty boys by him, would be an almost impossible position. He wants me to try and put the language in some shape Certainly I do not see how he is going to make much headway alone with such a tangle of dialects. . . . Nothing would be more to my mind than helping in gathering an elementary knowledge of Chikaonda.

" *March 12th.*—I am working at the Chikaonda now every day, and it is very like Luba, so I will be of some help. I could not have a task more congenial.

" To-day we crossed the Lenge and the Lufunyama in boats and waded waist deep for a mile or so. The people here insist that their name is ' the people of God,' and disclaim all connection with the tribes north and south of them. Walking through a clump of very long grass I found myself in the midst of a herd of wild animals sleeping. The snorting and stamping on every hand was most alarming, but I saw nothing, although some heavy animals like buffalo must have passed quite close to me. The growth of grass makes one feel very small, and only suitable for elephants Indeed in places the country is quite trodden down by these monsters, and the footpath we have to follow seems to be their favourite highway."

On March 20th, he writes to the boys at home : " Here we are in the wilds and wets, but beautifully cool. Rain has fallen daily and now that we are past the swamps we don't mind so much. Fancy trudging along at the rate of twelve miles a day, for that is really about our average. . . . I have left Mr. Bailey to do the shooting and have only killed a bush buck. They have very nicely shaped horns, so I am bringing these home with me. I have also a fine pair of boar's tusks to bring home. Mr. Bailey succeeded in killing a large antelope

so the men have plenty of meat. Mr. Bailey has lots of funny
stories. He has just told me of a boy who was asked to make
a sentence with ' toward ' in it. The boy wrote ' I toied my
pants.' Another was asked to write a sentence with ' boys,'
' bees ' and ' bear ' in it, thinking he would write about a bear
stealing a boy's honey. But lo! the sentence ran in the
exercise book : ' Boys bees bare when they are swimming.'
Another of his stories is about a little girl. The teacher asked
her to write a sentence containing the expression ' bitter end.'
She wrote, ' Our neighbour's dog chased my kitten, and just
as she ran under the porch he bit her end ' . . . Yesterday
a monkey came looking at us. My boy asked the loan of my
gun and shot her, for it was a little girl monkey, so to-day we
are teasing the men about eating their little sister "

On the way to Kansanshi the travellers stopped at Miamba,
on March 25th. The chief of the district, Miamba, came round
in the afternoon with another old man. " After looking a long
time with a long enquiring look," Arnot says, " he asked me if
I was Monare who had built between the chief Msidi's town and
Msidi's brother, Salushia, many years ago. I said I was, and
involuntarily we both stretched out our hands and half rubbed
and half slapped their palms together. ' Yes ! ' he said, ' and
I was there at the time. With all my people we lived by the
Bunkeya until the Belgians came, then we left and came here.'
So quite unwittingly we have come and built by a group of
Msidi's scattered people.

" *March 26th.*—Our camp is partly surrounded by a thicket
of tall trees, where baboons and monkeys find a retreat when
they come near the fields of ripening corn belonging to the
neighbouring village. Last night these trees were simply alive
with baboons, the branches swaying and bending as before a
strong wind We could almost hear the monkeys speak in
their endless chatter. At last night grew on and all seemed
to settle to sleep, for monkeys only raid in the daytime. My
men kept up a flow of jibing remarks at their hairy brothers
as one was heard jostling the other, or when a young monkey
was evidently being punished for his impudence, or when a
baby monkey would start up from a bad dream and scream,
when the mother's low soothing grunt would be distinctly
heard. Altogether it was one of the strangest nights I have
passed for a long time."

U

Arriving at the spot selected for the station, Arnot immediately took in hand the building of a house for Mr. Bailey. Having to see to walls, doors, windows, thatch, etc., he was unable to leave for some time. The house was built out of the material to hand in the forest.

He wrote to Mrs. Arnot on April 24th : " My last was written before going off for a day in the veldt, but I did not go far. Three or four miles does me up completely now, and I turned back before reaching the game. My heart seems to give out. I must try and sell Walter's bike, and stick to carriers. . . . We are still having rain here—so late in the season— and my bricks are not improving The door frames are all made and we are at window frames and if we only had a few dry days I would start the building. We have twenty men working, and I have only to direct them, but the house when finished will be really good. Two men are good at the pit saw, and all the door and window frames have been sawn out. I am making all the window casements. We had a good meeting at village to-day, over sixty attending and entreating us to go on. I think one of our boys has received something. He is very bright and quite a help already. . . . Do you know I have never been into Kansanshi yet, that gay city of thirty whites. I have kept to my work here steadily, and already with our boys, young and old, and day school, and midday service, and building going up, and piles of material, the forest has been transformed into a Mission Station."

To his daughter Winnie he writes : " I have found some perfect orchids growing here. One kind is not so large, but the flower has every shade of colour between light pink and purple blue. The other is in full flower just now, a lovely pure white, and about the size of a garden daisy. Although quite curious in shape, these white flowers hang in sprays about six to eight inches long, and they have a very sweet smell."

On the 14th of May he went to stay overnight at Kansanshi so that he could preach to the Europeans on Sunday, the 15th. Concerning this he wrote : " I had quite a good hearing. There is a fine open door here for Mr. Bailey. I stayed with the manager of the mine, and he put me up royally, only his dog chewed up my hat, so he sent down to the store for ' the best they had.' I have a very good new hat, so next time I go in I am going to look out a few other articles that may take the manager's dog's fancy and get a new fit out. . . . I am sending a python skin by this mail, and some pretty birds' wings. . . . I am sending too a parcel of really handsome orchids. I have seen nothing like these, and they ought to be valuable.

"*May 20th*, 1210.—We have just heard of King Edward's death and I have been asked to go in and hold a memorial service at Kansanshi, but Mr. Bailey is going instead, the distance is too far for me. . . . The King's death may change my plans and instead of going to Kalene, etc , I will go to Liwanika. A Mr Hazell has come here from the Barotse. He was chief magistrate there. He seems to think I ought to go as Liwanika has no one that he relies on to give him advice. Liwanika was going to meet the Prince of Wales at Livingstone ; now he is not likely to leave his capital. This would take me through a lot of new country.

" Mr. Bailey understands that I will not be able to remain with him after July 1st. By that time I hope to have his house finished. At Kansanshi the preaching services are improving ; beginning with fifteen, we have advanced to forty, some farmers and their families coming in on foot four miles, all Dutch. There are three small attempts at farming being made by three Dutchmen.

" The Koni friends are anxious to see me, but I must not overdo it. I have decided that I will go only where I am needed. Somehow I have so little reserve strength that I am going to pay no more friendly visits. I have finished seven door frames, so am taking a day off to-morrow. My poor hands will be glad of a rest from cuts and knocks and bruises—' when father carved the duck ' business—but a house had to be built.

" Mr Bishop, the acting magistrate at Kansanshi, has been telling us of a revolting case of witchcraft, or a feast connected with the crime of witchcraft that he had to look into and punish the chiefs involved. For some reason or other the body of a woman and child, who had recently died, were disinterred, and the heart of the woman when tasted was discarded as bitter ; but the heart of the child was sweet, so its corpse was danced round and eaten, and all who partook of this revolting feast, and had danced around with one of the child's bones in his or her mouth was made immune from all evil influences, and would have power to bewitch all their enemies. The ordeal of the boiling water test for witchcraft is still in vogue among the Vakonde.

" *May 26th* —Here I am again preparing for a move. All seems in train for my going to Liwanika. I can have as many men as I need for that route. . . . I have been three months and more with Bailey and have seen the house walls up and the roof fairly completed. I have also kept at the language study, and to-day have helped to plant a patch of potatoes. Tell the boys that the natives have brought me a mouse monkey about the size of my thumb, full grown. It has fingers and thumbs and looks so pretty. I am bringing it home in a tin like a milk tin.

" On Thursday, June 2nd, I left for Kasempa. We passed villages for the first and second day in fair numbers. Then came a long, desolate forest tramp for twenty miles, but the great trees were very fine to look on, and I shot a very large yellow pigeon, and another handsome bird of the parrot kind, both good eating—but together they represented almost every shade of colour. We crossed two large rivers full of water from the Congo watershed and camped at Kazembo's, the centre, I should say, of quite a district, and here I rested for Sunday. Not feeling over well either ; my old road trouble agrees neither with cycle riding nor hammock riding.

" *Kasempa, June 8th.*—Arrived at this delightful station late in the evening, and after paying off my men, moved into a room in the District Commissioner's house as Mr. Hazell's guest, so that I seem to be getting everything my own way again, and much too comfortable. Mr. Hazell has been H.M. Commissioner in the Barotse and friend of Liwanika's, and I think will help me all he can.

" *June 11th.*—Here I am awaiting carriers to turn up. I am right, I think, in doing a little exploring if I can in new districts, rather than in running home as my one bent is, pell-mell. The Lord must have our best, and the country west of here is almost unexplored, and plenty of people, they say. My plan is to take a detour west to the Zambesi, then south to Liwanika's. I am willing to help open fresh centres. Some may be stirred up to occupy the field.

" *June 19th.*—My ten days' wait at Kasempa has been made very pleasant by the constant kindness of Mr. Hazell. He has nearly all N.W. Rhodesia under his jurisdiction. Yesterday he surprised me by asking if twelve carriers would suit me as that number had come in that morning for work. When the carriers heard that the distant Barotse Valley was my destination they hesitated, and a few drew back. At last, after some talk among themselves, and a long look at me, they all came back saying they were willing to go with me, so I hastily packed up and left to-day, doing a good sixteen miles. I am quite excited at the thought of being back at my old field.

"*June 23rd.*—After five days fair travelling (about sixteen miles a day) I have arrived at the first place, Lutoba, that has seemed to attract me and might prove to be a suitable site for a Mission Station, not so much from the crowds of people found here, as from their homely welcome, from the headsman down to the children. All along villages have been close to one another, and the valley of the Dongwe, so far, is all that it is reported to be, a fairly populous district. It is difficult to name villages and headmen, however, and after having found the correct name of the headman, etc., it is still more difficult to find him at home, chiefly owing to the strange Kaonde custom that demands that when a man marries a woman he goes to live at the woman's village, and the children belong to her relatives, so in the case of chiefs and headmen they have so many villages to live in in different parts of the country as they have wives—a scattered household. At first it seemed impossible to believe that this custom was really in practice, but after hearing Mr. Hazell lecturing a company of chiefs in his district on the evils of the custom, and on the difficulties produced by it, I had no longer any doubt. The women, in fact, rule the Bakaonde, and this may account for the fact that the men are evidently home dwellers and do their full share of cultivation, although they have never been a strong tribe and have been preyed upon by their neighbours.

"*June 25th.*—To-day we have left the Kaonde villages behind, and are now in the country of the Bambunda, Liwanika's territory. The soil seems to have changed from a hard grey clay to Barotse sand, and an old man going along with a hoe and axe to sell, knelt down and gave me the regular Serotse greeting with his head bending down to the ground.

"*June 26th*—Quite refreshing to-day to arrive at a very well-peopled district. The chief, Kashinda, comes from the

Barotse, and he recognised me. His people are all Bambunda, and carry on the clever basket-making industry that has made the Barotse baskets famous. The men seemed to understand and speak Sekololo, but the women spoke the language of the Bambunda, which is a mixture of Umbunda and Luba, so that I understood all they said. One of my own Kaonde men gave them quite an address in their Bambunda language, not knowing that I was able to follow him. This, he said, pointing to me, is the great Monare who lived in the Barotse when you were all children. He has been away teaching the Lunda tribes, and Congo State people, and now they all can read and write and count shillings, and when these people come to the white men's stores they tell the white men that they can read and count shillings, and the white man does not cheat them, etc.

" It is interesting to notice change of custom, clothing and general appearance, as well as language, and the customs mixed up with other distant tribes as well as the language. They appear to have more in common with tribes living 300 or 400 miles away than with their immediate neighbours. But this is often the case. Here I met a woman carrying a basket on her back with a strap round her forehead. The Bachokwe women in West Central Africa are the only others I have seen doing the same, except our New Haven fish wives. The boys set rat-traps as the boys do in Bihé. I have not seen the same trap anywhere else, neither have I heard the word ' landa,' used for ' buy ' in any other tribe except among the Ovimbundu of Bihé districts, and here ; and the name for God amongst the Bambunda is Suka.

"*Long. 24° 40", E. Lat. 11° 35", S. Luena River, Monkoya country, June 27th*, 1910.—I have safely crossed the unexplored part of my journey from Kasempa and have struck Major Quick's route, my mapping being very close and has fitted in with his. Still I am six days off the capital. The bush has been very thick and trackless, but when almost at my wits' end for a guide a man came along with two children to say he was awaiting an opportunity of going to the Barotse and would I let him go with me as guide ; he had been there before. I am sticking to my hammock now as the country is more open   Indeed it is almost continuous plain now to Liwanika's. In my letter to him I say I am not going to remain long but will want a boat to take me to Livingstone. I am anxious to

be home. In spite of having a good cook my inside seems to
be hopelessly wrong. I am simply living on quinine, bismuth,
and tinned milk. Now I can buy cow's milk. When staying
at Kansanshi I was all right, and the week at Kasempa gave
me a respite. I must keep to the railway next trip and stay
in one place as much as possible. But oh ! for 100 missionaries
for the country I have just passed through. And what crowds
of children in their hidden forest homes. Our missionary
machinery seems all too heavy and cumbersome. We need
a new order of forest missionaries living in tents and taking
in wide circuits. . . . Tell the boys that I killed two geese
to-day with one rifle shot at 150 yards using the new Bisley
peep sight. But the country is so overgrown with grass and
forest that although there was plenty of game about I did
not hunt, and shot nothing. One night we seemed to sleep
in a regular zoological garden. We heard such a variety of
roars and howls and laughing howls, and antelopes calling
each other, and ducks and geese quacking as morning broke.
Yesterday an old man recognised me and was full of talk of
the old days, just on thirty years ago.

" On the 4th July I arrived at M. Coisson's and M. Voulet's
station. They gave me a hearty welcome, and said that they
were all going over to Sefula in two days' time to attend the
Annual Conference in connection with their Mission, when all
the missionaries would assemble for a week, as well as a fresh
party from home, and that I would be welcome. Well ! I saw
Liwanika that afternoon, and talked over all his plans and
private matters. He was exceedingly friendly, almost took
me in his arms.

" On the 6th I was able to come on to Sefula to the Conference, and called at the Chief Magistrate's post en route.
He gave me quite a welcome and talked over the history of the
Barotse country for several hours. His wife was a missionary
in the Livingstonia Mission.

" Sefula is the principal station of the Mission. Here M.
and Madame Coillard lie buried. The Sefula is the name of
a river flowing into the Zambesi, and provides water for the
Mission gardens and drives a water ram supplying the Station
with abundance of water. M. Bouchet's house too is quite a
fine affair and all enclosed with netting. There seem to be
plenty of people about too. Here I can have one of the

Mission boats to take me to within forty miles of Livingstone, so I was able to pay off my men, and here I am free again from carriers and for the next step. I cannot but feel, however, as if I had been guided in coming here just in time for the Conference.

" *Sefula, Barotse, July 6th,* 1910 —Here I am at last heading for home My diary tells you how I got along. And I am really very well, although tired. But sorry I wrote you from the Luena of my road troubles. It is my spleen, wabble wabbling, that seems to upset me. I am better already and the boat journey will be most enjoyable. . . . The French missionaries are very warm. They have welcomed us with plenty of compliments, and the natives are coming to see me as a sort of curio. The king's private business is he wants me to take messages direct to the High Commissioner in S. Africa and to take charge of two of his sons and have them educated in S. Africa. I was not able to encourage him with either proposal. However, I am glad I saw him again. He urged me again to begin mission work in his country and open up stations among the tribes to the N.E. We talked of the old days when he looked upon all the tribes to the north of the Barotse as ' his dogs.' Then he would not allow me to visit them. Now he is willing to do all in his power. M. A. Jalla, and the missionaries who have carried on M. Coillard's work, assured me of every assistance if I decided to make use of the Zambesi River again.

" *July* 11*th.*—I took leave of the friends at Sefula, M. and Md. Bouchet and their visitors ; and riding for two hours across the plain I came to the river, where I found my boxes already in the boat kindly provided to take me to Nalolo, where I arrived about sunset and was met by M. and Madame Lageard, the kindest of people

" *July* 12*th.*—Visited my old friend Mokwæ, the queen, in her very fine house. The central reception room would equal in elegance and good taste much that passes for artistic style in the houses of the rich. M Lageard and I were each shown to comfortable seats, and Her Majesty, who had on a straw hat with pink ribbon and aigrette plumes stuck all round, took her own chair, a very wide one, but even that was not wide enough. and when she wanted to rise I saw her husband had to half pull her out from between the arms of the chair. We were then invited to sit down to lunch, and this time Her Majesty's chair consisted of a settee sufficient for two people, which she filled admirably. She spread herself out with a contented smile between its wooden arms, like her own Zambesi River flowing comfortably between her banks. Wild duck, fish, brown bread, coffee and milk, were brought in by waiters, who knelt as they placed the dishes on the full-sized dining-room table with its white and pink damask cloth. All went well until the unfortunate husband spilled the jug of hot milk. The queen's smile instantly vanished, and a deep Kaffir a u—u brought in the waiters with a run, and woke up the courtyard outside, and several of the counsellors and cabinet ministers looked in at the door. But nothing very serious came of it. The husband saved his head by declaring that it wasn't he, but the sleeve of his coat that upset the milk. The waiters sopped it up, and the queen accepted the explanation, and the smile came back again. We then called on Mokwæ's daughter, who is a queen over a district and is visiting her mother. She looks quite a character, too, and in a fit of madness, the missionary Lageard told me, she ordered all the husbands and wives in her domain to change around, her chief idea being to try and make every person as unhappy as she herself was.

CHAPTER XXIII

IN January, 1911, Arnot, accompanied by his wife, started for the Zambesi to proceed through the Barotse Valley, to the Kabompo Valley, where he built a little three-roomed house at the junction of the Zambesi, the Kabompo and the Lungebungu rivers, which meet at one point like the three toes of a hen's foot and represent, at least, one thousand miles of water navigable by canoes. This district is called by the Chartered Company the Balovale. For a few happy months Arnot and his wife were the only white inhabitants in it, with the exception of Mr. Palmer, the Native Commissioner. Arnot wrote of this journey as follows ·

" Usually the dry season is the most suitable for travelling in South Central Africa, but the Zambesi is a river by itself. After the rainy season the marshes and lagoons remain wet, and the long grass and reeds damp and rotting until July. Then the river is low. August, September and October are very hot months, so that it is better to wait until the rains fall, when the weather is cooler and the river begins to rise. January is perhaps a little late. Unusually heavy rains were falling, compelling us to wait for two days in our gipsy tent. At last the clouds broke and our shivering canoe man scrambled up the dripping bank, landing our goods into the canoes and off for Shesheke, where we were warmly welcomed by Dr. Reuter. I was surprised to find Litia, the oldest son of Liwanika looking so old. Thirty-three years ago he was a boy of ten or twelve years of age, bringing me a supply of milk from his father's cows every morning, and now he is nearly bald. His life has not been an even one. He fled with his father towards Ngami when Mataha's revolution broke out. Afterwards under M. Coillard's teaching he professed conversion and bore a bright testimony; but a Mosutu ' evangelist,' who had been trusted by the French missionaries, taught him how easy it was for a king's son to live a double life, and secretly have more than one wife. Since those days Litia has tried again and again to pick himself out of the mud of polygamy, but only to sink deeper into the wretchedness of it. For from every point of view polygamy is an unhappy affair. In the old brutal days when a man could beat or even kill his wives, he was able to put down intrigue. But under milder, semi-civilised laws, his case is hopeless. Jealous women kill each other's children, or kill their own in embryo, as a protest against being isolated for two years or so during which time some miserable inferior reigns as queen of the compound. Litia had come to the decision, at the time of our visit, to dismiss all his wives, making thus a clean sweep of all his difficulties. And, ' if he did so,' he enquired of the missionaries, ' would they allow him to become a member of the Church again ? ' Against their advice he divorced all his wives, and, with his father's consent, married another, who was to be his ' one wife ' this time. But neither has this last move brought peace to his heart or hearth. Nine-tenths of the missionary's and the young convert's difficulties in Central Africa circle around the marriage question, and it cannot be settled by majority vote at a missionary conference.

"Sheshcke has been affected a good deal by the town Livingstone coming so near, and the railway, so that it is not the centre of population that it used to be. When we embarked again a crowd of school children saw us off, singing sweet old Waldensian and Huguenot airs. A spell of fine weather now set in. The Zambesi had risen just sufficiently to allow us to climb the rapids comfortably. And words cannot describe the pleasure of a canoe journey up the Zambesi under such circumstances. The river flows so clean and clear all the year round. White sand-banks covered with water-fowl, hundreds of islands studded with palm trees and clothed with verdure to the water's edge, and but for an occasional angry hippo, and man-eating crocodile, the scene might be laid in Paradise. As we approached the Gonye Falls the river became deep and rapid so that it was no easy matter steering our long, heavily laden canoes. The dimensions of the larger ones are 40 ft. long by 3 ft. wide and 14 inches deep, most outrageous measurements, and but for the skill of the canoe men there would be many more accidents. The men stand and pole their way along, only occasionally do they use the flattened end of their poles as paddles. When they fail to make headway in the rapids they either jump into the water and push the canoe up, or carry the end of a strong rope, made from palm fronds, to the bank and tow. The bow of the canoe is shaped like the head of an arrow, and the tow rope fastened above the barbs of the ' arrow-head ' cannot slip, and a combined force of twenty men often had to pull one canoe at a time through a torrent of raging water When close up to the Gonye Falls we found a span of twelve oxen awaiting us, by the king's orders, to draw our canoes overland, a distance of three miles, to the quieter water above.

" When walking across the hauling trail, imagine our surprise and delight at meeting our boy Dick, now looking quite old and grey He followed me on my first journey, and remained so true and faithful Pay or no pay was a matter of no moment to him. Night and day he served me. Once when tossing in a burning fever I longed for a hot bath, but there was no water in the camp, and the nearest water hole was fully three miles away, but when I called for Dick and told him how I thought a hot bath would relieve me, he at once shouldered the water keg and with his spear in hand strode off into the darkness of the forest in a lion-infested country. Leaving him with Mr. Swann in the Garenganze I found him, after my first six months' visit home, standing on the end of the Benguella jetty. He had travelled 1200 miles to meet us, not to figure as the ' white man's ' pet servant, but to carry the heaviest load he could find in the camp, of pots and cooking utensils for a party of eight missionaries. When the Barotse declared the liberation of all their slaves Dick thought he would like to return and spend the rest of his days among his own people. And King Liwanika, recognising his value as a faithful man, put him in charge of much valuable property He was still willing to come with us again, but as he was earning five times more money than I could think of paying him I advised him to remain where he was.

" As we paddled on, the wooded hills on each bank of the river began to widen out, and grassy plains appeared, until at last we had fairly entered the famous Barotse Valley, teeming with cattle and people. The river began to twist about now, making the journey long, and we were glad to reach Nalolo

the town of Mokwæ, Liwanika's sister, and the titular queen
of the country. She and her husband were old and tried
friends. They were delighted to see me, and invited us to
dine with them in the queen's wonderful palace. The large,
lofty reception room might ornament any country mansion.
Two rows of red iron-wood pillars supported the roof. A deep
fresco of ornamental mat work hung around, and down to the
level of the tops of the doorways that led into other apartments.
These doorways were curtained off by soft hanging lace work
The whole design and construction was native work. In the
centre of the room stood a large table covered with a snow-
white cloth ; the dishes and other appointments were all of the
best. Only, seeing native etiquette would not allow the queen's
waiters to stand when serving her, these menials had to drop
on their knees with dishes of roast duck and other delicacies
in their hands, and approach the table literally walking on
their knees. The queen is very fat as all African queens should
be, and she used a settee as a chair for comfort However, my
wife was to be the honoured guest. According to old native
ideas she would have been invited to sit on the queen's mat ;
and now, there was no help for it, she had to sit by Queen
Mokwæ on her settee.

"Mr. and Mrs. Lageard and Miss Smith were occupying the
Nalolo Mission Houses. They gave us a very warm welcome,
and every possible assistance. The Sunday services were well
attended, the queen coming to church in a large roomy canoe
drawn over the sand by four oxen. Nalolo is certainly one of
the most trying of the Barotse stations. The white and the
black ants seem to be always at war, the one driving the poor
people out of their houses, sometimes at dead of night, and the
other doing their utmost to pull the houses down. Snakes
and mosquitoes and dangerous crocodiles in the river complete
the catalogue.

"Two days' paddling brought us to Lealui. Here one
realises that the Barotse cannot be grouped with the usual
run of Bantu tribes. True they learned much from their
conquerors, the Basuto, but their skill at canal digging, at
heaping up artificial mounds, upon which to build their towns,
their sacred burial groves with priests in charge, where regular
forms of prayer with offerings are gone through, also their
ideas of pomp and pageantry, are quite their own. The royal

barge, or Nalinquanda, which was in use years ago, lay a wreck at the landing place, but still an interesting old hulk. One could see how up to the last every effort had been made to keep the raft-like barge together. The Royal Chartered Company took the occasion of the Duke of Connaught's visit to present Liwanika with a barge built at Putney on the Thames. Unfortunately the soft yellow pine planking could not stand the rough hauling by hundreds of natives over the rocks and rapids of the lower river, and already it was in sad need of repair. Liwanika gave us a hearty welcome, and proved as good as his word, for he supplied us with fresh canoes and canoe men, enabling us to proceed at once to the Kabompo. M. A. Jalla is in charge of M. Coillard's old station of Lealui. It was interesting to see the little house M. Coillard lived in before the present comfortable Mission House was built. The Station stands on the mound associated in my mind with executions and witch burnings. The site of my old hut, where I opened the first school north of the Zambesi, and where I suffered constantly from fever, rats and vermin of all sorts, is now occupied by a house built to entertain visiting princes. Liwanika's houses and enclosures stood exactly in the same positions as they were thirty years before, and the relative positions of the compounds of his nobles and headmen remain exactly the same. Only the town had grown considerably. Hardly anyone knew me but the king himself and Sopi, his Prime Minister, who was my cook boy for a time and my first African scholar. He is now the right hand man both of the king and the missionaries.

" The rains had begun to pour down again and the river rose daily so that we wished we had been one month earlier in our undertaking. However, the men were cheerful and we full of hope and joy in the prospect of at last being privileged to approach the Kabompo field. Our canoe men were daily, however, entertaining us with stories of the fierce hippos that made the navigation of that river impossible. We entered the Kabompo, however, and proceeded for some distance. But on seeing how the great forest trees bent over the deep water, forcing the canoes to keep to the centre of the stream and allowing the hippos to hide under the branches of the trees, one realised that until some of these ' rogue ' hippos were killed off, the river certainly would not be safe. So we

landed and began building on what appeared to be a very
suitable site between villages. However, one very heavy night
of rain turned our camping ground into something like a mound
of sinking mud. Down our cot-beds sank and the tent poles
and the boxes, and had we not with a great struggle, and in
pitch darkness, made a great effort to free ourselves, something
would have disappeared. Dark and wet as it was, my wife
and I had to turn out and escape to an adjoining ant-heap.
The natives gathered round in the morning professing to be
greatly distressed. When I asked them why they had not
told us the day before that the ground would sink whenever
the heavy rain came, they naively replied that ' they thought
we knew '

"At last, close by another village, I managed to build a
fairly comfortable camp, bushing it around with thorns, and
soon we were engaging fresh men to take us up the Kabompo
as far as Sekufelu's capital. Again the rains seemed to threaten
our progress, but we did not turn back As we proceeded
the number of Lunda villages on the north bank quite surprised
us. Indeed, we estimated that we passed through a group of
villages every twenty minutes, representing in each group a
population of 500 people. How the natives can manage to
endure the mosquitoes is a problem. The air was simply alive
with them night and day. As we travelled eastward the
country became more hilly and the timber heavier. These
are the forests that have supplied the Barotse with canoes,
probably for centuries. We saw a group of canoe carpenters
camped around a mahogany log that they had just felled. The
first season's work is to trim the outside roughly and hollow
it out while soft and green, leaving the sides of the canoe
about six inches thick, covering it over with leaves, branches
and grass. They have to season it for a year, then returning
with supplies of meal and snuff they camp out for weeks together.
The canoe gradually begins to take shape, and so soon as it is
light enough the owner's wife brews as much beer as she can
find pots for; invitations are sent to all the neighbouring villages,
and with the help of beer, songs. talk and laughter the canoe
is dragged over the mile or more that lies between its stump
in the forest and the river. But it is far from being of use yet;
but canoes are generally sold by the Lunda forest men in this
state to Bambowe experts. We allow it another year soaking

in the river before it is pulled up under the shade of a great tree and finished off, the sides varying in thickness from half an inch to an inch lower down. They tell me the big trees have been all cut down within hauling distance of the rivers. Some of the largest canoes now afloat were made during the reign of the chief Sepopo. And seeing that he died forty years ago these canoes must have been in use for a very long time. When Mission Stations are planted in these parts we will have to build long canoe-like barges for the transport of supplies. And I took care to cut down a few fine specimens of mazuri so that the wood might season for a year or two. The natives will never touch these fallen trees. Passing through a large Lunda village I saw a tall pole planted in the centre; a pot of medicine was tied to the top of it and bark cords hung in graceful curves between the top of the pole and the tops of the huts around, like the ribbons of a May-pole. This pole I was told was a lightning conductor, and the cords secured the safety of each hut to which they were attached.

" Leaving the Lunda villages, and their naked inhabitants, we visited many Bankoio and Bambundu villages. The inhabitants had a slightly superior air, they drank more beer and were better clothed. The garment of one woman, I must confess, rather puzzled us. It turned out to be the stomach of an elephant softened by rubbing. I had met many of the Bankoio in Barotseland and had passed through their country the year before. They are one of the 23 large tribes I was able to count up living around these parts who have no word of Scripture translated into their tongues.

" After travelling for fifty miles along the Kabompo, we arrived at the junction of the Ndongwe, and here we found ourselves on a high bluff looking over a vast expanse of country with the town and villages of people lying around and large fields of ripening millet corn extended on all sides. Sekufelu is the chief of this country. He is a thorn in the side of Liwanika. He belongs, he insists, to the original Barotse stock who at one time of the Makololo (Basuto) invasion refused to be conquered and fled north. In fact, while we were visiting his town he had succeeded so well in raising a scare of threatened trouble that the Chartered Company sent, at Liwanika's request, a force of Rhodesian police and a Maxim gun, to protect him. Our carriers became quite excited with all the talk of Sekufelu's people that they too began to be troublesome. They wanted their pay, beer for rations, and when the day came to return they refused to strike camp. However, better counsels prevailed. We put in a good day's march and were soon out of touch with Sekufelu's boastful young rebels. Seldom, however, have I seen such a tempting field for mission work. Sekufelu's people were so interesting and industrious. They brought us abundant supplies of every article of food-stuff grown in Central Africa, along with a basket or two of Irish potatoes, and a good sample of wheat. The chief had brought the seed of potatoes and wheat back with him from one of his journeys south. Then pottery, baskets, mats, canoes, fish traps were all being manufactured in the town the day we paid our formal visit, when all the petty chiefs assembled to hear our message.

" Returning to our depot camp by the Zambesi was a real home-coming Now our way seemed more clear. We would build a three-roomed house on a spot of land that divides the Kabompo from the Zambesi, spend the remainder of our time evangelising among the Bambowe, and make a short exploratory trip by canoes up the Lungebungu.

" When I called for men to cut poles and make bricks about 500 responded, out of which we employed thirteen at 5s. per month. We soon had four men sawing out planks with a pit saw, others making bricks and fetching hard wood poles and rafters, and the cottage was a great success. Also a kitchen garden dug over and fenced, and a fruit tree garden cleared and fenced around in the bush by us, gave our surroundings an air of respectability, not to speak of the street of native huts and shelters springing up at a safe distance behind our house. The Bambowe responded delightfully to our visits, and several young men gave much promise. All these activities, however, were brought to a close by a sudden illness overtaking me. My wife had now to take charge, and within a week she had me gliding down the Zambesi in one of the canoes we had brought up for the Lungebungu expedition. Fortunately we met Dr. Reuter in the Barotse Valley. He ordered me south at once."

x

CHAPTER XXIV

AFTER resting for some months in Johannesburg Arnot made a second attempt in 1912 to take up the work in the Kabompo Valley, but was turned back again by another breakdown in health. He had already forwarded his baggage to Livingstone, and arranged with his paddlers from the Kabompo to meet him there at a certain date. Then he went to Kimberley for a week-end, intending to join the Zambesi express at that place. The day before he should have left he was taken seriously ill. After a fortnight in hospital he sadly retraced his steps to Johannesburg.

Loath to relinquish the work to which he had devoted his life Arnot decided to visit the homeland to consult with specialists, although the local doctors were against the proposal. He left for England in January, 1913, and returned at the end of the year, having undergone a three months' course of open-air treatment. Three doctors were consulted and neither saw any reason why he should not return to his field of labour provided he lived carefully.

Returning to Johannesburg he met there Mr. Suckling from Kalene Hill and Mr. T. L. Rogers from home. These brethren expressed their willingness to accompany him to the Kabompo. As he was then feeling strong and well it seemed to Arnot that the call to proceed north was clear.

Leaving the Golden City on November 21st, the three missionaries journeyed to Shesheke on the Zambesi, where six canoes, in charge of twenty-five paddlers, were waiting for them.

To his son Robert, Arnot wrote from the Zambesi on December 2nd : " When we left Livingstone to go to the river, where we met the canoes, I shot a partridge. But there are plenty of them. Then the waggon was too heavy, and stuck in the mud again and again, so we had enough to do. Then we came on here, and I am sitting looking at the Zambesi.

322

Yesterday a big crocodile came and lay out on a rock, greatly to Mr. Rogers' amusement. Then he opened his mouth as wide as he could and kept it open while a bird walked in and picked his teeth. Rogers wanted to shoot the croc., but there was a village on the other side, and we were afraid of killing someone. The man told me that this croc. had already eaten his ox and his dog."

To his son Arthur, Arnot wrote on December 3rd : " I am surprised at the number of new villages up here and the number of children. Africa certainly wants not so much more missionaries as more active missionaries. The people never see or hear a missionary except when he passes them on journeys. Then I met an old friend from the Mobabe who tells me that the Bushmen are very numerous, and the Basubia on the Mobabe. I wish I was a boy like you again. I would roll up my sleeves and begin again, and learn my lessons better than ever I did, and work for a bursary, and then set out like John the Baptist into the wilderness and eat locusts and wild honey and preach to the Bushmen. How happy one would be in heaven with a thousand Bushmen round you. Just such another sight could not be seen anywhere in heaven for no missionary has really been the Bushman's missionary.

" On December 14th we left Shesheke and slept by some cattle kraals. In the evening a sweeping storm came up, driving us into our tents, but my dome tent stood well. The next day we camped early at Katonga, to await two men I had left behind to bring on the mail. Having a few hours to spare, Rogers and I took our seine net to a sand-bank. We duly cast it, apparently catching nothing, but when one of the men stepped into the water to throw the bag of the net on the shore, he sprang back in terror, for a crocodile was lying quietly in the sack, and immediately showed its teeth and dashed about. Rogers shot it with his rifle. Then there was a roar of laughter and hand-clapping among the natives. The crocodile was quite young, only measuring nine feet. The net was none the worse, and we afterwards had a good catch of fish. The next day brought us to the foot of the first rapids. Here, on the German bank, we found two men in partnership, building boats and barges, and selling them to the British traders for fifty or sixty pounds each. They seem to be just what we want. We camped in the forest near, where I shot a little antelope

behind the camp. Suckling shot one, too, and Rogers shot a
guinea-fowl ; so we were quite set up with game meat. That
night we slept at Ngambe, where we had to pull the canoes
overland a short way. Next day we passed dozens of our old
friends the hippos.

" The 20th of December we shall long remember. Landing on
an island we put up our tents and seemed to be very comfortable when a peculiar colour began to appear in the sky, volumes
of white clouds forming. Behind these in a half-circle was a
very dark, leaden cloud ; then banks of light ash-coloured
clouds formed up, and behind them all was pitch black, while
a red copper glow filled the air. In spite of the dead calm we
all rushed to the tent ropes, and piled up stones around the
pegs. I shouted to a trader pitched 200 yards below us, but
all too late ; his strong, heavy tent suddenly filled out like a
balloon and rose skyward, an extraordinary sight ! Then
Rogers' tent tipped over end-ways, snapping the iron pegs of
the tops of the poles. Fortunately my tent held, with the help
of six men. We put all our goods into it pell-mell, and so for
about an hour we were in one of the biggest storms I ever
experienced. The lightning flashed every second and seemed
to run like liquid fire round the iron-stone rock which composed
the island.

" The next day being Sunday, we had intended remaining but with one consent we moved on. How we longed
for the shelter of trees ! But when after an hour or two
we camped by the Kalle Rapids, we saw that the forests
had their dangers, for huge branches lay strewn over the
ground. I had a nice afternoon with my boys, giving them a
lesson to repeat. We had great Bible and book talks, and made
great plans for the future. '

At Lealui Ainot had a bad attack of fever for two days and
was very low in spirits as he thought his old trouble was on
him again, but this passed and he felt quite himself again.

The narrative proceeds :

" *Jan. 6th,* 1914.—After being again held up by the rain,
and spending an hour at a trader's little store, we were rather
late in overtaking Suckling's boat To-day, just at dusk, our
men called out that a flock of ducks were on a sandbank close
by. Rogers lifted his shot gun and fired among them, dropping
the weapon, muzzle down on to his left foot, whiled he craned

his neck to see the results of his shot. I was standing close to him. Eight men stood all around the bow of barge when the second barrel of his gun went off. It was loaded with buck shot. A thrill passed up my leg A big hole was made on the top of Rogers' boot, and again an exit hole to the left. The shot had refused to penetrate the thick sole of his boot. In the shortest possible time we had the boot and sock off and a bucket of disinfectant prepared and the wound washed, but it was too dark to see anything. Suckling was canoed across the river. As soon as possible we had Rogers up to my tent, all dressing and instruments available laid out. Rogers had all these handily by him in a bag, and with the best camp light I dressed the foot, finding, strange to say, that most of the charge had passed between the two small toes of the foot The top of the little toe was hanging by a thread. The bone of the next toe was splintered. But there seemed to be a break across the toe. After an injection of morphia, I removed the splintered bone, cleaned and put back the hanging little toe. We all went to bed. Rogers was very plucky.

" *Jan 7th.*—This morning, with better light, we undid the toe, managed to get the wound cleaner, and set the little toe more correctly. Began our journey at 10.15. Camped by Mamboure Village.

" *Jan. 8th.*—Rogers had fair night ; temperature normal. The little toe has stuck on ; wounds quite sweet.

" On January 11th we reached Njonjolo's, on the Kabompo River, our very trying journey over, and our goods all being there. The little house that I built two years and a half ago seemed to be exactly as we left it ; nothing had given way, and only a few drops came through the roof after a heavy rain the first night, but the bush had all grown thick again. The people were very glad to see us.

" On the 12th Mr. Suckling left to seek a suitable site for a station among the Balunda. I began the day by clearing the yard, then took Offiey, one of the boys, to the lake and taught him how to wash the clothes. This was followed by two hours' gardening, and I then came back to lunch, which consisted of fresh fish from our traps and thick milk. I had Kaffir corn ground, and made a loaf of bread, half of flour and half of sifted mealie meal ; the result was excellent.

" The same day I began school with seven little boys,

and by the 17th it had increased by leaps and bounds. The people *did* listen. I was tied up with little duties from morning till night—baking, cooking, buying, talking, gardening, farming, house repairing, storekeeping and butter making—yet I felt the place a perfect haven of rest, the house being cool and pleasant, with no white ants or rats about.

" However, ' Man proposes but God disposes ' On the 25th I was smitten down as by a sword thrust. My spleen, which had given me much trouble in years gone by, and was surcharged with the refuse of many fevers, suddenly ruptured and filled my abdominal cavity with blood, although this was not discovered until I had arrived in Johannesburg six weeks later. How I recovered from the first shock and endured the long journey cannot be explained or told here. It was to me a thousand miles of miracle in miniature.

" Messrs. Suckling and Rogers had no hesitation in deciding to remain on. May the Lord's richest blessing rest upon them and on all the heroic band of missionaries throughout Central Africa who have put their hands to the plough and have not drawn back."

Miss Ray Arnot, Arnot's eldest daughter, wrote the following account of her father's return from his last journey .

" Father was taken ill on January 24th. The Commissioner, Mr. Thwaites, who had come up to the station in his barge with the mail, had only been in the house five minutes before father complained of great pain. They put him to bed and the next day hurried him off to the doctor at Mongu. All the Commissioner's things were bundled out of the barge, and Messrs. Thwaites and Rogers took father a five days' journey in two days, through terrible storms of thunder and rain, travelling night and day. When Mr. Suckling, who had camped twenty miles further on, heard of father's illness, he walked that distance in one night through a country infested with wild animals. He arrived just in time to see them off and to fling into the barge his good eiderdown quilt, which proved a great comfort. The doctor was kindness itself to father, and nursed him night and day. After a fortnight at Mongu, father picked up wonderfully, and was well enough to travel south. Dr. Dickson came with him part of the way and then gave him his own boy (trained as a cook as well as a nurse) to go with him the rest of the journey. The Ellenbergers, French missionaries from the Barotse Valley, happened to be going on furlough, so this fitted in very nicely, and they joined parties at Lealui. The three weeks' journey from Lealui to Kazungula down the Zambesi was one ' series of miracles,' to quote father's words. It would rain all night and clear up just in time for their start off in the morning ; of course, they could not travel when it was raining. At night, when the pain was very bad, God drew near to His suffering servant and filled his soul with peace and with perfect resignation to His will. At times His presence so filled the tent that the whole place seemed lit with His glory. They stopped at Sheshcke for a day or two, and messengers were sent from there overland to Livingstone to ask for a waggon to be sent to meet the party. Unhappily none of these messengers could get through, as the roads were made impassable by heavy floods. Before reaching Shesheke one interesting little incident took place. They were in need of meat one time, so the canoes were stopped while M. Ellenberger took aim at two or three guinea-fowl that were on the bank and shot one. Before they could land, however, to their astonishment they saw a lion suddenly seize the shot guinea-fowl and make off with it. The lion had been lying, unperceived by the party, behind a bush near, eating a baboon. The other guinea-fowl had seen the lion, and did not move when the gun went off, but waited to see what the lion would do. The lion evidently preferred the flesh of the guinea-fowl to that of the baboon.

" They did not know how long they would have to wait at Kazungula for the waggon—perhaps a week, perhaps a fortnight —as no message had got through. What was their surprise, therefore, to hear the crack of a whip in the distance half an hour after they disembarked ! M. Jalla had heard a rumour of a party coming down the river, so sent the waggon on spec. Father was carried overland in a hammock, while the other missionaries and the goods went in the waggon. One day the waggon driver said he wanted to push on for two hours longer that evening before camping for the night, as he was afraid a river, now low, would fill in a few hours. They looked towards its source and saw heavy black clouds in that direction. They pushed on, hoping for the best ; what was their relief to find the river quite low ! They had hardly crossed when they heard a roar behind them, and down came the water, carrying all

before it and flooding both banks of the river. If they had
been on the wrong side of the flood, it would have kept them a
week or ten days at the least. When they arrived at Livingstone, father looked up the first train for Johannesburg. Some
wanted him to wait for the quick train, which left a day later
but arrived before the slow one. But father would take the
slow, stopping train, which in the end proved the quickest,
as the other was delayed seventeen hours by a wash-away.
Dr. Berry ordered him off to the Nursing Home the day after
he arrived, astonished that he was still alive, and that the blood
from the ruptured spleen had not turned septic."

Several weeks of suffering faced the tired missionary on his
return to Johannesburg. But time and energy were found for
the revision of the proofs of one more book. Arnot had been
repeatedly urged to republish *Garenganze*, but as he felt that
much of its contents were out of date he decided to rewrite the
story of his pioneering journeys. This he did during 1913.
In the preface to this his last work, *Missionary Travels in
Central Africa*, Arnot said he would not attempt " to give a
history of the missionary work that had been carried on so
successfully by the brethren and sisters whose names appear in
our Appendix." This list contained the names of sixty-one
missionaries, labouring on sixteen stations scattered over five
mission fields. These fields are described by Arnot as follows :

" 1. The Bihé plateaus are homes now of native churches
that go a long way to support their own out-stations, schools
and evangelists.

" 2. The Chokwe is still a field full of peril and privation.

" 3. Again, further east, in the Lovale-Lunda countries
with their fine stations, ' light has sprung up ' to many, and of
Kavungu the missionaries write of a ' continued stream of
blessing.'

" 4. The old Garenganze field, now called Katanga, has
passed through most unusual vicissitudes, the history of which
would require a book to itself, but much that appeared to have
been lost has been gathered up within the last ten years. Msidi's
old capital at Bankeya has been rebuilt ; Muenda, the chief,
is a most generous helper, and the Belgian Government has
loyally kept the field open for our brethren, only reinforce-
ments at the four stations now occupied are sadly wanted.

" 5. The Vemba mission field is in British territory, and

is traversed in all directions by the paths that Livingstone trod during the years of his ' Last Journey.' "

The sixty-one missionaries referred to above were all living when the list was compiled, and did not include those who had also dedicated their lives to the same fields, but had "fallen on sleep " at their posts. What a cheering vision this number of workers must have been for the missionary to contemplate in his last days. Thirty-two years earlier the whole of the vast fields, now occupied at strategic points by these, was a blank, and heathen darkness reigned supreme from end to end. But Arnot never boasted. A few days before he passed away he said to a friend that the words of the Apostle Paul : " I have fought a good fight, I have finished my course," were words he could not use. But just as a drummer boy could say he had fought in a great battle so he felt he could take these words of Paul's and adapt them to himself and say, " I have fought *in* the good fight."

As Arnot became worse it was decided that nothing but a serious operation could relieve him. This was performed, and all appeared to be going well till May 14th, when, his wife wrote · " He had a sudden attack of the heart and terrible pain. Though he became easier he steadily sank. When I told him the doctor said he was sinking, he seemed quite peaceful and happy, and told me to cable home, ' Fred at rest.' Then he said, ' Have the funeral as simple as possible,' and named those whom he wished to be invited. As his breath became slower, I quoted to him, ' When thou passest through the waters, I will be with thee.' He tried to say something, and nodded his head brightly. After that he went away so quietly ; it was like a little child falling asleep."

On May 15th, 1914, Arnot entered into rest, at the age of fifty-five. His body was buried in the Brixton Cemetery, Johannesburg. A large number of people were present. Mr. Laurie Hamilton, one of the leaders of " The Brethren," conducted the service. The Rev. Canon Berry, of the Church of England, read the committal sentences, and addresses were given by the author of this book and by Mr. Hamilton.

A memorial service, largely attended, was held a few days later in the Johannesburg Baptist Church, when representatives of various evangelical churches paid tributes to Arnot's memory.

Arnot left a wife and seven children to mourn their loss, but also to rejoice in a fragrant and precious memory. Of these Ray, the eldest daughter, heard the call to the Mission Field, and proceeded to Bunkeya, her father's old station, in 1916, but malarial fever forced her back again. Nigel, Cyril and Alec, the three eldest sons, volunteered for service in the Great War. Nigel fought under General Botha in the campaign in German South-West Africa, and came through unscathed. A serious motor cycle accident, which befell him in Johannesburg afterwards, hindered his acceptance for Flanders, but at the time of writing, he was engaged in " munition work " in Britain. Cyril enlisted in the 3rd South African Brigade, and fell in the fight for the Menin Road on September 24th, 1917. Alec was in one of the flying corps.

Map showing
Mr ARNOT'S ROUTES

Benguela to Garenganze ....
Benguela to Durban . — — —
R. Zambesi to Luanza . —·—·—·

Scale of Miles

INDEX

Lucalla, R , and town, 285
Luena, R , 163
Lufiia, R , 186
Lunda, Villages, 294
Lutoba, Marriage customs at, 309

M

Makoffee, 82
Mala, of Secumba, 97
Malonda, 97
Mamwia, 81
Mangetti tribe, 83
Maritzbuig, 22
Marriage, Compulsory, 84
Mary, Princess, 234
Masaioa Bushmen, 41
Mbova, 54
Men, Barotse, woik of, 85
Mentality of the native, 96
Mosanga, 83
Millet, Destructive method of grow-
ing, 262
Misho-Misho, 265
Missionaries, Married and un-
married, 135
Mistaken methods with the African,
91
Moffat, Dr , 81
Mokwæ, Queen, 312
Molenga, 180
Moleni, 83
"Monaie," 100
Monkobe, 189
Monona, 218
Monsoia, 26
Morris, Mr.
Mosibe, 159
Msidi, 119, 181, 183, 191, 202
Mukurru, 182, 202
Muller's Orphanages, 284
Muiray, Dr A , 267
Mweru, L , 264

N

Nalolo, 317
Nambi, The spirit, 122
Nana Kandundu, 174, 249
Native etiquette, 317
Nest, A curious, 282
Ngoi, Rescue of, 249
Nyassa, L , 260

O

Obea men, 269
Olohosi, 176
Operation in the bush, An, 227

Orchids, 306
Ordeal, Boiling water, 87
Ordeals, 89
Osore, L., 105
Ovimbundu carriers, 152
Ox-riding, Difficulties of, 105

P

Panda-ma-tenka, 51
Parrot, An entertaining, 152
Peho, 161
Poisonous spider, A, 286
Polygamy, 203, 287
Porto, Senhoi, 116, 244
Portuguese, Trouble with the, 244
Portuguese in Africa, The, 288
Post, A welcome, 228
Potchefstroom, 24
Poverty, 191
Preparing for the great work, 19
Present, An embarrassing, 171
Price, Dr., 81
Printing press, A, 139
Protéges at Msidi's, 193

Q

Quarantine, In, 182

R

Radstock, Loid, 234
Raided countiy, A, 156
Raids by Garenganze, 195
Rains, 200
Ramosi, 36
Rebuke for temper, A, 170
Religions and beliefs, 122
Reviews, 235
Rhine, The, 272
Rhodes, Cecil, 256
Rivers, Difficulties of crossing, 137
Rogue hippos, 318
Rough fellow travelleis, 301
Royal barge, A, 318
Royal Geographical Society, The,
232

S

Saddle, A, 146
Sanders, Mr and Mrs , 118
Sceneiy on the Kwando R , 111
Scripture, Translating, 293
Sefula, 311
Segunda, 192
Sekufelu, 320
Sekulu, 144
Selous, F C , 25

Printed in Great Britain at
The Mayflower Press, Plymouth
William Brendon & Son Ltd
1920

CPSIA information can be obtained
at www.ICGtesting.com
Printed in the USA
LVHW082027011222
734418LV00005B/195